CASS LIBRARY OF AFRICAN STUDIES

GENERAL STUDIES

No. 152

Editorial Adviser: JOHN RALPH WILLIS
Department of History, University of California, Berkeley

The Southern Sudan

The Southern Sudan

The Problem of National Integration

Edited by
DUNSTAN M. WAI

FRANK CASS : LONDON

First published 1973 *in Great Britain by*
FRANK CASS AND COMPANY LIMITED
67 Great Russell Street, London WC1B 3BT, England

and in United States of America by
FRANK CASS AND COMPANY LIMITED
c/o International Scholarly Book Services, Inc.
P.O. Box 4347, Portland, Oregon 97208

ISBN 0 7146 2985 5

Library of Congress Catalog Card No. 72-92980

Printed in Great Britain
at the St Ann's Press, Park Road, Altrincham

Contents

Maps

Notes on the Contributors

Muddathir 'Abd Al-Rahim, B.A. (Khartoum and Nottingham), Ph.D. (Manchester), Director of Research, CAFRAD, Tangier. Born in Al-Damar, Sudan. He taught at the University of Manchester for five years, and was Head of the Department of Political Science at the University of Khartoum, 1965-69. He was offered the Professorship and Chair in the Department of Political Science, University of Zambia, in 1970, and was Visiting Professor of Political Science at Makerere University, Kampala, 1970-71. His major fields of interest are political theory and political institutions. He is the author of *Imperialism and Nationalism in the Sudan: A Study in Constitutional and Political Development, 1899-1956*; *Human Rights in Theory and Practice* (in Arabic); *Ahmad Khair's Kifah Jil* (a history of the Sudanese Graduate Congress Movement); and has written many articles for learned journals.

Abel Alier, LL.B. (Khartoum), LL.M. (Yale), President of the Regional Government in the Southern Sudan, Vice-President of the Sudan. Born in Bor District, Upper Nile Province, Southern Sudan. In 1961-62 he was a Research Fellow in Land Law in the School of Advanced Legal Studies, University of London. He worked as district judge in El-Obeid, Wad-Medani and Khartoum, and was a member of the Sudan Judiciary in the High Court in 1965 when he resigned to take an active part in the politics of the Southern Sudan. He took part in the 1965 Round Table Conference, which laid down a basis for a solution of the Southern Sudan Question, and was a member of the Twelve-Man Committee appointed by the Conference to recommend a constitutional and administrative solution to the Southern problem. He was also a member of the Political Parties Conference on the South; of the Constitution Commission 1966-68; of the Board of Directors of the Industrial Planning Corporation; of the National Scholarship Board; and Secretary General of the Southern Front. He is a distinguished advocate, and has travelled widely.

Donald Denoon, B.A.(Natal), Ph.D.(Cambridge), Lecturer in History at Makerere University, Kampala. He has lectured at the Universities of Toronto and Ibadan; has written various articles on South and East African history; and is writing on South Africa since 1800, and Uganda before 1900. He was Chairman of the World University Service at Makerere, 1967-69.

Joseph U. Garang, LL.B.(Khartoum). Born near Wau, Bahr-el-Ghazal Province in the Southern Sudan, he practised as an advocate. He joined the Sudan Communist Party and was a member of the Central Committee. In May 1969 he was appointed Minister of Supply and then Minister of State for Southern Affairs until his execution in July 1971.

A. G. G. Gingyera-Pinycwa, B.A.(Makerere), M.A.(Chicago), Lecturer in the Department of Political Science and Public Administration at Makerere University, Kampala. Born in Jonam County, West Nile District, Uganda. He served as an Assistant District Commissioner and an Acting Town Clerk in the Central Government of Uganda before embarking on graduate studies. His major fields of specialization and interest are international relations and East African political systems.

Ali A. Mazrui, B.A.(Manchester), M.A.(Columbia, New York), D.Phil.(Oxford), Professor and Head of the Department of Political Science and Public Administration at Makerere University, Kampala. He was Dean of the Social Sciences at Makerere from 1967-69 and has been Visiting Professorial Scholar at the Universities of Chicago, California (Los Angeles), Harvard and Singapore, and at the Indian School of International Studies, New Delhi. He has lectured in America, Europe, Asia and Africa; and has been associated with many international journals both as editor and contributor. A Kenyan, he is the author of *Towards a Pax Africana; The Anglo-African Commonwealth; On Heroes and Uguru Worship; Violence and Thought; Cultural Engineering and Nation-Building*, and is co-editor, with Robert I. Rotberg, of *Protest and Power in Black Africa*. He has written numerous scholarly articles.

Storrs McCall, B.A.(McGill), B.Phil and D.Phil(Oxford). He lectured at McGill University from 1955-63, and since then has been commuting back and forth between Pittsburgh and Makerere Universities. He is the author of *Aristotle's Model Syllogisms* and editor of *Polish Logic*.

Peter H. Russell, B.A.(Toronto and Oxford), is Professor of Political Economy and Principal of Innis College in the University of Toronto. He was Visiting Professor of Political Science at Makerere University from 1969-71, and is the author of many books and scholarly articles on political theory, constitutional law and the judiciary.

Dunstan M. Wai is a student at St. John's College, Oxford. Born in Kajo-Kaji, Yei River District in the Southern Sudan, he fled to Uganda in October 1962 during the climax of General Abboud's military brutalities in the South, and lived in a refugee camp for eighteen months. He was reading for a degree in Political Science at Makerere University when he won a St. John's/Trinity Junior Common Room Refugee Scholarship. While at Makerere he was elected member of the Guild Representative Council, and of the Guild Secretariat. He was also President of the Southern Sudanese Makerere Students' Union.

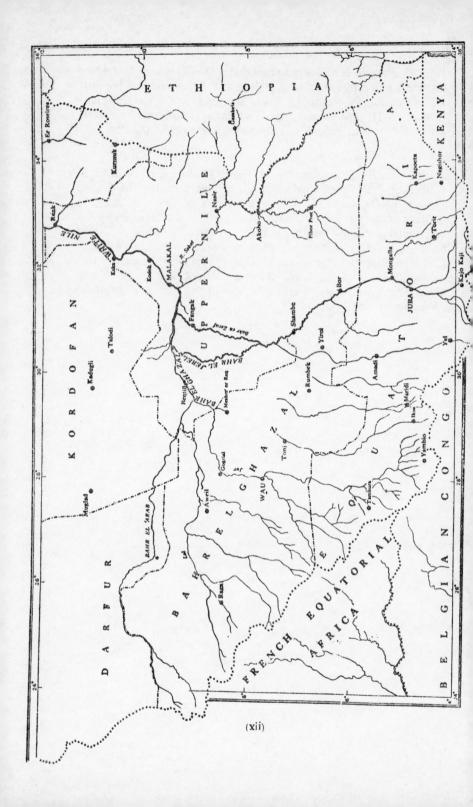

(xii)

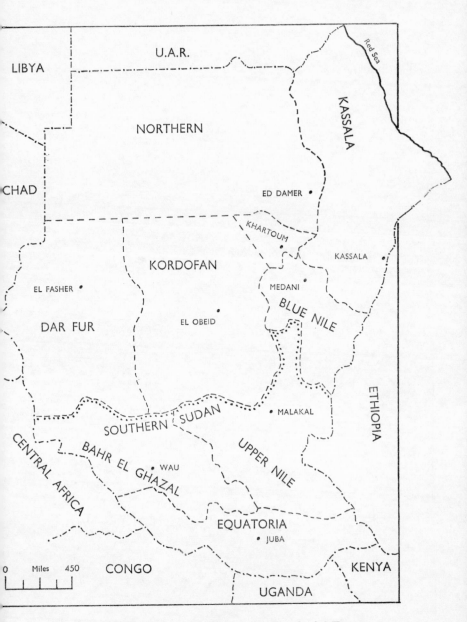

Political Map of the Sudan with Provincial Towns

(xiii)

INTRODUCTION

The purpose of this book is to try to further understanding of the problems of the Southern Sudan, which have often been unfairly equated with the prevalent problems of national integration facing post-Colonial Africa. For greater understanding of the history and the contemporary manifestations of the conflict between North and South in the Sudan, the focus here is upon the generic aspects of the problem:

1) the environmental differences between the two regions;
2) the antecedents in their historical hostility;
3) the racial, cultural, social and religious differences of the peoples of North and South;
4) the economic inequalities;
5) the assimilative and repressive policies of independent Northern-dominated governments in the South;
6) the possibilities of foreign intervention in the conflict.

The authors in general have attempted to look at the Southern Sudan question introspectively and in perspective. Being committed to no one belief, they have felt free to cast their net wide. As a result, the attitudes of the contributions may seem very diverse to the reader. On the other hand, he cannot fail to notice certain similarities. For example, all agree that the North and the South are two culturally and denominationally different regions which have their own historical developments; that imperialism and colonialism, having brought them together, failed to integrate them into a nation or at least into a territorially and administratively unified entity; that independent governments have failed to face the reality of the situation and refused to offer a workable compromise; and that peace should be fully maintained without the support of violence.

The history of the conflict in the Sudan is full of tales of invasions, enslavement and exploitation of the South by the North. Group consciousness in the Sudan has been founded on race, culture and religion and these factors have been powerful in accentuating inter-group relations in many plural societies. Moreover, in the Sudan, the Northern Sudanese have deliberately disregarded tradition in the

South. While they tend more towards western civilization, the course of change for the South is consciously being diverted to Arab-Islamic civilization, before western modernization. Thus African culture in the South is subjected to two stereotyped notions of modernization; Arabization and westernization. As Dr. Francis Mading Deng has put it:

> "Traditional decision makers are exploited to ensure the dominance of the National decision-makers and their Arab-Islamic civilization."[1]

But the Southern Sudanese people's memories of their past created in them a strong need for autonomy, the need to throw off the external control of the Northern Sudanese, whose position of superiority is satisfying their own need to dominate. The peoples of the two regions looked at independence from the British in different ways. The point involved is well expressed by two students of African international relations:

> "Two ethnic communities can suffer joint domination from an external colonial power, particularly when there is no immediate hope for either of them to attain independence. When prospects for independence do materialize, each may define its limits of self-determination. In the Sudan, the Northerners, because in the majority and with better prospects of taking over as successors of the British, defined self-determination for the entire Sudan as one entity. The Southerners, because in the minority and apprehensive of domination by the Arabs of the North, defined self-determination to mean separate independence for the North and the South. The clash between the two was, therefore, inevitable."[2]

The language of the conflict is heavily charged with emotion. Each party has irrational goals, based on mutual feelings of suspicion, fear, and hatred. During the course of the deterioration of relations between the two regions, there has been a tendency for goals to become even less rational and compatible. The persistent call by successive Northern Sudanese governments for the unconditional surrender of the Anya-Nya, and the Anya-Nya declaration to fight relentlessly for secession of the South, are the expressed aims of the contesting parties. It is true that in many conflicts such manifest goals are unreasonable and the parties concerned cannot unfortunately be convinced by argument of their irrationality. It could, however, be argued that where expressed goals are not compatible but basic goals are, conflict will end if this fundamental compatibility is perceived by both parties.

The Southern Sudanese have four basic needs: autonomy; affiliation and identity; dominance and self-assertion in the Southern Sudan; protection and self-preservation. Freud has argued that inability to meet these needs in any society leads to frustration, and may therefore be the cause of civil wars.[3]

This is true in the case of the Southern Sudan. The history of the South shows basic needs, and persistent refusals to accept any foreigner in the territory. Just as the South did not welcome British and Egyptian colonialism, so it has been opposed to subjection in the political, economic, educational, and religious systems being forged for the Sudan by successive Northern governments. Independent governments have obstinately pursued a rigorous policy of repression of the South, including attempts to Islamize and culturally assimilate the region into the Northern fold. Freedom of action, as defined by the values and ends of the African culture, has been denied in the South. The Southern Sudanese see these policies as a calculated attempt to thwart the need for their self-preservation and development in their own African cultural traits. Indeed, these policies were the immediate precipitants of the mutiny of 1955 and the civil war. As the Cotran Commission of Inquiry into the Mutiny of 1955 points out, careless and thoughtless governmental measures were instrumental in the mounting tension and feelings of frustration in the South.

Political leaders in the Northern Sudan have often pinned the tragedy of the Southern Sudan on the British Colonial administration They have argued that the colonial policies of separate development and administration of the two regions, and the exclusion of Islam in the South, are responsible for the acute difficulties of integrating the two regions after independence. The Sudanese Arabs, however, cannot continue to take refuge behind colonial idiocies. As George W. Shepherd has persuasively argued:

"While British and missionary policy clearly militated against the emergence of a modern, national consensus for unity in the South, it would be a simplification to see in this the sole reason. The cultural, racial and historical reasons for differences have a continuity over a long period of time. If the British had attempted to press integration, it is possible that they, rather than the new Sudanese nation, would have faced the problem of revolt in the South. Their greatest error was in their ambivalence and failure to accept the necessity for integration much earlier than they did, and their consequent failure to provide the kind of social development and constitutional transition that might have had some chance of safe-guarding and integrating the interests of the two major sections of the country."[4]

B

The misfortune of the Sudan is that most politicians in the North are sectarian and reactionary. Some even look on the South as a colony and treat it as such. It is also true that some previous politicians from the South offered their votes for sale, now to the semi-feudal parties, and now to the business parties of the North, with the result of diluting the expression of the grievances of the South. They forgot their main mission to the National Assembly in Khartoum. They were outmanoeuvred and rendered ineffective by the political machinations in the North. The Southern question, then, has been used by the conservative parties in the North for balancing power against each other. It was not to be solved but to be perpetuated at the expense of many lives in the South, which has been virtually under the rule of "security forces" since the war began. The Sudan has yet to learn that a society cannot really have social order without social justice.

As the authors have shown in their analyses, no outsider can help the Sudanese resolve their problem. They must do this themselves. The Sudan must demonstrate her ability to settle her own problems free from dictation by outside vested interests. In the past, it has failed to do this and the problem has been exacerbated by the lack of understanding, or refusal to accept, the historical and social factors, and the failure to recognize the weakness of national consensus between the North and the South. It is hoped that present and future leaders will address themselves honestly to this agonizing problem.

This introduction is not the place for a summary of the views advanced in the book. Much value lies in their diversity and it is for the reader to draw his own conclusions, however tentative these may be. A collaborative book of this kind inevitably raises the question of collective responsibility. As editor, I am responsible for soliciting the individual articles that make up this book. My only criterion in choosing contributors was a genuine respect for their intellectual integrity. I do not necessarily agree with all that they have written, nor indeed does each of them necessarily find himself in agreement with other contributors. Each author is responsible for his own article, and for his own article alone; I am accountable for my own articles. I personally welcome a diversity of interpretations regarding the problem of the Southern Sudan; and all the authors sincerely hope that Sudanese leaders, both from the North and the South, present and future, will find this book useful in their search for an acceptable and lasting solution to the conflict.

It remains for me to thank all those who have given so generously of their time and energy to this undertaking. I would in particular like to thank Professor Ali A. Mazrui and Dr. Y. Tandon for the initial encouragement they gave me in undertaking this project while I was their student at Makerere University. I first discussed the feasibility of such an endeavour with Mr. Okello-Oculi and I am grateful to him for his invaluable advice. I am also indebted to Miss Eunice N. Kagondu and Mr. James Oporia-Ekwaro, colleagues and friends, for their continued counsel and encouragement.

I started the project for this book while at Makerere, where controversial discussions on the Southern Sudan question among my fellow Southern Sudanese students in a way prompted me to begin. The trust and the unfailing confidence they have shown in me and the help they gave various researchers proved invaluable. To Messrs. R. A. Hargreaves and R. O. Windsor, once my school teachers and still loyal friends, I am deeply grateful for reading the manuscript in detail and correcting errors in English.

Finally, I would like to thank Mr. Anthony Doniger of New York, my colleague and friend at Oxford, for his generous assistance which enabled me to have the manuscript typed.

Dunstan M. Wai

St. John's College,
Oxford
January, 1972

REFERENCES

1 Francis Mading Deng, *Tradition and Modernization: A Challenge for Law among the Dinka of the Sudan* (Yale, 1971), p. 334.
2 Tandon and Gingyera-Pinycwa, "Uganda-Sudan Relations and Uganda-Congo Relations, 1962-66: A Comparative Examination", Paper for the University of East Africa, Social Science Conference, December 1966 (unpublished), pp. 1-3.
3 See S. Freud, "Why War?" (Letter to Professor Einstein, 1932) in *Collected Papers*, edited by J. Strachey (London, 1956-57), Vol. V, quoted in Ogbolu M. Okonji, "The Psychological Causes of Civil Wars: the Sudanese Case" (unpublished, 1970), p. 11.
4 See George W. Shepherd, Jr., "National Integration and the Southern Sudan", in *Journal of Modern African Studies*, 4, 2 (1966), p. 198.

1

THE SOUTHERN SUDAN: THE COUNTRY AND THE PEOPLE

Dunstan M. Wai

Position

The Democratic Republic of the Sudan is the largest country in the continent of Africa. It extends from Latitude $3\frac{1}{2}°$N on the border with the Republic of Uganda at Nimule to Latitude 23°N on the Red Sea Coast just north of Halaib and from Longitude $21\frac{3}{4}°$E to Longitude $38\frac{1}{2}°$E. It is 1,070 miles (1,722 km) from west to east and 1,245 miles (2,003 km) from north to south. It covers an area of 967,500 square miles, approximately 8.3% of the entire area of the continent of Africa.

The Southern Sudan is that part of the country which lies south of Latitude 10°N and extends as far south as Kajo-Kaji and Nimule on the Uganda border. It consists of the three provinces of Upper Nile, Bahr el Ghazal and Equatoria. The area of the Southern Sudan is about 250,000 square miles, just over one-fourth of the total area of the Republic. The boundaries of Southern Sudan and the neighbouring countries of Ethiopia, Kenya, Uganda, Zaire and the Central African Republic were arbitrarily drawn by the imperial powers that colonized the Sudan and her neighbours. Thus one finds that some tribes in the Southern Sudan spill over the border into the neighbouring countries.

Climate

The climate of the Sudan may be described as tropical continental. But whereas the country merges into desert in the north, it runs into an equatorial belt (rainy climate) in the south. One could say that the climatic regime in the Southern Sudan lies between the tropical and the equatorial. When the north wind blows over the Southern Sudan, there is, however, a dry season lasting for about three months. But although the expected rains at this time are often less than 1.2 inches, the humidity is quite high. The season between January and 15th March is the hottest of the year, the mean daily temperature in Juba in February and March being 84.2°F and 84.6°F respectively. August is the coolest month and in Juba there is a mean daily temperature of 77.5°F. This gives an annual range of 7.2°F in Juba, much less than Khartoum's 18.7°F.

The rainy season lasts for five to eight months in the south and for one to three months in certain parts of Northern Sudan. August is the rainiest month in the whole country. In the south, the annual total rainfall exceeds 40 inches but in some areas lengthy periods with little rain may be recorded. There are some local rainfall variations; for example, Eastern Equatoria receives an annual rainfall which is scanty for the latitude: whereas Yambio in the midst of the plateau in the west receives a rainfall amounting to 51 inches, Torit further east in the same latitude, receives 40 inches, and Kapoeta in the north-east receives only 32 inches.

The Physical Features

The diminution of rainfall eastwards is matched by changes in vegetation and soils and this also accounts for the variability in tribal economies, ranging from those that are basically agricultural, to agricultural mixed with pastoral, and then finally to predominantly or exclusively pastoral economies. Close to the borders of Uganda and the Congo, there are hills and plateaux which have been systematically moulded by the weathering and denudation processes characteristic of high temperatures and frequent rainfall. The region shows a clear dendritic drainage pattern and there is also a deep mantle of weathered rock and soil. Professor Lebon has conveniently divided the Southern Sudan into two principal vegetational zones: the deciduous high woodland savanna and swamp grasslands extending from 5°N to 10°N and the modified tropical rain forests of the southern borderlands which extend roughly from 3½°N to 5°N. The Toposa area in Eastern Equatoria, is however, on the whole "grassland alternating with stands of Acacia mallicera" resembling thorny scrub and therefore does not fall within the two zones. South of Malakal is the floating swampy papyrus vegetation and this is known as the Sudd area. The highest mountains in the south are the Imatong and Dongotona — about 4,500 feet. The vegetation on both these mountains is degraded tropical rainforest.

Communications

Communications and transport are not highly developed in the Southern Sudan. Rivers provide the major system of communications and there is a steamer line between Juba and Kosti linking the north and the south. A railway line has also been extended from Western Sudan to Wau in Bahr el Ghazel, and Sudan Airways has recently increased its flights to the Southern provincial headquarters of

Malakal, Juba and Wau. Roads have been developed but they are rough and difficult to use during the rainy season.

Economic Viability

The Southern Sudan is potentially an agricultural country. Shifting cultivation is widely practised and crops such as maize, dura, duldam, groundnuts, cassava, simsim, sweet potatoes and beans are grown. Cotton, tobacco, coffee, rice and sugar cane could be developed on a large scale and some areas have cocoa, tea and sisal. Hunting and fishing are two of the main activities of the people. Some of the fish is sold. Cattle are reared mainly by the Nilotes and it was estimated as early as 1954 that the number of cattle in the Southern Sudan was 2,397,150 and the number of sheep and goats 12,562,100.

Some minerals such as copper, gold and iron ore have been discovered. But although the Southern Sudan is an economically viable area, these riches have not been exploited. The cash economy has been retarded by the long distances from the main markets, and the lack of efficient means of transportation. Most of the traders are from the northern part of the country with a few Greek and Syrian merchants. It was not the intention of the colonial and independent governments (until 1969) to encourage and assist the Southern Sudanese to participate in commerce. The main exports from the south are simsim, groundnuts, timber, peppers, hides, skins, honey, gum and ginned cotton, mangoes and other fruits, coffee, sugar and cattle. Manufactured goods and fuel are the main imports. The recent fighting, however, has made the south dependent on the north, and even grain which could be grown in the south is now brought from the north. Yet on the whole, the south is potentially an agriculturally wealthy area.

The People of the Southern Sudan

Whereas the Northern Sudanese defy any distinct racial classification, the inhabitants of the Southern Sudan are undoubtedly Negroid Africans. They may be divided into three main groups: the Nilotes, the Nilo-Hamites and the Western Sudanic tribes. These groups in turn have their sub-divisions and the total number of tribes and sub-groups in the whole of the Southern Sudan is reckoned to be 572. But the ethnic heterogeneity in the area should not be exaggerated, as all these tribes have a shared feeling of belonging to the Southern Sudan and consider themselves as "one people" of the area.

The Nilotes comprise the Dinka, Nuer, Shilluk, Anuak, Burun, Bor Balanda, Jur, Shilluk Luo and Acholi. The Dinka form the largest single tribe, numbering over a million, and occupy a larger area than any other tribe in the Southern Sudan. They are divided into a number of sub-tribes, for example, the Cic, Bor, Aliab, Agur, and Atot. Most of the Nilotes have an absorbing interest in cattle, which have been given a position of reverence in their customs and traditions.

The Nilo-Hamites have been divided into three major groups based allegedly on cultural affinities and apparent relationships. The Southern Sudanese Nilo-Hamites fall into the northern group and these are the Bari, Mundari, Nyangwara, Pojulu, Kakwa, Kuku, Nyepu, Lokoya, Luluba, Latuko, Lopit and the Ligo. This group may further be divided into three groups based on traditional cultural traits and relationships between them. One group constitutes the Bari, Mundari, Nyangwara, Pojulu, Kakwa, Nyepu and Kuku; the second group is composed of the Lokoya and Luluba and the third group comprises the Latuko and the Lango. The central Nilo-Hamites are represented by the Toposa, Donyiro, Jiye and Turkana but of these the Toposa live only in the Southern Sudan in the Kapoeta district, north of the Didinga hills, while the others spill over the borders. The main occupation of the Nilo-Hamites is cultivation, with some pastoralism. They attach great importance to the existence of rain-chiefs and rain-making.

In the extreme south-west of the country, are the Sudanic tribes who are composed of the Azande (they are actually a group of tribes rather than a single people), the Ndogosere group, the Moru-Madi and the Bongo-Baka groups. The Ndogo-Sere group live near Wau while the Moro-Madi group is divided linguistically into three sub-groups: the Moru, who occupy the Meridi and Amadi districts; the Avukaya and the Kaliko, who live in Yei District, extending into the Congo and Uganda; and the Madi, who inhabit the Opari and Nimule areas spilling over into Uganda. Some of these tribes keep a few animals but the Azande are exclusively cultivators.

REFERENCES

K. M. Barbour, *The Republic of the Sudan: A Regional Geography* (London, 1961).
J. H. G. Lebon, *Land Use in Sudan* (London, 1965).

2

THE SOUTHERN SUDAN QUESTION*

Abel Alier

It is perhaps proper to ask the question: What is the problem of the Southern Sudan? What is the Southern Question? I could answer it in a few lines but this would diminish its complexity and one would not be in a position to judge for oneself what ought to be done, or what has been done, to solve it. Some of the aspects of this problem are historical, others are cultural and yet others are economic. Some of it has become psychological. But the problem was essentially one of neglect by the British administration between 1898 and 1952 to develop the Southern Sudan.

To get a total view it is necessary to focus attention on a summary of the past and recent history of the Southern Sudan. Three distinct historical phases are relevant to this topic. First, the Turco-Egyptian activities and the Mahdia in the Southern Sudan; second, the British re-occupation of the Southern Sudan and finally, post-independence rule of the Southern Sudan.

I. THE TURCO-EGYPTIAN ACTIVITIES AND THE MAHDIA IN THE SUDAN

Looking briefly into the first phase, we notice that the first important foreigner to visit the Southern Sudan was an official of the Turco-Egyptian Government, one Captain Selim. He penetrated the Sudd and reached Gondokoro for the second time during his visit in about 1841. His mission was to explore the country for commerce and for strategic spots that could be useful in times of occupation of the Southern Sudan and further exploration into the source of the Nile in East and Central Africa. The idea came from Mohamed Ali, Viceroy of Turkey in Egypt, whose imperial ambitions to obtain colonies in Africa could not have been less than those of his contemporaries in Belgium and Britain. Selim's sojourn was followed by increased visits to the Southern Sudan, all arranged by the

* This is a final integrated version of speeches of Mr. Abel Alier.

Khartoum Government and aimed at collecting ivory and other available wealth to enhance the dwindling resources of the Egyptian treasury. This effort was later improved upon, and on to the scene came people like Baker, Gordon and Emin. With the news of opportunities for commerce in the Southern Sudan spreading to the Northern Sudan, Europe and what is the present Middle East, the merchant class came into the South. The rush made ivory scarce, so slavery and cattle raiding became handy substitutes. Rivalry sprang up between the merchants and the Government. Several merchants attempted to establish pseudo-governments within their trading domains. At the time of the appearance of the Egyptian Government agent and the merchant, the missionary, too, came on to the scene. This was the period of Christian zeal to preach the word of God to the heathen and make the native soft and submissive, for easy colonial management. What then was the reaction of the Southern Sudan to this sudden and unceremonious appearance of the foreigner? What was the attitude of the different foreigners towards the people of the Southern Sudan; in other words, what was the opinion of the people of the Northern Sudan, the Turco-Egyptians, the missionary, and the British like Baker and Gordon, and other Europeans? There is abundant evidence that this attitude was not complimentary and it is, I think, well summarized by a distinguished British commentator who stands high in the esteem of those Sudanese who know him: Mr. K. D. D. Henderson. He describes so precisely the attitude of different foreigners towards the people of the Southern Sudan:

"One thing they shared, a common contempt for the Southerner as an inferior being, coupled with complete indifference to his religious ideas, ethics and standard of behaviour, his social and tribal pattern."[1]

What reaction did the Southerner have to the foreigner in 1841 and subsequently? When Captain Selim arrived among the Shilluk and later on among the Dinka and Cic near Shamba in Bahr el Ghazal Province, he was welcomed courteously, and with a great deal of curiosity, and supplied with plenty of food according to the orders of the Reith (Shilluk King), and the Dinka chiefs respectively. But none of these tribal leaders gave Captain Selim audience since his mission was obscure and he did not perhaps match the high social status of these tribal leaders!

Again, neither Baker nor Gordon found sufficient co-operation among the Bari, Lokoya, Latuko and Dinka Bor to make their plans for administration, and settlement in the Southern Sudan a success.

Both Baker and Gordon were compelled by circumstances to steal cattle. There was thus a definite and calculated resistance against them and their successors, and this resistance at times made the tribes overlook inter-tribal feuds. The same reaction and resistance applies to the Mahdia rule. One reads, for instance, of the Nuer annihilation of Arab forces near Tonj in 1895, or of the Mahdist forces recovering from their defeat at the hands of the Dinka.

In short, then, it may be said that five significant trends are noticeable between 1841 and 1898. First, the main concern of the foreigner in the Southern Sudan was trade, either in ivory or slaves. His second preoccupation was to secure a free waterway to the heart of East and Central Africa. Lord Cromer, British representative in Cairo, expressed the position as follows:

> "Although I somewhat regret to say so, we cannot on purely humanitarian ground afford to lose sight of the main British and Egyptian interest . . . That interest as I have frequently stated, appears to me to be that both banks of the Nile from Lake Albert Nyanza to the sea, should be in British or Anglo-Egyptian hands. The good government of the wild tribes in the interior, even the possession of districts which may be commercially productive, are, relatively speaking, of minor importance."[2]

Third, the period is characterized by the lack of a government presence with effective control over the Southern Sudan. This applies both to the Turco-Egyptian and the Mahdist periods. Fourth, a definite clash of cultures, beliefs and general ways of life of the foreigners on the one hand and the Southern people on the other intensified the conflict between the two groups. Fifth, there was unremitting resistance by the people of the Southern Sudan to foreign influence. This resistance was a reaction against the slave trade, plundering property, stealing animals and burning dwellings, the occupation of land contrary to local customs and beliefs and introduction and the imposition of alien customs and beliefs into tribal life.

II THE ANGLO-EGYPTIAN COLONIAL RULE AND THE SOUTHERN SUDAN

The second phase in the brief history relevant to this is the period between 1898 and 1952. The Sudan was reconquered and the sole task of the British in the Southern Sudan was to establish law and order. Unlike the Northern Sudan, which had accepted defeat and its implications and felt, wisely, that it was a better policy, or at least a convenient one, to settle and develop economically and oscially, the Southern Sudan continued to defy British authority. Mr. Duncan, writing in 1956 after serving in posts in the Sudan

political service in different parts of the country, said in defence of
the British and the Northern Sudan and in justification of the
backwardness of the Southern Sudan, that the Southerner lagged
behind the Northerner, not because the British did not work for
him, but because of the *"obstinacy of his forebears"*.[3]

Mr. Duncan meant what he said and a brief account of some events
in the Southern Sudan and some inner thoughts of the Southerner
bear him out rather well. For instance, and to mention only a few
clashes between condominium administration and some tribes and
personalities in the Southern Sudan: in 1912, the Anuak in Upper
Nile Province killed 47 soldiers including five officers; in 1919 the
Aliab Dinka in Bahr El Ghazal killed Governor Chauncey Stigand;
in 1927 the Nuer killed their District Commissioner, Mr. Vere
Ferguson; and as recently as 1941 Mr. Wilson, District
Commissioner of Tonj, was severely wounded with a spear by one
of his subjects in the district; up to 1933 the Baris still entertained
the happy belief that the foreigner who was building Juba would
disappear just as his predecessor who built Gondokoro, Rejaf and
Mongalla had left Bari land. To the Bari, the supposedly temporary
huts the tribe occupied were in fact more permanent than the
grandiose building of the foreigner. The foreigner, whatever
buildings he put up, was there only temporarily and could have no
legitimate claim over Bari land. This might be regarded as a very
simple, unsophisticated expression of a vain optimist, but I believe
it is one that clearly and truthfully expresses an entrenched resentment against a guest who did not come to his host's home with clean
hands. The facts of history generated this resentment and rejection.

May one not conclude that the British did not develop the
Southern Sudan as a punishment for "the obstinacy" of the Southern
people, to use the phrase of Mr. Duncan?

However, in fairness to the British, the problems facing the
Anglo-Egyptian administration were perhaps not fully realized by
many people and particularly by the people of the Southern Sudan.
The slave trade, which had increased in the 1870s, was assuming
unprecedented proportions in subsequent years prior to re-
occupation of the country. For although people like Zubeir Pasha
were no longer on the scene, Mohammed Aggad, Ismail Zubeir
and others were active. The traffic was also undertaken by petty
traders and it continued despite all the precautions taken and
attempts to stamp it out. Herein lies the origin and occasion for the
declaration of the Southern policy of 1930, which cemented a social
and commercial barrier between the people of the Southern Sudan
and the people of the Northern Sudan.

Southern Policy

The immediate reasons prompting the Southern policy could be defended. Those who were trading in the Southern Sudan from the time it was opened up until the time of reconquest had been somewhat ruthless in their dealings with the local people. Cattle raiding and the plundering of dura and other foodstuff were very common. In addition to this, most of these traders were generally associated with the slave trade. At the time the Southern policy was announced, secret trade routes of slave traffic were discovered in Bahr El Ghazal. Finally, and most importantly, the South and North were two different regions whose political and economic unification had hitherto not been successfully achieved by any administration. It seemed, therefore, legitimate for the administration of 1898 to enforce restrictions that were thought necessary in all circumstances and particularly in respect of security. It is, however, difficult to defend the whole of this policy and the way it was executed. The prohibition of Arabic, the abolition of Arab names, the wholesale accusations against all Northerners of being slave dealers, and the advantage given to Christian missionaries over Moslem preachers, made the whole policy look somewhat ridiculous. It is in the interest of anyone (and the Southerner is no exception) to know as many foreign languages as he is able to learn. The prohibition of Arabic in the Southern Sudan was not in any conceivable manner in the interest of the people, whether they were ultimately to be independent, or to throw their lot in with the North or East Africa. As for names, it is the private business of the father and the mother to choose a name for their child and for a grown-up to change his. A Government which thus engaged in the prohibition of particular names betrayed its own inherent inadequacy.

All these provisions marred the essential merits of the policy which were the attempt to preserve the cultures of the people of the Southern Sudan; the need to give time to the people of the Southern Sudan to regain their self-assurance, which had been shaken during the second half of the nineteenth century; the stamping out of the slave trade, which was flourishing in spite of official prohibition; and the prevention of a situation obtaining in East Africa where the Indian controlled both petty trade and farming to the exclusion of the indigenous people. The importance of the Southern policy to the present topic lies in the reaction it provoked during the national rule. Apart from literature written on the subject (or perhaps because of this literature), the official policy after independence has amounted to a confirmation of the British fear about the future of the people of the Southern Sudan in the hands of Northern-dominated bureaucracy and government. For instance, post-independence development of languages and cultures in the South has been stopped. Not only that, these languages have been abolished in schools and replaced by Arabic, English and French. Teachers who could only teach in Southern languages lost their jobs if they did not pass a course in Arabic.

In 1959-64 wholesale propaganda in the South and especially in Equatoria Province was spread against Christian names and in favour of Arabic names. In Meridi and Lui, lists were drawn up every morning and posted on the official notice boards by local Government inspectors and Medical Officers, of Government officials who had rejected the "foreign names" of "John" or "Barnabas" and the "foreign religion" in favour of the "national names" of "Ibrahim" or "Abbas" and the "national religion". The Missionary Societies Act of 1962 was passed to limit and discourage the expansion of Christianity, and a department of religious affairs was created in the Ministry of Education for the encouragement and spread of Islam. No similar department existed for the Christian religion till the May 1969 military coup. A department of Christian affairs has now been set up and is manned by Southern and Northern Sudanese Christians. Most Southern officials were transferred to and kept in the North in the interest of security during the Abboud regime. However, during the October Government,[4] many Southerners were transferred back to the South. But they were returned to the North after the fall of the October Government in June 1965. The May Revolutionary Government has, with relief, adopted the October policy, and many Southerners are being sent back to serve in the South.

The Juba Conference

The second major event after the Southern policy is, of course, the Juba conference of 1947. There are two commonly accepted opinions about this conference. The first is that the conference was about whether or not the South should unite with the North. The second is that the majority of Southerners in that conference had decided for unity with the North.

One's reading of the proceedings of the conference does not lead one to accept either of these popular positions. The Civil Secretary had decided on the unity of the South and North before the conference was even thought of. His decision on unity was made in 1946 and he was encouraged by the Sudan administration conference recommendations of March 31st, 1947, to formulate a public statement of the new policy for the Southern Sudan. In June 1946 members of the Sudan Administrative Conference, which was discussing the next step in the devolution of power at the centre, flew to Juba to get a swift impression of the South. A demand for fusion of the North and South and for representation of both in the proposed new legislative Assembly followed, and the new Civil Secretary, J. W Robertson, made up his mind that separation was no longer practicable. The Conference of Juba, then, was not about "Unity". This was decided for the South by the Civil Secretary. It was about whether the South should be represented in the Legislative Assembly. The view that the majority of Southerners at the conference were in favour of one legislative assembly is not borne out by the proceedings. On the first day of the conference, all the Southerners objected to one assembly On the second day, six spoke in favour of one assembly, four spoke against it. The rest were not given a chance to talk and there was no voting to show whether or not they had changed their stand of the previous day. The proceedings do not indicate that the six who spoke in favour of one legislative assembly spoke on behalf of the other, silent, seven. It is therefore clear from the proceedings that the majority of Southerners were not in favour of one legislative assembly. But, of course, the Civil Secretary, having already decided on "Unity", would not stand for a contradiction of his view. It was, after all, not his idea to have this conference. To him, two legislative assemblies, one for the North, the other for the South, or an assembly where the South was not represented, virtually meant continuing the status quo between North and South and this would be contrary to the position already taken by the Civil Secretary. So he made his position known to the conference the following day and rejected the idea of an Advisory Council for the South in preference to Provincial Councils. He emphasized that this was what the North would readily accept. What the Civil Secretary said must have had a fundamental influence on the six who spoke in favour of one legislative assembly. It is also possible that the six had entertained the belief that the South would fare better in the proposed system than they had done under the British. Mohammed Saleh Shengeiti and his colleagues, representing the North, spared no effort to make a South-North union attractive to the Southern representatives. He lived long enough to appreciate the increasing claims of the South for political and cultural recognition and for equality of opportunity in participating in the formulation of state policies. Shengeiti was disturbed in 1967 when he learned that Chief Lolik Lado, a member of the 1947 Juba conference and a member of the Board of Enquiry into the Southern Disturbances of 1955, had in 1966 narrowly escaped with his life from the Sudan army at Liria, Eastern Equatoria in the South. Lolik had in the 1947 conference pleaded caution in establishing a unified administration between South and North. He recalled the violent relations between the North and South of the past and thought it might be difficult to expect any change for the better. He was, however, prepared to observe closely the new generation of Northerners before the South made up its mind about its future relations with the North. He is quoted in the Minutes of the conference as having said:

"A girl who had been asked to marry a young man usually wanted time to hear reports of that young man from other people before consenting; likewise Southerners before coming to any fixed decisions about their relations with the Northerners need time. The ancestors of the Northern Sudanese were not peace-loving and domesticated like cows. The younger generation said that they meant no harm, but time would show what they would in fact do."[5]

Two points are clear in the Juba conference. The first is that the Southerners indicated sufficiently their fear and suspicion of the North, though they also recognized that they had received equal treatment with the North at the hands of the British Administration. Second, the stand of the Southerner in the conference has been misunderstood by those whose overwhelming desire was to see "Unity" established between South and North in the shortest possible time and without regard to the gap — economic, social and political — that existed between the two regions.

Prelude to Independence

The next phase is the Anglo-Egyptian Agreement of 1952. The South was, of course, left out of the negotiations. There are some good arguments justifying the non-representation of the South. It is said the South had no political organizations to send representatives to Cairo. Unity was established between the North and South in 1947 so it was quite legitimate for the Northern politicians to represent the Sudanese as a people and the Sudan as a political unit. These may be sound arguments; but their soundness is based on what was clearly a mistake. The Southerners hold this point against both the Northern politicians of the time and the British particularly. Southerners needed safeguards in a new Sudan and they were the best people to press for safeguards in the 1952 Anglo-Egyptian negotiations.

Perhaps the next most vivid events of pre-independence were Sudanization (nationalization of jobs), the mutiny and the move to independence. A brief account of each of these events is thus necessary in so far as it relates to our discussion.

Sudanization

That the South was dissatisfied with Sudanization is no longer in dispute. The Cotran Report did not hesitate to state that one of the causes of the mutiny was the failure of the government of the time to keep some of its election promises; another was the attitude of some

Northern administrators who chose to assume the arrogant air of
rulers. Sudanization brought friction between the then Prime
Minister, the late Ismail El Azhari, and the only two staunch
Southern supporters of the government, Sayed Bullen Alier and
Sayed Dak Dei. They were those on whom depended the task of
assuring Southerners of the good intentions of the Northern
Administration; with them thrown out of the cabinet, the gap
between South and North widened. The failure of the government to
give special attention to the South thus increased the fears and
suspicions of Southerners in a United Sudan. The voice of the
intellegentsia began now to be heard in offices, politically-organized
groups, and in schools. In 1954 the Liberal Party conference in Juba
condemned the way Sudanization was carried out and demanded
federal status for the South. The Juba Training Centre organized a
boycott of the Prime Minister in the Southern Club in Juba; and
enlightened Southern opinion put pressure on Southern members
of Parliament in the government to leave.

The Mutiny

The mutiny of 1955 had many causes, which are well summarized
in the Cotran Report. But in short, the mutiny was due to the
increasing fear and suspicion which had come about as the result of
the situation described above. However, its effect on both Northerners and Southerners was far-reaching in terms of the future political
relations between the two parts of the country. The Northerners
witnessed the tragic deaths of some of their fellow countrymen and
close relatives. Most of these persons were unarmed and unaware
that their death was imminent; some of them had the best of
intentions for the South and its people; some of them were women
and children who, in the best traditions of both primitive and modern
warfare, should not have been touched. In 1965 it was the turn of the
South to witness similar tragedies. The events of 1955 were still fresh
in mind, and those given the responsibility of maintaining security
in the South from July 1965 had either personally witnessed the
mutiny of 1955 or had lost a friend or a relative. Given the freedom
to decide and act in the light of the facts on the spot, it was not
surprising that those security officials permitted the tragic events of
Wau and Juba in July 1965, and other towns and villages
subsequently.

Independence

Independence came as a result of agreement between North and
South based on a firm pledge on the part of the North to work out a
federal relationship as a safeguard against cultural assimilation, the
monopoly of policy-making, of jobs, social services and economic
development plans, and also to eliminate the Southerners' fear and

C

suspicion of the North, as expressed at the 1947 Juba conference.

III. POST-INDEPENDENCE RULE AND THE SOUTHERN SUDAN

The Military Regime

The military government of General Abboud brought the relationship between the North and South near to disaster. The bottling-up of political ideas and freedom was bad in the North and South alike. But the South had more to suffer and more to be aggrieved about. A Southern policy, in reaction to that of 1930, was initiated. The Southerner, whatever his position, was suspect, and most of the Southern employees were transferred to the North. Their stay in the North, supporting families and paying rents which were quite high, and put in offices where they did practically nothing because of the lack of a working knowledge of Arabic, created frustration and sometimes left bitterness. The passing of the Missionary Societies Act in 1962 restricted the activity of the Christian church in winning more converts in the South. The imprisonment of schoolboys who protested against the abolition of Sunday as a public holiday, an act that had had no parallel in the North, was yet another grievance. Physical violence by government agents in remote areas of the South drove many people into exile and led to the taking up of arms by some Southern dissidents; sizeable numbers of sub-grade teachers, who had for years been teaching school children through the medium of their local languages, lost their jobs on the introduction of Arabic as the medium of instruction; the almost complete cessation of recruitment of Southerners to police, military and prison colleges was, again, another grievance. The recruitment of policemen in Blue Nile and Kordofan Provinces for training and later posting to the Southern Provinces became an accepted practice; and it was out of the question of course to have Southern recruits. Those few Southerners who got into the army did so as a gesture from the individual military officials and strictly on a personal basis. It requires special mention that the recruitment of police and army was not fundamentally changed till after the May Revolution. Between 1959 and 1964 a total number of 352 cadets were recruited to the military college. Only four of these were Southerners. From 1965 to May 25th, 1969, a total number of 366 cadets were recruited: only six were Southerners. Over three-quarters of the police recruited for the Southern provinces used to come from Blue Nile, Kordofan and Darfur Provinces till this practice was changed after the May Revolution. Recruitment of police for the South is now done in the South and from Southerners. About 650 Southern policemen have been recruited in the South alone between June 1969 and July 1970. This number excludes those Southerners recruited in the Northern Sudan to serve there. In October 1968 Equatoria Province had three hundred recruits. Of these, only 68 were Southerners. Decisions in all these areas of action were not just the work of the military regime. All except a very few Northern officials in the South and at the centre of decision-making in Khartoum participated willingly and with approval in the formulation and execution of these policies. One understands why some of these policies were adopted then. The Southerner could not be trusted. Given a sensitive job, or otherwise put in some responsible position, he might use this position to the detriment of the state. And this suspicion and fear are based on reasonable grounds. Some Southern policemen and soldiers have killed Northern Sudanese or fled with their rifles. From 1960 similar treatment has been meted out to Southerners by Northern soldiers. But what does all this prove except that increased suspicion and fear of one another has affected both the South and North, and this increased distrust has now become a part of the Southern problem.

The Post-Military Regime

The story of the fall of the reactionary military regime of General Abboud is familiar, together with claims by many in the South and North to credit for the overthrow of that regime. What is of interest here are the events following the government of General Abboud. We confine ourselves to what affects the Southern Sudan alone. Grim and forbidding though the military rule might have been, it gave the Southern intelligensia an opportunity to play a unique role in exposing to the world, particularly the African world, what kind of future the people of the Southern Sudan faced, physically, culturally, economically and politically, and one might add, morally, as a result of the repressive measures of that regime against the South, and as a result of a clash of cultures and ways of life of indigenous negro-Africans and Afro-Arabs in the Sudan — as a result, in fact, of the refusal to recognize the facts of diversity in the Sudan; and as a result of the refusal to share power and wealth among the peoples of both regions.

What was being done in the Sudan in all the departments of state activity (education, religion, economics, culture, language, politics, etc.), was analysed and disseminated abroad, and literature was composed and distributed by a Southern elite appearing for the first time in the 1960s. The period of General Abboud's regime is not only notable for awakening the Southern elite to serious political work; it also witnessed the replacement of the old by a new set of political leaders who would measure up to the intellect of the old guard in the North, though sometimes lacking the wealth and experience of the latter.

Round Table Conference, March, 1965

Viewing, then, all the grievances of the South up to the time of the October Revolution in 1964, the issues facing the October government were somewhat clearer. Could political accommodation be found for the South in one United Sudan? And what was the nature of this accommodation? It was the desire to search for a solution that led to the convening of the Round Table Conference in March, 1965. This was attended by Southern representatives from inside the country and from outside. The positions taken by Southern representatives were threefold: self-determination, separation and federation. Those who claimed separation had not mentioned why. The speech of Aggrey Jaden (the President of Southerners in exile) may be summarized into two arguments. First, in the past the South and North were not one country politically and whatever political union may exist now came without the consent of the South — James Robertson decided Union alone in 1946; the 1953 Anglo-Egyptian Agreement leading to self-government status was an agreement between Britain, Egypt and the Northern Sudan; the 1955 "Independence motion" was based on a *quid pro quo*. That is, the South agreed on the "independence motion" moved by the North provided, and on a clear understanding, that the South and North should be two federal states. The North dishonoured its part of the agreement in 1958 when it rejected federation in the 1957 Draft constitution (so runs the argument); thus the South is not bound to respect its part. The other part of the argument was simple: that separation could be effected by agreement. The federalists argued very simply and logically. The undertaking of the North on December 19th, 1955, to create federal states, of which the South would be one, should now be reaffirmed by the North. Those who stood for self-determination had been misunderstood, partly because many people did not quite understand the term "self-determination", and partly because the position taken allowed very little room for the Northern political leaders to avoid facing the Southern problem. Many thought (wrongly, of course) that this stand meant separation. In a way, those who equated separation with self-determination might also have been right, but only because they suspected that the result of free choice by Southerners might be separation.

The argument of the Southern Front in the conference was that history had shown that the South and North were two different countries. The South had not been asked to make its own conscious decision about its political and economic future. It should now be given this chance to make up its own mind. It had now become reasonably conscious about its pre-Anglo-Egyptian position in relation to the North; its Anglo-Egyptian position in relation to the North; and the period between 1954—1964 in partnership with the North. Self-determination might be the affirmation of the *status quo* obtaining after December 31st, 1955, but separation, federation, and regional autonomy were alternative and plausible ranges of choice. This position was framed for three reasons (i) the facts of history, given above; (ii) to answer the current argument among Northern politicians that all Southerners wanted unity and only a handful of adventurers wished to disturb the *status quo;* (iii) the group representing this latter view thought that the events of 1955, where much blood had been tragically shed in many places in the South, induced repulsion and the temptation to take revenge upon Northerners. They also thought the violence of the reactionary military regime in the South and the Sunday incident of December 6th, 1964, indicated the volcanic future of North-South relations. The Sudan was a country where relations were deteriorating fast instead of improving, because the majority looked upon the other group as inferior and because mutual suspicion and fear existed. No recognition was being made of the cultures, languages, and ways of life of one group by another. Such a country might in future explode irreparably and it would be a wiser and more humane policy to reconsider the political ties and the basis of this nation-state, bearing these problems in mind. The group at a disadvantage should on moral grounds be entitled to decide its destiny.

The tragedies beginning in July 1965 in the South confirmed the Southern Front analysis of the South-North relations. The incident of December 6th, 1964, had demonstrated the continued existence of North-South tension.[6]

However, the Round Table Conference has its other, unique, importance in the political history of the Southern Sudan. Its place will be alongside the Juba conference of 1947 and the Independence motion of 1955. Ten years after independence the South showed increased concern about its future. Its fears were no longer based on the slave trade, although Aggrey Jaden might quote this in extension of his more immediate reasons, but on the experience of ten years of independence. The Round Table Conference did, however, find some tentative solution to remove the fears of the South in a United Sudan. The answers are the recommendations of the twelve-man committee appointed by the Round Table Conference. After extensive work over more than a year, the committee recommend that the existing arrangement of heavy centralization was unsuitable. It also said that the South need not separate from the North. It recommended a detailed system of regional autonomy for the Sudan. Recruitment of police was to be done locally; district officers were to be appointed from the region; there would be a regional legislature and a regional Commissioner who should be a citizen of the region; education was to be shared by the Central Government and the region; local culture would be preserved and encouraged and local languages would be taught in schools; and there would be a regional economic planning committee. No agreement was reached on two points. The first was the number of regions that would constitute the South. Southern representatives in the Committee wanted one region; Northern representatives wanted three. The second point was whether the regional commissioner should be elected by the region or nominated by the Head of State. Again, the Southern representatives preferred election while the Northern representatives wanted nomination by the Head of State.

The recommendations of the twelve-man committee were welcome in the South and there was optimism that a basis had been found to ensure national unity, and hence the stability on which depends development and advancement. There were, however, increased fears immediately after the committee's recommendations and quite a sizeable section in the Northern Sudan, especially the professional administrators and the merchants, did not welcome them. Obvious pressures were being brought to bear on some of the Northern political parties to shelve the recommendations of the twelve-man committee, even after their endorsement by all Sudanese political parties at the conference of 1957 and on the National Draft Constitution Committee of 1967.

The Islamic Constitution and the Southern Sudan

In 1967, a new element of especially grave concern among Southerners, as well as the Socialists and liberals in the North, appeared. It was the vigorous drive for an Islamic constitution. The element became markedly apparent after the October Revolution had handed over power to the elected Assembly in 1965. The various aspects of the Islamic constitution were stated in Sayed Saddiq El Mahdi's maiden address as Premier to the constituent Assembly in October 1966, when he said:

> "The dominant feature of our nation is an Islamic one and its over-powering expression is Arab, and this Nation will not have its entity identified and its prestige and pride preserved except under an Islamic revival."[7]

Dr. Hassan Turabi, the youthful leader of the then Islamic Charter Front had on several occasions expressed himself in similar vein. He argued that the South had no culture, so this vacuum would necessarily be filled by Arab culture under an Islamic revival. This view dominated the discussion of the first and second constitution commissions in 1967 and 1968.

With the Arab revival successfully enshrined in the Islamic constitution, the Southerner would remain an outsider, useful only because his number would add to the prestige and status of his Northern counterpart. Thus the people of the Southern Sudan saw in the Islamic constitution the supreme expression of a way of life, of a culture, of a mystique known as the "Arab Nation".

Because of the overriding religio-racial components of the constitution, Christian, Moslem and pagan Afro-Negro Southerners appeared unanimous in their rejection of such a document. In this situation the Southern representatives, for whom I had the honour to be spokesman, left the constitution commission at the end of December 1968. We did not wish to be party to a document that emphazised the Arab race, Islamic religion and Arab culture to the exclusion of other existing races, religions and culture. It would have made nonsense of a regional autonomy anyway. The people of the Southern Sudan have learnt something of the religions of Christianity and Islam. But these religions have not affected the way of life and the indigenous cultures of the people of the Southern Sudan up to this moment. A person still has the option to follow his religion and preserve his culture and identity. In being told to accept the rule of a constitution based on religion, the Southerners were being told they would become aliens in the Arab world and its cultures, exiles from the negro-African world. They were being told to say goodbye to their cultures and their general way of life. They also saw in the Islamic constitution a legal instrument of state discrimination against non-Moslems. One might therefore agree with Professor Arnold Toynbee, who sees the problem as a conflict between two Africas: Negro-Africa and Afro-Arab-Africa. Throughout the years, the role played by the Arab world in the South-North conflict has been in favour of the North. This has provoked concern for the South. It should provoke similar concern for the other Afro-negroes in East, Central and West Africa.

The May Revolution

On the 25th day of May 1969, the Chairman of the Revolutionary Council, Major-General Jaafar Mohammed Nimeiry, outlined the reasons that had led him and other members of the Revolutionary Council to take over power in the country. Two significant reasons relevant to the Southern question were mentioned. The first was that the Revolutionary Government was to work for social justice and self-sufficiency for the people, especially those underprivileged living in the rural areas. The Southern Sudan falls, of course, under this general category. In the last fourteen years what little development there had been was concentrated in Khartoum, with the result that citizens were abandoning their livelihoods to go to Khartoum for jobs. The second point mentioned in the statement was the failure of previous governments to solve the Southern problem. On June 9th, after several days of combined meetings of the Revolutionary Council and Council of Ministers, a policy for the Southern Sudan was announced. The statement recognized: (i) the existence of the Southern problem; (ii) the cultural and historical differences between North and South; (iii) the right of the Southern people to develop their separate cultures and traditions and (iv) the right of the Southern people to regional self-government. The Revolutionary Government laid down a six-point programme of work:

1. Continuation and extension of the amnesty law of 1967. It was extended in October 1969 for another year.
2. Economic, social and cultural development of the South.
3. Appointment of a Minister for Southern Affairs.
4. Training of personnel to help in the administration of the South.
5. Creation of a special economic planning board.
6. A special budget for the South.

The statement emphasized two important points. The first was that the Revolution was a continuation of October 1964. The October Government had recognized for the first time the existence of the Southern problem and the need to solve it. If the October revolutionaries had not been ousted from power by the forces of reaction in 1965, the problem of the Southern Sudan would have been happily regarded as history today. But the revolutionary forces could not withstand the tide of reaction. The first group to be forgotten were the Free Officers who refused to open fire on demonstrators at the Republican Palace in October, and compelled General Abboud to dissolve the council of ministers and the council for the armed forces. The next to go were the socialists. It was the Free Officers of October 1964 who staged the Revolution of May 1969.

The second important point is that the Revolutionary Government called upon all Southerners abroad, in the bush and at home to see that peace and stability prevailed and life returned to normal; all in order to assist the Government in carrying out the programme for the South.

Observers may say that they do not think such a solution is adequate. It seems to me, if my assessment of public opinion is correct for the South, that the policy and the solution proposed is acceptable. I witnessed both the events of October 1964 and the June 9th, 1969 announcement in Khartoum, and I do not think the

Southerners received the October Revolution as they received the announcement of the policy on June 9th. Others may say that such statements are easy to make, and ask what guarantee there is that this government is different from those in power before and after October. To this question, one can only say that all that is wanted from both the observer and the participant in this situation is their goodwill and patience. Time is merciful, and it is very important that this process should be peaceful and that armed conflict should be abandoned as undesirable, destructive and self-defeating. The time is not very far away, I believe, when the people of the Southern Sudan will make their contribution to the development and well-being of the Sudan, and to the cause of the continent of Africa and humanity at large.

At the time of writing (9th February 1970), the following steps had been taken by the Government in pursuance of its policy:

(i) A Ministry of Southern Affairs had been set up.

(ii) An Indemnity (amendment) Act was passed in 1969 effective for a further year under which all Southerners who came back would not be subject to any inquiry or prosecution.

(iii) £4 million was appropriated in 1970 for the development of health, sugar cane, coffee and tea plantations, and agricultural experiments—fish, fruit and vegetable, and water development.

(iv) 644 Southern policemen had been recruited, 17 Southern Officer cadets went to the Military Colleges and Southern Sudanese had been appointed to responsible positions, e.g. Foreign Affairs.

(v) An economic planning board had been set up in Juba.

(vi) A third senior secondary school had been opened in Mallakal.

(vii) A Department of Christian Affairs had been set up in the Ministry of Education.

REFERENCES

1 K. D. D. Henderson, *Sudan Republic* (London, 1965), Chapter 10, p. 153.

2 Muddathir 'Abd Al-Rahim, "Fourteen Documents on the Problems of the Southern Sudan", Ministry of Foreign Affairs, Khartoum, 1965.

3 See J. S. R. Duncan, *The Sudan: A Record of Achievement* (Edinburgh and London, 1952), Chapters II and III.

4 Referred to the civilian government that replaced the military junta in October, 1964.

5 See Mohammed Omer Beshir, *The Southern Sudan, Background to Conflict* (London, 1968), Appendix 9, p. 143.

6 This incident was touched off by Southern demonstrators in Khartoum but followed by Northern excesses in which some 200 Southerners were killed.

7 See *Proceedings of the Sudan Constituent Assembly*, October, 1966.

3

ARABISM, AFRICANISM, AND SELF-IDENTIFICATION IN THE SUDAN

Muddathir 'Abd Al-Rahim*

Physically, culturally, and ethnically the Republic of the Sudan is a microcosm of Africa. Its achievements, problems, and potentialities are in many respects typical of those of other African or Afro-Asian countries — particularly the belt of 'Sudanic' states which runs across the continent from the Horn and the Red Sea in the East to the Atlantic Ocean in the West. Thus, like the great majority of Afro-Asian countries, the Sudan has been subjected to alien rule for considerable periods during its modern history; its existing boundaries, administrative institutions, and cultural outlook have been largely moulded by its colonial masters; it developed a nationalist movement whose primary objective was the achievement of independence; and, since the fulfilment of that objective, it has been faced with a host of problems, chief amongst which is the erosion of nationalism, in the sense of loyalty to the homeland as a whole, and the resurgence or development of a variety of particularistic tendencies, loyalty to which has in some cases equalled or even surpassed loyalty to the nationalism under whose banner independence was won.

In at least one respect, however, the Sudan is unique among African countries and differs from even those 'Sudanic' states which it resembles most: it is at one and the same time both 'African' and 'Arab', the combination being present — especially in the six northern provinces — to a degree and in a manner which are not paralleled in any other country. All Sudanic states share the attribute, frequently associated with the Nilotic Sudan, of forming a bridge between what are usually referred to as 'Arab' or North Africa and 'Black' or Sub-Saharan Africa and, as a rule, experience tensions

* This article is a revised version of a paper presented at the international conference on "The Sudan in Africa" (convened by the University of Khartoum's Sudan Research Unit in 1968), and subsequently published in the *Journal of Modern Africa Studies*, 8, 2 (1970).

between their northern regions — which are predominantly Islamic in character and outlook — and their southern, mainly 'pagan' or Christian regions. But none of them can be said to constitute an Arab-African entity in the same sense or to the same extent as the Sudan. This is obvious for Somalia, Chad, Niger, Mali, Nigeria, and Senegal, for instance, all of which are to a greater or lesser degree Islamic, and, therefore, closely connected with the Arab world, but none of which is either wholly or partly Arabic-speaking like the Sudan. It is true, but for the reverse reason, even of Mauritania, whose southern regions, unlike those of the Sudan, are almost completely Islamized and Arabized, while its northern regions are practically inseparable from the main body of Maghrebi culture and society.

ARABIZATION AND AFRICANIZATION: GROWTH OF A SYNTHESIS

The fact that the Sudan in general and its northern provinces, in particular, constitute a unique meeting point of Arabism and Africanism is the result of the geography and history of the land. The country is located in the north-eastern part of the continent so that it is separated from Arabia by the Red Sea (which has been crossed, particularly at its narrow southern end, since man was first able to devise rafts and boats); it directly borders on Egypt, to which it is also linked by the Nile, while, at the same time, it stretches deep into the heart of Africa. With its one million square miles (an area as vast as that of Spain, Italy, France, the United Kingdom, Portugal, Sweden, Norway, Denmark, and Belgium put together), it is the largest country in Africa and incorporates large sub-Saharan as well as Saharan areas. Finally, the Nile and its tributaries, which link the Sudan with East and Central Africa as well as Egypt in the North, is, for the most part, easily navigable throughout the year.[1]

Considering these factors, it is not surprising that the Sudan, though deeply entrenched in Africa, has had a long history of close contact with the worlds of the Mediterranean and the Middle East, particularly Egypt and Arabia. The Bible, Pharaonic scriptures, and monuments — both in Egypt and the Sudan[2] — as well as the historians and chroniclers of ancient Greece and Rome, have all testified to the involvement of the 'Cushites' or 'Nubians', as the indigenous ancestors of the Northern Sudanese were called, in the affairs of Egypt, Palestine, Syria, and Arabia. The most outstanding instance of such involvement in ancient times was the conquest of Egypt by the Cushites under King Piankhy (751-716 B.C.), where they founded the twenty-fifth Pharaonic dynasty and thence proceeded to conquer Syria and Palestine under the leadership of their celebrated King Taharqa (668-663 B.C.), whose name is mentioned in the Bible in more than one passage.[3] In most cases, however, the trend of conquest or political domination — usually channelled through Egypt, the most important link between the Sudan and the outside world, especially after the rise of Islam — ran in the opposite direction, both in ancient and modern times. Thus the Pharaohs, the Persians, the Greeks, the Romans, the Arabs, the Turks, and the British — all those who governed or conquered Egypt in the past — have, in turns, found it either necessary or desirable to try (with different degrees of success) to extend their influence if not their power beyond the traditional boundaries of Egypt, between the first and the second cataracts, into the lands which now constitute the Republic of the Sudan.

Of all those conquerors and would-be conquerors, the Muslim Arabs were the most successful; their culture and religion, having replaced those of Rome, Greece and ancient Egypt, have been of lasting effect in the Sudan.

Relations between the Sudan and Arabia, as indicated above, have existed since the dawn of history. But the process of Arabization of the Sudan, as of Egypt, North Africa, and much of Western Asia, did not start until the rise of Islam in the seventh century and was a direct produce of Islamization: the twin processes being closely linked ever since — not only in the Sudan, but throughout the Muslim world, both Arab and non-Arab, and in the minds of the modern Arabs in general, whether they happen to be Christian or Muslim.

As with several other countries, both in Africa and in Asia, the Arabization and Islamization of the Sudan was not primarily the result of military conquest.[4] It was mainly brought about through the agency of Muslim Arab immigrants, who — coming from Arabia across the Red Sea, from Egypt after the conquest of 641, and, at a later stage, from the Maghreb — gradually infiltrated the Christian kingdoms of Nubia. Their readiness to mix, coupled with the matriarchal system of the Nubians on the one hand, and the Arabian patriarchal organization of the family and the tribe on the other, had the effect not only of facilitating the assimilation of the immigrants and the spreading of their culture and religion, but also of giving them the reins of power and political leadership in the host society. Ibn Khaldun, writing about the major immigrant groups in the fifteenth century, summarizes the situation with characteristic clarity:

"various tribes of Juhayna Arabs spread over the country, settled in it and made it their own ... At first the Nubian kings tried to resist, but failed. Later on they tried to win them [the Arabs] over by giving them their daughters in marriage. But this led to the passing of power to some of the sons of Juhayna in accordance with the custom of [the Nubians⁵] which vests the right of succession in sisters and their sons. Thus did the Nubians lose their kingdom and their lands passed to the bedouins of Juhayna."⁶

The result of the social and cultural revolution which had thus been effected by the end of the fourteenth and the beginning of the fifteenth centuries was the total transformation of Nubia and the establishment, in 1504, of the Islamic kingdom of the Funj, which lasted until 1821.

With the added advantage of political control over the central Sudan, the by now largely Africanized Arabs were able to penetrate the remoter parts of the land, including areas which were, geographically speaking, decidedly less similar than the central Sudan to Arabia. But they were barred from entering the South by swamps, flies, and tropical humidity, none of which were suitable for camel breeding or attractive to desert people. Some of them, therefore, turned eastwards, entered Abyssinia and settled there, while others moved westwards into Kordofan and Darfur and, moving further west, reached as far as Lake Chad and Bornu in West Central Africa.⁷

The further they went, it seems, the better conditioned they became to their new environment and the greater became their influence through the twin media of racial assimilation and Islamization — which owed a great deal to the religious fraternities or *Tariqas*. The extent of the adaptation of the immigrants to their new African environment and the resulting Arabization of the indigenous population — or, to look at it from the opposite angle, of the Africanization of the immigrant Arabs — can perhaps best be illustrated by reference to the Baggara (i.e. "cattle-men" as distinct from "camel-men" or *jammala*) Arabs, many of whom are ebony-black in colour and who, in order to cope with the wet and muddy conditions of Kordofan and Darfur, have deserted the camel for the bull, which, however, they ride upon and generally treat as if it were a camel.⁸

THE VOCABULARY OF TRADITIONAL POLITICS

In so far as the modern Sudan is concerned, the outstanding result of the historical and social processes outlined in the preceding section has been the Islamization — and to a large, though lesser, extent also the Arabization — of the areas which now constitute the six Northern provinces of the Republic; while the South remained virtually untouched by these influences until the nineteenth century. But neither this, nor the fact that the Arabized sections of the population were simultaneously Arab and African, became the subject of serious dispute or even comment before the establishment of the Anglo-Egyptian regime in 1898 and the subsequent growth and development of modern nationalism in the Sudan.

One reason for this is the fact that the Sudan, as a clearly defined entity and as an object of national loyalty, did not exist before this century. The words *Sudan* and *Sudani*, or Sudanese, were indeed familiar and frequently used, but in the old sense of the original Arabic meaning "Black" as distinct from *Bidan* or "White". Thus medieval Arabs used the expression *Bilad al-Sudan* to denote in general "the lands of the Blacks", and in particular the territories which today roughly correspond to the "Sudanic" group of African states — very much in the same way as the term "Ethiopia" was used by Homer and Herodotus with reference to those lands whose inhabitants were "Ethiops", i.e. "burnt-faced", or "Black". In this sense the terms *Sudan* and *Sudani* are still sometimes used, especially by members of the older generation among the Northern Sudanese, with reference to the non-Muslim and non-Arabized sections of the population, particularly in the Southern provinces. The expression "Sudan" did not even begin to acquire its modern sense, referring to the territories which now constitute the Republic of the Sudan, until well after the beginning of the nineteenth century. Thus the Firman granted to Muhammad Ali Pasha by the Sublime Porte in 1841 refers to the "States of Nubia, Darfur, and Kordofan and Sinnar" as individual and separate entities; nor does the term "Sudan" appear in the Firman of 1866, whereby the viceroyalty of Egypt and those "territories and dependencies" which belonged to it was vested in Khedive Isma'il and his descendants.[9] And when the expression began to be habitually used in official and other statements, during the last third of the century, it signified a loosely defined area which extended as far as the Great Lakes in central Africa and included considerable areas of the Horn and the Somali coast.[10]

Thus neither the word nor the country as we now know them existed before this century.[11] It is obvious therefore that the question of national loyalty could not arise. Nor indeed had the concept of nationalism, as that elusive notion is now generally understood, been introduced into the country or the political vocabulary of its inhabitants at that time. Until at least the beginning of this century, the "Sudanese" identified themselves as members of different tribes and sub-tribes, adherents to various *Tariqas* or religious fraternities, belonging to this or that religion of the country, and (especially the

Northern Sudanese, when thinking of wider affiliation) as Muslim and/or Arab people. But they never thought of themselves as "Sudanese", unless they happened to belong to what were regarded as the less sophisticated, non-Islamized and non-Arabized sections of the population.

Of these four modes of self-identification, tribalism and regionalism, often closely associated if not identical, are the oldest; the main divisions along these lines being, as the Pharaohs of Egypt knew, between the Negroid peoples of the southern hinterlands and the Brown races which inhabited the territories bordering on Egypt on the one hand, and on the other, within the Brown groups themselves, between the Nubians of the central Sudan and the "Blemmyes" or Bejas of the Red Sea Hills. These three main groups were further divided along Tribal and regional lines. The coming of the Arabs, themselves divided into several tribes and sub-tribes, may, from a certain angle, be regarded as having confirmed and accentuated the indigenous pattern of tribal and regional loyalties. Arab tribal divisions, however, existed within the context of the Arabic language and culture, which superseded these divisions, put them on an entirely different plane and perspective from indigenous tribal divisions, and indeed gave the Nubian, Beja, and Negroid peoples of the Sudan what it had already given the Arabs of Arabia: a unifying cultural bond which they had not possessed before.

Islam, the chief motive force behind Arabization, also cut across tribal frontiers and with its strong emphasis on the brotherhood of all Muslims, irrespective of racial or linguistic differences, cemented the Arabized sections of the population among themselves on the one hand, while, on the other, uniting them with those sections of the population — mainly in the eastern, southern, and western fringes of the central Sudan — who accepted Islam but were not likewise Arabized. The unifying processes of Islamization and Arabization have gone so far that, especially by comparison with the Southern Sudan, those tribal differences which still exist in the Northern provinces today are "mainly superficial", as Nadler put it in 1935; that was, significantly, during the hey-day of Native Administration. Consequently, he wrote, "the District Commissioner who is transferred from Berber to Bara, from Kassala to Kordofan, finds that he is dealing, in different local conditions, with the same kind of people, the same mental outlook. Once he has accustomed himself to the differences caused by a varying mode of life, he knows what to expect."[12]

Although Islamization and Arabization have brought about a remarkable degree of cultural unity and social cohesion, they have not, however, been totally devoid of divisive particularism. For the

Islamization of the Sudan (which, as we have already noted, was not brought about by means of military conquest) was largely the product of the missionary activities of a wide spectrum of popular religious fraternities, or *Sufi Tariqas*, each of which was centred around the personality and teachings of a particular saint, Shaikh, or master.

It should perhaps be emphazised that these *Tariqas* did not in any sense constitute religious "sects", like Catholicism or Protestantism in Christianity; nor did they represent such serious cleavages within Sudanese Islam as existed between *Shia'a* and *Sunni* Muslims elsewhere. They operated, by and large, as they still do, within the bounds of Islam as it is generally understood and practised throughout the world, i.e. *Sunni* Islam as distinct from *Shiism* (which, incidentally, is not known in the Sudan); but varying degrees of emphasis on communal worship of a *Sufi*, or mystical, type were recommended by the founding Sheikh and his more important disciples.[13] *Tariqas*, as popular, open and proselytizing associations, have cut across tribal boundaries and, by emphasizing and encouraging mutual sympathy and cooperation among their followers, have also achieved a remarkable degree of unity of purpose and outlook among their adherents. This, however, coupled with the fact that there have been many *Tariqas* in the country, sometimes with numerous sub-*Tariqas* as well, and that religion and politics have traditionally been closely linked in Muslim societies, has resulted in the growth of important, sometimes even bitter, rivalries between some of these *Tariqas*.

Partly for this reason, and partly because he aspired to reform Islam (in the Sudan and elsewhere) by leading Muslims back to the universally accepted and, as it were, untainted original sources, i.e. the *Qur'an* and the *Sunna*, Muhammed Ahmed al-Mahdi tried, among other things, to abolish all *Tariqas* — including those in which he had received his apprenticeship as a religious novice. As might be expected Mahdist puritanism was met by stiff resistance and hostility on the part of the *Tariqas* and was particularly disliked by the Khatmiyya, whose principal leader, Sayyid 'Ali al-Mirghani, was forced to lead the life of an exile in Egypt until the end of the Mahdiyya in 1898. The overthrow of the Mahdist state was, naturally, followed by a revival of Sufism in general and a resurgence of the principal *Tariqas* — Qadiriyya, Summaniyya, Shadhaliyya, and, of course, the Khatmiyya in particular.

Reporting on the increase of the *Tariqas* and their activities in 1901, Lt.-Gen. Reginald Wingate, who was well aware of the relationship between the religious feelings and institutions of the people and their resistance to the new regime, and knew that the

D

Mahdi had himself been nurtured in the *Tariqas*, told Cromer that he hoped to deal with them quietly but firmly, using, among other things, an official *Council of 'Ulama* which he had then established.[14] Henceforth, under the Anglo-Egyptian administration, "official Islam" — mainly Sunni in character, but carefully tamed and kept under close watch by the Government — became an additional factor in the socio-political set-up of the country. As an instrument of the administration, it was used for the double purpose of controlling — usually on a selective basis — the *Sufi Tariqas* and counteracting Mahdism, which stood apart from all the *Tariqas*. Thus, the fact that the Mahdiyya had failed to stamp out the *Tariqas* and the excessively harsh measures used by the new regime, at least until the First World War, in order to crush Mahdism, resulted in the development of the situation where Mahdism — which rejected Sufism and wished to abolish the *Tariqas* — itself became, in fact if not in theory, a new and militant *Tariqa*.

NATIONALISM AND THE SEARCH FOR SUDANESE IDENTITY

It was in this context and against this background that modern Sudanese nationalism was born and developed. We are not concerned here with Sudanese nationalism in general; the subject has, in any case, been dealt with in some detail elsewhere.[15] Suffice it to note in this connexion that the idea of Sudanese nationalism as such (i.e. as a patriotic sentiment that would unite all the inhabitants of the Sudan, irrespective of tribal, religious, or regional differences, foster among them a sense of loyalty to the Sudan as a fatherland and a political entity, and mobilize the Sudanese for the purpose of achieving independence and socio-economic advancement) did not appear until after the end of the First World War. Its appearance and subsequent development, very much under the wings of the *Tariqas*, were greatly influenced, first by close contacts with Egypt — through her Arabic press and publications, through her personal working in the Sudan, through Sudanese traders and students (especially at al-Azhar University), and, above all, through the example of Egyptian nationalism, all of which proved to be strong stimulants to Sudanese nationalism — and, secondly, by the policies of successive Egyptian Governments, which claimed that the Sudan was an Egyptian territory, and aimed to achieve "the Unity of the Nile Valley under the Egyptian crown", and which thus constituted a negation of Sudanese nationalism.[15]

An equally important influence was British policy, which deliberately fostered Sudanese nationalism during certain stages of its development — especially after the outbreak of the Egyptian revolution of 1919 — mainly in order to keep the Egyptians out of the country, so as to maintain Britain's control over the Sudan. The Anglo-Egyptian dispute over the Sudan, combined with the older rivalries and hostilities between the *Tariqas* — especially the Mahdists and the Khatmiyya — had the effect of splitting the Sudanese nationalist movement into two major camps, even before the establishment in 1938 of the Graduates' Congress, its chief vehicle of expression.

As Sudanese nationalists, the two groups held similar views on a number of issues and indeed were united, for example, in opposing Native Administration, involving as it did the encouragement and, in some cases, the re-creation of tribalism, which — by contrast with the *Tariqas* — had been greatly weakened by the Mahdiyya — especially in the Northern Sudan. They were also united in opposing the government's "Southern Policy", introduced in the 1920s and vigorously pursued during the 1930s and early 1940s (up to 1946); this was aimed at the elimination, by administrative means, of all traces of Muslim-Arabic culture in the South and the substitution of tribal customs, Christianity, and the English language, with the ultimate objective of giving the three Southern provinces a character and outlook different from that of the country as a whole and even, possibly, separating them from the main body of the Sudan and "lumping" them together with other "possessions" further south, in order to form a great East African Federation under British control.[16]

Although Sudanese nationalists were united in their rejection of policies such as native administration and the "Southern Policy", because they fed separatist particularism instead of Sudanese nationalism, they could not help being themselves divided over the chief question they had to face up to the end of the Anglo-Egyptian regime in 1955, namely, the future of the Sudan. One camp, fearful of Egyptian domination over the Sudan and consisting mainly of Mahdist elements, stood for the independence of the country by means of cooperation with British as against Egypt. The other consisted in the main of non-Mahdist elements and was supported, for the most part, by the Khatmiyya (who never forgot the Mahdiyya and, at least until the early 1950s, were fearful that their opponents were intent on imposing a Mahdist monarchy in the Sudan). This camp stood for the "Unity of the Nile Valley", either as an end in itself, or as a political lever against the Mahdists on the one hand and the British on the other; the majority, including the Khatmiyya, ultimately revealed the latter as their aim.

Both the agreements and the disagreements of these two groups were reflected in the writings of the more articulate among them, particularly by the poets, as in other Arabic-speaking countries, where practically everything of public importance, from the opening of a national bank to the celebration of the anniversary of the Prophet's birthday, is greeted with a spate of poems. Some of these were able to express their views with remarkable precision of argument as well as intensity of feeling.

A dominant theme in the writings and verbal utterances of the *literate*, as might be expected, was the need for unity and solidarity. During the first two or three decades of the century, however (but to a lesser extent afterwards), the principles on which unity was sought were those of Islamism and Arabism rather than Sudanese nationalism as such. In a brilliant study of literary trends in the modern Sudan, Professor Muhammad al-Nuwayhi discusses the attachment of the earlier generation of Sudanese poets and writers to the values of traditional Islam and the forms of classical Arabic literature to the almost complete exclusion of their African heritage and environment. Explaining this fact, Professor Nuwayhi argues that the Sudanese, having been defeated and humiliated by the Anglo-Egyptian forces, needed psychological reassurance, which they could not find either in their African past or in the realities of contemporary Africa. Instead of helping them to regain their lost self-confidence, Africa would have the effect of accentuating their feeling of inferiority *vis-à-vis* both the British and their nominal partners in the new régime, the Egyptians. Almost involuntarily, therefore, the Sudanese, according to Professor Nuwayhi, turned their backs on Africa and became passionately attached to the glorious past of Islam, which, together with the richness of classical Arabic culture and thought, provided the necessary psychological prod.[17]

Professor Nuwayhi is an able student of Arabic literature and is well known for his efforts in applying the techniques of modern psychology to the analysis of his subject. There can be little doubt of the soundness of his opinion that the past glories of Islam and the Arabs were used by many Sudanese poets and writers of the first two or three decades of this century as an escape from the harsh realities of their contemporary world and as a compensation for the misery of their existence — particularly, as far as the Mahdists were concerned, during the difficult years from 1898 to the outbreak of the First World War, and after the collapse of the pro-Egyptian rebellion of 1924 as far as the non-Mahdists in general were concerned.

The strong attachment of Northern, or Muslim and Arabic-speaking, Sudanese at that time to the historical glories of Islam and the medieval Arabs was, however, like that of other Muslims and

Arabic-speaking peoples, especially in the rest of North Africa, a complex historical and political fact, which cannot be entirely or satisfactorily explained in psychological terms alone. It was essentially a result of the fact that, by the turn of the nineteenth century and the beginning of the twentieth, Islam was still, for most people, the basic bond to which they owed allegiance — not only within each of the "national" entities into which the Arab world was gradually carved up between 1830 — when the French took Algeria — and the First World War — when they shared the remaining Arab provinces of the Ottoman Empire in Western Asia with the British — but also and, more significantly, between Muslim and Arabic-speaking peoples across these new and arbitrarily defined boundaries. In those days, nationalism as such was either not known at all or, where the term was known and used, it was generally regarded (perhaps somewhat confusedly) as an extension of Islam rather than as a potentially alternative form of association. In other words, most people saw themselves primarily as Muslims and, to the extent that they thought of themselves as Arabs, their Arabism was for them inseparable from Islam.[18]

It was for these reasons that the African past of the Sudanese — like the Pharaonic history of the Egyptians, the Phoenician ancestry of the Lebanese, and the Assyrian background of the Iraqis — was not regarded as an object of glorification or seen as a source of self-gratification by politically conscious Sudanese. Their non-Islamic present, like their pre-Islamic past, was for them a part of the *Jahiliyya*, the "Age of Ignorance" or "World of Darkness", and they could not therefore identify themselves with either, any more than the Muslim and Arab populations of, say, Egypt or Iraq could identify themselves with theirs. Islam, as a religion, a civilization, a way of life, and a polity, was the central fact in life and the main object of loyalty. It was through its association with Islam that Arabism also had become a subject of pride, not only among the Arabs but throughout the Muslim world, including places as far apart as Indonesia and Mali or Nigeria, where, to this day, some people may be found who would proudly explain their Arab connexions and ancestry (true or imagined) as well as their Islamic identity.

As nationalism, especially secular nationalism, gradually spread into the Muslim-Arab world, and in one country after another became the accepted basis of political organization in place of the international brotherhood of all Muslims, so the pre-Islamic or non-Islamic aspects of the Sudan, as well as of other parts of the Muslim-Arab world, were, by stages, rediscovered and reasserted.[19] And just as in Egypt, for example, some nationalists began to identify themselves as children of the Pharaohs, rather than as Muslims or Arabs — the writer, Taha Husain, declared that Egypt was, after all, part of the Mediterranean world of Europe rather than of the Middle East or the Arab world — so did some Sudanese begin to take pride in Piankhy and Taharqa;[20] while a Muslim Arabic-speaking poet from the Northern Sudan (Muhammed Miftah al-Faytoury, who is discussed at some length by Professor Nuwayhi) identified himself as an African and nothing but an African.

Thus, whereas four or five decades ago Faytoury's predecessors identified themselves exclusively as Muslims and Arabs, there are now at least some Sudanese (Northerners as well as Southerners) who, in this age of nationalism and pan-Africanism, have come to take the reverse position, identifying themselves in purely African terms to the exclusion of Arabic and Islamic influences. But neither of these two trends, as we shall try to show, was entirely correct in its assessment of the state of being Sudanese.

SYNTHESIS OR CONFRONTATION?

In the light of the preceding paragraphs it is not surprising that the "unionists", such as Sheikh Muhammed Sa'id al-'Abbasi and 'Abdalla 'Abd al-Rahman, strongly opposed the Mahdists when, as the champions of independence, they began advocating Sudanese nationalism (mainly through *Hararat al-Sudan*, the first Sudanese political newspaper, from June 1920 onwards) and propagating the motto, "The Sudan for the Sudanese", as opposed to "Unity of the Nile Valley under the Egyptian crown". As might be expected, the opposition was chiefly couched in terms of traditional Islamism and Arabism, not merely out of inertia or force of habit, but because, politically speaking, the unionists correctly suspected that Sudanese nationalism was, at any rate at that stage and in that form, at least partly inspired by the British: not because they genuinely believed that the Sudan should be for the Sudanese, but in order to keep the Egyptians out of the Sudan and thus be better able to keep the Sudan under British control. By emphasizing Islamism and Arabism as opposed to Sudanese nationalism they were, furthermore, positively contributing to the strengthening of bonds which were common to Egypt and the Sudan.

In the circumstances, it was natural that the first coherent statement on the nature of Sudanese nationalism should have been made by a champion of independence who was of Mahdist background but, having studied at Gordon College in the early 1920s — a time of intense nationalist activity both in Egypt and the Sudan — had the incentive and the training as well as the ability to begin such an undertaking. Having discussed the subject in public lectures at the Graduates' Club in Omdurman and in articles which were published in *al-Fajr*, the principal Sudanese journal of the 1930s, Muhammad Ahmad Mahgoub concluded that Sudanese nationalism must be firmly based on Islam, Arabic culture, and African soil and traditions, and that it should be open to and freely interact with international currents of thought. Sudanese culture, he said, would have close friendly relations with the neighbouring Egyptian culture, but would be independent of it; it would retain its own distinct character, but would learn from the culture and thought of all other nations, both ancient and modern.[21] On the subject of the goals and character of the literary movement in the Sudan, he wrote in 1941:

"The objective towards which the literary movement in this country should be directed is to establish an Islamic Arabic culture supported and enriched by European thought and aimed at developing a truly national literature which derives its character and its inspiration from the character and traditions of the people of this country, its deserts and jungles, its bright skies and fertile valleys ... By giving an increasingly more prominent place to political studies of a kind more directly concerned with our problems and ambitions, this movement should then be transformed from a cultural to a political movement whose final goal should be the achievement of the political, social, and cultural independence of this country."[22]

Being chiefly concerned with questions of practical politics rather than with social or political theory, Mahgoub himself, like other advocates of Sudanese nationalism and, of course, the unionists, was unable to elaborate or substantially add to his own description of Sudanese nationalism in the 1930s. Political developments, however, especially after the achievement of independence on January 1st, 1956, obliged the Sudanese to resume thinking about the goals and nature of their nationalism. The principal factors in this development were the emergence of the Southern Sudanese as active agents in national politics after the termination of the separatist "Southern Policy" of the (British) Sudan Government in 1946 and the development, at a later stage, of pan-Arabism and pan-Africanism as regional forces with a strong appeal to the Sudanese and important implications for the Sudan.

The termination of the "Southern Policy", a result of many factors both internal and external, was a great victory for the Sudanese nationalists, who, as already noted, were unanimously opposed to it, particularly as it was aimed at the systematic elimination of Islam and the Arabic language and culture from the Southern provinces. But the Southern Sudanese, who emerged after the removal of the restrictions of the "Southern Policy" in 1946 and who, two years later, made their début in national politics as members of the Legislative Assembly, were naturally very much the product of "Southern Policy". This had had the effect of almost completely eliminating the cultural and religious bonds which had previously existed between the Northern and Southern provinces. Under the influence of this policy, furthermore, many Southerners, especially those who had been to mission schools as distinct from tribal chiefs and elders, had been imbued with a spirit, not only of strong local patriotism, but of bitter hostility towards their Northern compatriots.

We are not concerned here with the nature and development of the problem of the Southern Sudan in general.[23] Suffice it to say that, in the above-indicated circumstances, many Southern Sudanese — mostly graduates of Christian missionary schools — came to regard themselves as a different people or "nation" from the Northerners and, as such, believed that they should have their own independent state; if some link with the Northern Sudan had to be maintained, they felt it should be in the form of a weak federal, or confederal, arrangement.[24] Exasperated by the length and intensity of the debate over the rights and the wrongs of the subject, some Northerners, including several who have held or now hold responsible government posts, have come to similar conclusions;[25] they argue in, addition, that the Southern Provinces are a "drag" or a "liability" on the North, and advocate that the South should be severed from the main body of the country at the earliest possible opportunity and be given the independent status which some Southerners at any rate say that they wish to have.

These views (whatever their merits) are ultimately based on the differences between the Northern and Southern provinces, which are often summarized in the by now stereotyped statement that the Northern Sudan is predominantly Muslim and Arab, while the Southern Sudan is African and mainly "pagan" or Christian: that the two, therefore, are separate entities and cannot, in any shape or form, constitute a single state.

No one who knows the Sudan, or is interested in an objective assessment of its problems, would wish to minimize either the many and important differences that exist between the Northern and Southern parts of the country or the extent to which they have contributed, and still contribute, to the tensions which mar the mutual relations of the two regions. It must be pointed out, however, that the above simple and almost conventional description of the differences between them, though it may be useful in giving a quick over-all idea of the nature of the country, is based on certain misleading generalizations and assumptions which cannot be accepted in any serious discussion of the subject[26] Thus "Arabism" is normally equated with the North while "Africanism" is used with reference to the South; and the terms are popularly regarded as having a racial content and being mutually exclusive.

In fact, however, Arabism, which is a basic attribute of the majority of the population of the Sudan and of several other African countries, is not a racial bond which unites the members of a certain ethnic group. It is a cultural, linguistic, and non-racial link that binds together numerous races — black, white, and brown.[27] Had Arabism been anything else but this, most modern Arabs, both African and Asian, including the entire population of the Northern Sudan, would cease to be "Arab" at all. And just as Arabism is a cultural and non-racial bond, so Africanism is a geographical, political and cultural — but non-racial — link which binds together the various peoples of Africa irrespective of differences of race, colour, or language.[28] Hence the close association between Arabism and Africanism, not only within the bounds of Africa itself but on interregional and international levels as well.

In the Sudan, which, as already noted, is a microcosm of Africa with all its physical, racial, and cultural diversities, Arabism and Africanism have become so completely merged in the Northern provinces that it is impossible to distinguish between the two, even from the most abstract point of view; the great majority of the population rightly feel that they are Arab and African at the same time, to an equal degree, and without any sense of tension or contradiction. The fact that they are predominantly Muslim and Arab does indeed distinguish the Northern Sudanese from their Southern compatriots, who are mainly "pagan" and, to a much less extent, either Christian or Muslim; but it does not mean that they are not African. As the only region in the continent — and indeed the world — in which the physical, racial, and cultural diversities of Africa as a whole are not merely represented but synthesized into a unique and unparalleled entity, the Northern Sudan may in fact be described as more representative of Africa as a whole than any other country or region, including the Southern Sudan.

Nevertheless, the Northern Sudan differs from the South in that it is predominantly Muslim and Arab, while the latter is mainly "pagan" and only to a much lesser extent either Muslim or Christian. This, though it may correctly be regarded as an adequate ground for claiming a special status for the South within the framework of a united Sudan, does not constitute a sound argument for the splitting of the Sudan into two independent sovereign states. For the modern state, especially in Africa, is not and could not be founded on religious, racial, or even cultural homogeneity. It is based, above all, on the community of interests and objectives of peoples who, different though they may be in certain respects, have met across continental and not merely tribal or regional boundaries. In the present age Africa, of which the Sudan constitutes an integral part and a uniquely representative cross-section, is moving towards unity and close association rather than in the direction of separation and Balkanization. Viewed against this background, the splitting of the Sudan into two (or more probably, in that case, several) parts would not only be unnecessary and undesirable as a matter of principle; it would also have serious practical repercussions on Africa as a whole, and — in an age when the race question is becoming of increasingly great importance — it might, from a world-wide point of view, be a most tragic event.

REFERENCES

1 Before embarking on the conquest of Cush, the Emperor Nero (A.D. 54-68) despatched two centurions with some Praetorian troops to report on the country. The troops seem to have travelled as far as the Sudd region in the Southern Sudan, where they encountered "some marshes of enormous extent [where] the muddy water was covered over with an entangled mass of weeds, which it was impossible to wade through or sail over". W. Budge, *The Egyptian Sudan* (London, 1908), Vol. II, p. 172.

2 According to Sir Douglas Newbold, the number of pyramids in the Sudan is greater than in Egypt. See K. D. D. Henderson (ed.), *The Making of the Modern Sudan* (London, 1953), p. 481.

3 Isaiah, XXXVII, 9, and Kings, XVIII and XIX.

4 On the wider theme, see T. Arnold, *The Preaching of Islam* (London, 1935); on the Sudan, Yousif Fadl Hasan, *The Arabs and the Sudan* (Edinburgh, 1967).

5 Ibn Khaldun uses the expression '*Aajim*, which Lane Poole, among others, translates as "infidels". But this is obviously wrong since the word '*Aajim* literally means non-Arabic speaking people, and is used with reference to non-Arabic speaking Muslims as well as others. "Barbarians" as used by the Greeks comes closer to the Arabic expression.

6 Ibn Khaldun, *Tarikh* (Cairo, n.d.), Vol. V, p. 429.

7 A. J. Arkell, *A History of the Sudan from the Earliest Times to 1821* (London, 1955), p. 199.

8 For an excellent study of these people see I. Cunnison, *Baggara Arabs* (Oxford, 1966).

9 See the relevant texts in *Al-Sudan Min 13 Fabrayir 1841 ila 12 Fabrayir 1953* (Cairo, 1953), pp. 1-2.

10 'Abd al-Rahmán al-Rafi'i, *Misr wal-Sudan* (Cairo, 1948), p. 83.

11 In 1899 only the northern boundary of the Sudan was defined with any degree of precision. Until 1910, the Lado enclave was administered by the Belgians, and Darfur did not become part of the Sudan until 1916. More important in this connexion is the fact that the idea of fixed and well-defined boundaries was itself unknown in the Sudan before the present century.

12 L. F. Nadler, "The Two Sudans", in J. A. Hamilton (ed.), *The Sudan from Within* (London, 1935), pp. 94-5.

13 Tabaqat wad Daif-Alla is still the best source on Sufism in the Sudan. See also 'Abd al-Majid 'Aabdin, *Tarikh al-Thaqafa al-'Arabiyya Fil-Sudan* (Cairo, 1953).

14 Letter of 13th January, 1901, from Wingate to Cromer; the Wingate papers, School of Oriental Studies, University of Durham.

15 See Muddathir 'Abd al-Rahim, *Imperialism and Nationalism in the Sudan* (Oxford, 1969).

16 See Muddathir 'Abd al-Rahim, "The Development of British Policy in the Southern Sudan", in *Middle Eastern Studies* (London), IV, 3, April 1966. The same paper, together with six appendices, has been published as a booklet by Khartoum University Press, 1968.

17 See Muhammad al-Nuwayhi, *al-Ittijahat al-Shi'iriyya Fil-Sudan* (Cairo, 1957), particularly Chs. 2 and 8.

18 On this theme, see Zeine N. Zeine, *Arab-Turkish Relations and the Rise of Arab-Nationalism* (Beirut, 1958), particularly the last chapter; 'Umar al-Daghagh, *al-Ittijah al-Qawmi Fil-Shi'ir al-'Araby al-Hadith* (Halab, 1963), especially pp. 35-72; and Anis al-Maqdisy, *al-Ittijahat al-Adabiyya Fil'Aalam-al 'Arabi al-Hadith*" (Beirut, 1952).

19 See, for example, Hazim Zaki Nuseibeh, *The Ideas of Arab Nationalism* (Cornell, 1959), and al-Daghagh, op. cit., pp. 105-52.

20 Although this sentiment has never assumed in the Sudan the proportions of, for instance, Pharaoism in Egypt, traces of it can be clearly seen in the works of some Sudanese journalists and writers of popular histories.

21 *al-Fajr* (Khartoum), 1st April, 1935, pp. 857-64, and 16th January, 1935, pp. 1040-5.

22 al-Haraka al-Fikriyya Fil-Sudan (Khartoum, 1941).

23 For the author's view of the nature and development of the problem of the Southern Sudan in general, see *The Development of British Policy in the Southern Sudan* (Khartoum, 1968), App. VI.

24 Cf. the proposals submitted to the Round Table Conference, March 1965, and subsequently to the Twelve-Man Committee by the representatives of S.A.N.U. and the Southern Front, in the author's "Fourteen Documents On the Problems of the Southern Sudan", (Khartoum, 1965, mimeo.). The Documents in question were subsequently reproduced as appendices to M. O. Beshir's *The Southern Sudan—Background To Conflict* (London, 1968).

25 This sort of view has been expressed, on several occasions, by a number of public figures from the Northern Sudan, including the former Minister of Local Government, Sayyid Hasan Mahjoub, and the late Ambassador Yusif Mustafa al-Tinay.

26 The substance of this argument was first stated by the author in connexion with the Round Table Conference on the Southern Sudan. Cf. *The Development of British Policy in the Southern Sudan*, App. VI.

27 See, for example, Nuseibeh, op. cit., especially pp. 51 and 65-6; and Edward Atiyah, *The Arabs* (London, 1958), pp. 7-9.

28 See, for example, Colin Legum, *Pan-Africanism* (London, 1962) particularly on the concepts of negritude and the African Personality.

4

THE BLACK ARABS IN COMPARATIVE PERSPECTIVE: THE POLITICAL SOCIOLOGY OF RACE MIXTURE

Ali A. Mazrui

In discussing the spread of Islam in the Nuba Mountains of the Republic of the Sudan, Mr. R. C. Stevenson referred to two parallel processes of social change — "one linguistic and cultural, by which the people of the land acquired Arabic as their language and certain Islamic cultural conceptions and became connected with the Arab tribal system; and the other racial, by which the incoming Arab stock was absorbed in varying degrees, so that today a modicum of Arab blood flows in their veins".[1]

It is this combination of acculturation and inter-mating between races which might be called a process of *bio-cultural assimilation*. Some degree of integration between groups is achieved by the process of mixing blood and fusing cultural patterns.

SYMMETRY IN BIO-CULTURAL ASSIMILATION

There are two concepts here which need to be further refined. One is the concept of symmetrical acculturation and the other is the concept of symmetrical miscegenation. Symmetrical acculturation arises when a dominant group not only passes on its culture to the groups it dominates but is also significantly receptive to the cultural influence of its subjects or captives. Symmetrical acculturation is arrived at when cultural transmission is a two-way affair. Complete symmetry is impossible to achieve, and even if achieved, would be impossible to measure. What needs to be approximated is a significant reciprocal influence.

There have been occasions in history when acculturation has been asymmetrical, and yet the receiving group has been the politically dominant. The classic example is that of Greek influence on the Roman conquerors. After the decline of Greece and the rise of Rome, Greek subjects succeeded in partially Hellenizing the Roman conquerors.[2]

A more common example is the kind of asymmetry in which the politically dominant culture transmits itself to its subjects and captives and receives little in return. The British cultural influence in much of Africa has been of the second category. We might call this descending asymmetry, and call the Greek-Roman example a model of ascending asymmetry.

As for symmetrical miscegenation, this would arise in a situation where two racial communities inter-marry and produce a comparable number of both men and women who crossed the racial boundary to seek partners from another community. In very isolated circumstances, and even there with some qualifications, such symmetry is conceivable. It may be conceivable in a situation where one race or ethnic group is patrilineal and the other is matrilineal. The matrilineal group might not mind its women crossing the border and marrying men from the other country. The patrilineal group, in like manner, might permit the men to be exogamous. But in such situations claims as to whether the mother or the father has first priority to the children, and how descent is to be determined, might become an issue as soon as the married couple appear to be on the verge of separating. For as long as they are together, it is conceivable for a child to enjoy dual racial citizenship. To the matrilineal race the child is regarded as sharing the race of its mother; while the patrilineal wing recognizes the child's racial affinity to its father. Tensions in such situations are conceivable, precisely in the duality of citizenship and the pulls of potentially conflicting loyalties. Symmetrical miscegenation in such an instance could indeed be approximated.

A much more prevalent phenomenon is that of *asymmetrical* miscegenation. Certainly, in the great majority of cases where black people have inter-married with non-black people, a lack of symmetry has been a continuing characteristic.

In this article, we shall pay special attention to racial mixture as between the Arabs and black Africans. We intend to do this in a broad comparative perspective, relating the Afro-Arab experience to the different histories of racial mixture in the United States, in Latin America and in South Africa. These three, when combined with the Afro-Arab model, provide four distinct patterns of the relationship between miscegenation and social structure.[3]

All four models of miscegenation are asymmetrical but in significantly different ways. In each case the dominant ethnic group has produced many more husbands in the racial mixture than wives. Over seventy per cent of the so-called black population of the United States has white blood. But overwhelmingly the white blood has come through white males rather than white females. Until recently, mating between whites and blacks in North America usually meant white men and black women.

The Latin American model is less straightforward, but it is still basically asymmetrical. It is the fairer-skinned males that have easy access to darker-skinned females, rather than the other way round. A factor which has in some respects accentuated the asymmetry in Brazil is the sexual prestige of the mulatto girl among white Portuguese.

"Gilberto Freyre has written that prolonged contact with the Saracens led to the idealization among the Portuguese of the type of the 'enchanting Mooress', a seductive ideal with dark eyes, enveloped in sexual mysticism . . . Freyre suggests that dark-skinned women were preferred by the Portuguese for love, or at least for physical love."[4]

Within the African continent the asymmetry in miscegenation originated partly in the phenomenon of slavery itself. Both in South Africa and in Arabized black Africa, slavery was the breeding ground of asymmetrical miscegenation. The Boers in the Cape, and the Arabs in Zanzibar and the Sudan, helped themselves to female African slaves and produced children. The transmission of Afrikaner blood in South Africa and of Arab blood in Zanzibar and the Sudan was definitely through the dominant Afrikaner or Arab male.

But in spite of the fact that all the four models of race relations that we are going to discuss are based on asymmetrical miscegenation the fate of the children varies in fundamental ways among those four models. Do the children of a mixed marriage between a dominant race and an under-privileged race follow the father into the amenities of dominance or do they follow the mother into the handicaps of under-privilege? Or do they in fact become a class apart?

It is the contention of this paper that the answers to these questions are different in each case when we are looking at the North American, the Latin American, the South African, or the Afro-Arab models. The precise fate of children in mixed unions has a great deal of relevance for the whole issue of a biological approach to national integration. Does racial mixture reduce cleavages between groups and in what way? The answers differ in the four models, and their pertinence to the integrative process has to be correspondingly differentiated.

Before we look at the four models let us examine more closely the Arab presence in Africa, as a whole, before we examine more specifically those Arabs who have intermingled directly with black Africans.

I have already argued elsewhere that Egypt is at once the least African of the Arab countries within the African continent, and the most pan-African among them. She is the least African because of her longer exposure to Western influences. Egypt is in many ways the most Westernized of all African countries apart from South Africa, and her capital city, Cairo, is among the most cosmopolitan.

Yet, in spite of being the least African of the Arab countries in the continent, Egypt can still be described as the most pan-African. The initiative for this status was derived from Nasser's foresight and leadership. Nasser's pan-Africanism consisted in granting scholarships to African students, allowing Cairo to become the first major centre of refuge for nationalists from colonial Africa, converting Cairo Radio into an instrument of anti-colonialism in Africa as well as the Arab world, involving himself in the conference diplomacy of African states, establishing cultural links with Muslims elsewhere in the continent, undertaking the responsibility of looking after illustrious destitutes, like the children of Lumumba on Lumumba's death, and participating in the struggle to make Africa an effective component of the movement of the non-aligned.

In general, among all Arab states within the African continent, it is quite clear that Egypt has been more involved in many more African enterprises than any other Arab state. To that extent it has proved its credentials for pan-African involvement. It has even gone as far as to participate in the Nigerian civil war, on the side of those who wanted to maintain Nigerian unity.

In many ways, Egypt is less African than Algeria, or Morocco or even Tunisia. Egypt's pull towards the rest of the Arab world, and her status as the largest country in the Arab world, came to enforce upon her an outward-looking perspective, which reduces her roots within the African continent. She is pan-African by ideology and sympathy rather than by historical roots.

What all this confirms is that there are *degrees* of African-ness. In any case, the Arabs in the north might be natives of Africa even if they are not fully "Africans". Yet by what criterion are they to be regarded as natives of the continent. One answer I have heard given in Ghana is the following:

"The Arabs by now must be recognized as natives of Africa because they have been in Africa since the seventh century."[5]

But sometimes even more important than duration of stay is rapidity and depth of assimilation and extent of intermingling with the local population.

It is sometimes too readily assumed that the population of Egypt today consists mainly of descendants of Arab conquerors who arrived there thirteen hundred years ago. Of course, such an assumption about the actual racial composition of Egypt is, to say the least, naive. It is perhaps still true to say that the most dominant "racial" strain in the population of Egypt today is descended from the indigenous Egyptian inhabitants — the societies that produced the Pharaohs and Cleopatra. As we know, there have been other races immigrating into Egypt in the last thirteen hundred years. This is typical of the Mediterranean as a whole and its capacity for migrations. But the important fact to grasp is that the bulk of the population of Egypt is Arab by cultural assimilation and not by blood descent from Arab conquerors. The numbers of the conquerors at that time were a small fraction of the population of Egypt. It is true that the population of Egypt itself then was modest, but the few Arabs from the deserts of the Arabian peninsula who exercised authority over this former province of the Byzantine empire were little more than a fraction of the subjects over whom they exercised that power.

The Muslim conquests of the sixth century had taken on two mighty empires simultaneously. The Byzantine empire of which Egypt was a province, and the Persian empire. Egypt and Persia were conquered at roughly the same time in the first wave of Muslim expansionism from the peninsula. The Persians were converted to Islam, but the Persian language survived as a separate language. The strength of Persian civilization withstood the Arab impact, absorbing religious aspects and interacting with others, but still retaining a distinctive personality as Iranian rather than Arab.

The Arab conquest of Egypt, on the other hand, succeeded not only in Islamizing the people they found there, but also in gradually Arabizing them. In Egypt there was cultural asymmetry, as the conquering civilization exerted its dominance over the population, and finally made Egyptians feel that they were indeed Arabs.

In Persia, on the other hand, the interaction between Iranian civilization and the new Arabism and Islam was more symmetrical. Persia has made an impressive contribution to Islamic civilization. The range is from architecture to the *Arabian Nights*, from Persian carpets to poetry. At the same time Persia became deeply Islamized, and because of that, partially Arabized. In the Persian case the two mighty civilizations, ancient Iranian and Islamic, interacted substantially on a level of balance and reciprocity.

In Egypt, on the other hand, the new wave of Islam and its original language, Arabic, found an old civilization in decay — tired and petty in its sectarian squabbles. Over a period of time the Egyptians became Arabs.

Is what is going on in the Sudan today a repetition of what went on in Egypt earlier, a gradual conversion of a country to Arabism

E

through bio-cultural assimilation? The answer once again has to be sought in a wider comparative framework.

MISCEGENATION: DESCENDING, AMBIVALENT AND DIVERGENT

We must again remind overselves that acculturation and inter-marriage do not necessarily result in social intermingling between the races or even in a system of desegregation. It very much depends upon the precise systems of descent observed by the race in question, and by the general racial attitudes of the dominant race in a particular society.

One might say that there are four active models of relationship between blood mixture and social structure at large. One is the North American model. Within this model, whenever there is mating between a white person and a black person, the offspring is invariably "black". We may call this the model of *descending miscegenation*. Over three-quarters of black Americans have Caucasian blood flowing in their veins, and yet they are categorized as Negroes or blacks. Until recently, there were states in the United States which presumed to characterize a person's race according to calculation of how much Negro blood the person had. Certainly the law of white-dominated Florida used to define a Negro as recently as the 1960s as a person with "one-eighth or more of African or Negro blood". And the laws of Forida, like the laws of eighteen other states in the American union in 1963, specifically prohibited "miscegenation".[6]

The second model of racial mixture in relation to social structure is that of Latin America. In Brazil especially, the offspring of mating between a black person and a white person produces a mulatto or mestizo, but the mestizo could either enjoy the same rights as the white person or the same handicaps as the black person depending partly on the actual colour he inherits from his parents. We may call this the model of *ambivalent miscegenation*. In other words, much of the prejudice in Latin America is colour prejudice rather than race prejudice. Of course, very often the two coincide, but they need not. And even where they coincide a different emphasis can often be discerned. Class stratification in Brazil does correlate substantially with the shades of skin colour — the fairer your child is the better are its chances of social success in the future.

This does contrast with model number one of North America where the emphasis is on purity of blood, regardless of how fair the child is. Indeed, a person might have a skin which is indisputably white, but if the legal calculators of blood in Florida were to discover that one-eighth of this white man's blood was "African or Negro blood" the white-skinned person would become re-classified as a black man.[7]

During the colonial phase of Brazil's history, Francisco Manuel de Melo once noted that "Brazil is the Inferno of Negroes, the Purgatory of White Men, and the Paradise of Mulattoes of both sexes."[8]

It is unlikely that de Melo was ever right in this formulation. Brazil might indeed have been, and to some extent still remains, an inferno for Negroes. But it is clearly the white men that are in paradise, and the mulattoes that are in purgatory. The mulatto, a person of mixed parentage, could either end up in the hell of the black people or in the paradise of the white people, depending upon the precise shade of his colour.

Census figures in Brazil have tended to adopt the three categories of whites, Negroes and "mestizos", the mixed group that allows also for the inclusion of Indian blood. But Brazilian census figures in these terms have always been bedevilled precisely by this phenomenon of racial mobility — the capacity of a person to move upwards in race classification if his physical features and skin-colour permit it.

> "Many light mulattoes, refined, educated, and of good appearance, must appear to be white. Mestizos appearing to be white are included as whites, contrary to the practise in the United States, where one eighth of Negro blood classifies one as Negro."[9]

This important distinction has struck other writers too. Donald Pierson has noted that while the American criterion was based on racial descent, the Brazilian was based on physical appearance. Pierson draws attention to the phenomenon of many Negro grand-parents having grand-children who are "white".

It is this consideration which leads to the conclusion that while in the United States the progeny of mixed marriages is classified as belonging to the less privileged group, the progeny of mixed marriages in Brazil could be classified either with the privileged or with the under-privileged depending upon physical features and colour of skin.

> "In the white group, then, one finds not only true whites but also white phenotypes, that is, Afro-white and Indian-white mestizoes reverting to white type. In the Negro group there are Negroes and Negro-phenotypes and *cafuzos* [Indian-Negro] reverting to Negro type. Finally, the mestizo classification shows the greatest lack of precision, for mulattoes, mixtures of Negro and white, are not distinguished from *caboclos*, mixtures of Indian and white."[10]

And then we come more specifically to the African continent in our quest for categories of relationship between racial mixture and social structure.

In South Africa we see a third category. In the case of South Africa the progeny of mixed marriages between whites and blacks are neither automatically black, as they are in the United States, nor are they entitled to upward mobility if physical features permit, as they are in Brazil. The South African model decrees that the progeny of a mixed marriage between white and black belongs to a group apart. The group is that of the Coloureds. We might call this the model of *divergent miscegenation.*

Over three-quarters of the Coloured population of South Africa live in the Cape. The concentration of this mixed population coincides roughly with the settled districts of the Western Cape during the slave period. The Coloureds have been defined as "the product of a dual process of Westernization and miscegenation between Whites, Hottentots and slaves."

The total subordination of the woman slave to the whims of her master, and the interest of the master in producing highly prized mulatto slaves, promoted a good deal of racial intermingling. In culture the bulk of the coloured population is a sub-group of the Afrikaner culture. Indeed, the great majority are native Afrikaans-speakers.

Under the conditions of the United States the Coloureds would have belonged more firmly to the "Black" population. Any mixture of blood follows the line of less privilege. Under Latin-American conditions the Coloured population of South Africa would have been divided between the blacks and the whites, according to physical features inherited from the parental groups. Some coloureds would definitely have been accepted fully as part of the Afrikaner population, while others would have had to find solidarity with the black population. But since South Africa is neither the United States nor Latin America, the Coloureds have remained a group apart, distinct both from the pinnacle of racial privilege and from the base at the bottom of the pyramid.[11]

ASCENDING MISCEGENATION: THE FOURTH MODEL

The fourth model of assimilation would bring us at last to the phenomenon of places like the Sudan and Zanzibar. The population of the Sudan as estimated on January 17th, 1956, was 10,262,536. At the time of the census 39% of the total population was deemed to be *racially* Arab. The racial definition of Arab was in terms of membership, or claimed membership, of an Arab tribe. This constituted biological intermingling between the races, real or claimed.

But in a country like the Sudan there is also the linguistic definition of Arab to be taken into account. By this linguistic definition a person is an Arab if his mother tongue is Arabic. Muddathir 'Abd Al-Rahim has estimated that 51 % of the Sudanese speak Arabic as their first language and must, according to the census figures, be deemed to be Arabs. The linguistic definition hinges not on biological integration but on cultural or linguistic assimilation.

But, although 'Abd Al-Rahim emphasizes the linguistic definition of Arab, he does draw attention to the remarkable racial inter-mingling in many parts of the Sudan. The two southern provinces of Bahr al-Ghazal and the Upper Nile are almost exclusively populated by Nilotics. There are also relatively unmixed communities, in the biological sense, in parts of Northern Sudan. But the central parts of the country illustrate considerable genetic mixture.

"Although Arab tribes predominate in the provinces of Khartoum, Blue Nile, Kordofan, and Northern Province, the Beja in Kasala, Westerners in Darfur, and the Nilo-Hamites in Equatoria, it is obvious that considerable racial mixing has taken place, particularly in the central parts of the country. A clear indication of this is the wide range of colours and features among the Sudanese Arabs (over half of the total population) who are, on the whole, much darker than other Arabic-speaking peoples north of the Sahara and across the sea in Arabia."[12]

If in the Sudan the utilization of the linguistic definition of Arab increases the number of Arabs from 39 % of the population to 51 % of the population, in revolutionary Zanzibar a linguistic definition of Arab would have nearly *halved* the Arab population. In other words, while the Sudan has more native Arab speakers than it has people with Arab blood, pre-revolutionary Zanzibar had more people with Arab blood than it had native Arabic speakers. Many Arabs in pre-revolutionary Zanzibar were native speakers of Swahili, a Bantu language.

What all these differences indicate is that the distinction between Arabs and Black Africans is not dichotomous but has the complexity of a continuum. That was one reason why the Organization of African Unity was born as a multi-pigmentational enterprise. The Arabs as a race defy straight pigmentational classification. They vary in colour from the white Arabs of Syria and Lebanon, the brown Arabs of the Hadhramout to the black Arabs of much of the Sudan and of some of the Eastern parts of the Arabian peninsular. Within Africa itself the range of colour among the Arabs is indeed from white to black also, though each colour cannot as smoothly be allocated to a specific geographical area. Even within Egypt on its own the range of colour is virtually as wide as it is in the Arab world as a whole.

This is what brings us to the relevance of this model of Afro-Arab intermingling, as contrasted with the model of Afro-Saxon intermingling in the United States, and with the Afro-Latin intermingling in Brazil and the Afro-Afrikaner intermingling in South Africa. With the Arabs the idea of "half-caste" is relatively alien. If the father is Arab, the child is Arab without reservations. If we visualize an Arab marrying a Nilotic woman in the fourteenth century and visualize the son being born, the son would be Arab. If we imagined in turn that the son again married a Nilotic woman who bore a son — this son, too, would be an Arab. If we then assumed that the process is repeated, generation after generation, until a child is born in the second half of the twentieth century with only a drop of his blood still ostensibly of Arab derivation and the rest of his blood indubitably Nilotic, the twentieth century child is still an Arab.[13]

It is this phenomenon which has saved the Arab-Negro division in Africa from being a dichotomous gulf — and converted it instead into a racial continuum of merging relationships.

In Pan-African literature it has been more the Afro-Americans than either the Arabs or the Black Africans that have grasped this fact of the racial continuum. Edward Blyden, the nineteenth century Liberian intellectual of West Indian birth, put it in the following terms:

"With every wish, no doubt, to the contrary, the European seldom or never gets over the feeling of distance, if not of repulsion, which he experiences on first seeing the Negro . . . The Arab missionary, on the other hand, often of the same complexion as his hearer, does not 'require any long habit to reconcile the eye to him'. He takes up his abode in Negroland, often for life, and, mingling his blood with that of the inhabitants, succeeds in the most natural manner, in engrafting Mohammedan religion and learning upon the ignorance and simplicity of the people."[14]

Blyden here captures the paternalism which characterized missionary work both by Arabs and by Europeans. But the essential contrast here is between the repulsion reluctantly felt by well-meaning Europeans, on the one hand, and the Arab capacity for "mingling his blood with that of the inhabitants", on the other.

What Blyden has also captured is the difference between the social distance purposefully created by European missionaries in the areas in which they worked, and the more integrative approach to proselytism adopted by Muslim missionaries. The Christian missionary even today may indeed walk among the people to comfort the sick, educate the ignorant, convert the heathen, and reform the sinner. But he does not mix his blood with them. If he is a Protestant, and has already been ordained, he has probably taken the precaution of getting himself a wife from home prior to coming to Africa in any case. According to the dominant interpretations of the religion, Christianity favours either the self-discipline of no wife at all (celibacy) or the "faithfulness" of one wife only (the more prevalent principle of monogamy). The Catholic missionary, a celibate, is a biological specimen apart in the village in which he is proselytizing. The ordained Protestant missionary has a wife, carefully obtained from home both as an assistant in the great enterprise of spreading the gospel and serving the unfortunate in distant lands, and as a safeguard against the temptations of Satan in the loneliless of life among the heathens.

By contrast, Muslim missionaries did not have to be monogamous, and were hardly ever celibate. Nor did they regard it as necessary to arm themselves with a wife from their own community before venturing into the darkness of Africa. In the words of Blyden:

> "The Muslim missionary often brought to the aid of his preaching the influence of social and domestic relationships — an influence which in all efforts to convert a people is not to be entirely ignored."[15]

What Blyden here is suggesting is the efficacy of biological integration as a method of cultural assimilation. He even quotes Dean Stanley's assertion:

> "The conversion of the Russian nation was effected, not by the preaching of the Byzantine clergy, but by the marriage of a Byzantine princess."[16]

It is arguable that the three most important ways of spreading a culture to other lands are, firstly, by purposeful cultural transmission and proselytization, secondly, by the flow of trade and its incidental consequences in the field of culture contact, and thirdly, by actual migration of people from one land to settle in another. It is arguable that imperialism is a means towards a means. Conquest and imperialism help to determine the magnitude of trade, cultural transmission, or migration.

TRADERS, FARMERS AND MARRIAGE

Special emphasis needs to be placed on the phenomenon of trade and the incidence of culture contact caused by trade. In the impact of Europe on Africa, the missionary and the trader were distinct specimens, though often in alliance. But in the case of the impact of Islam and Arab civilization on Africa the missionary and the trader were often the same person.

Islam very often spread casually as a result of contact between individuals, and as a result of ordinary social intermingling between a Muslim and a non-Muslim. The Arab shopkeeper in a small town in Tanzania or the Sudan could converse about Islam to his animistic customers, and sometimes influence them towards conversion. The Arab shopkeeper may marry among the same alien people he serves commercially, and through the influence of kinship and marriage he may at the same time unofficially proselytize for Islam. Or the Arab trader may be a nomadic business man, moving from town to town selling his wares. Again migratory trade has often served the function of being a mobile mission in Islam at the same time.

But in the European penetration of Africa the missionary has tended to precede the trader, and both in turn have helped to prepare the way for the Flag.

William C. McLeod once discussed the trader and inter-marriage in a context related to the subject of this paper. McLeod put forward the hypothesis that a trading man was more ready than a settler to get married to groups other than his own. He referred to those analysts who insisted that there was a difference between the Nordic and Latin races in their attitudes to non-white peoples. The standard assertion has been that the Nordic Germanic peoples, by their very cultural background, tend to be racially endogamous and rather averse to "miscegenation". The Latin peoples, partly because of their cultural universalism, are less exclusive in their social and matrimonial habits. Certainly the difference between the North American model we discussed of descending miscegenation, and our Latin American model of ambivalent miscegenation, has sometimes been explained in terms of the differences in *culture* between universalistic Latins and more socially exclusive Germanic peoples.

But McLeod argues that the comparison has been based on a fallacy :

"In contrasting the French and the English, [popular writers] make the cardinal error of comparing French traders not with British traders but with British agriculturists; and the needs of a French colonial regime which never developed to the point where the trading interests lost control with the needs of dominantly agricultural settlements. French and British traders alike married Indian women and gave rise to numbers of half-breeds; and both groups were able to adapt themselves to Indian ways of life and the Indian manner of thinking."[17]

As for the Spaniards and the Portuguese, McLeod asserts that they are indeed capable of intense racial prejudice. But their attachment to religion has tended to make the religious differences a greater barrier to adequate social intercourse than racial differences.

"The Moor and the Jew in Spain and Portugal were hated only so long as they refused to become Christians; Christianized they were racially absorbed by both the aristocratic and the commoner strata of the population."[18]

And yet in conceding the relevance of Iberian Christianity to their racial attitudes, McLeod was beginning to concede the relevance of Latin culture at large for differential behaviour as between the Latin and the Germanic peoples.

But what McLeod's analysis wishes to emphasize is the relevance of those aspects of culture which are to do with cooking, keeping house, and general domestic arrangements. McLeod's theoretical thrust in this hypothesis is that these very mundane aspects of culture, often determined by whether the man has settled in one place for good or regards himself as a transient nomad, have been far more important in determining racial orientations in matrimonial matters than the wider concepts of culture concerned with God and values.

"Farmers needed wives who knew the ways of European housekeeping and husbandry, who knew how to milk cows, fry eggs, and so on. Indian women would not do. The farmer, even in Virginia, so late as 1632, often preferred to pay the expense of importing women of questionable repute from the European cities, at considerable cost, than to take Indian women who would be helpless on a farmer's homestead. Champlain offered one hundred and fifty franks as a dowry to each French Canadian farmer who would marry an Indian girl, but his offer was in vain."[19]

Herbert Moller, writing more than a decade later, re-affirmed McLeod's thesis. Moller took the position that the greater extent of inter-racial mingling in Spanish and Portuguese America could not be attributed to an inherently different attitude on the part of the Latin peoples in their relations with "the natives". The history of race relations in New France would, according to Moller, be an effective witness against such a position. During the second half of the seventeenth century, when the early French colonists had an exceedingly high sex ratio, there was no prejudice against alliances with Indian women. Only four marriages between French men and Indians were recorded at the time, but "left-handed marriages are known to have been frequent". But by the turn of the century, the sex ratio in the eastern parts of Canada was beginning to be fairly balanced, partly because the number of males was not radically increased by new immigration. With the balance came a decline in mixed marriages in Canada.

On the other hand, the western parts of Canada still remained strongly masculine, and so did Louisiana. "There concubinage with young Indian squaws was the rule through the eighteenth century."

Similarly, argues Moller, British colonists had relatively easy ideas about miscegenation for as long as there was a great shortage of white women, and moral attitudes had not been deeply influenced by white women.

There is an underlying suggestion sometimes in Moller's analysis that the predicament of the new colonists, still unsure of the future and even of survival in very strange new circumstances, is sociologically comparable to the position of the trader settling in a village and being guided by the likely impermanence of his abode.

But once the agricultural pattern of life began to gain roots and the people were at last settlers, the aversion to mixed marriages began to rise perceptibly among North American colonists. Moller asserts that the kind of racial prejudices which grew up in North America were not imported from Europe. Such antipathies were, according to the writer, virtually non-existent in the Europe of the seventeenth and eighteenth centuries. Racial aversions of the form which was found in subsequent decades of North American history, were, so to speak, native to the American experience.

"The most plausible explanation, so far, for the increasing avoidance of inter-racial marriage in the British colonies has been the need of agriculturalists and tradesmen for wives 'who knew the ways of European housekeeping and husbandry', whereas traders, both French and British could afford to marry Indian women."[20]

Moller's own important contribution to the debate was his thesis regarding the influence of the white woman on racial attitudes. There has been a lot of literature so far emphasizing sexual insecurity in the white male as a major reason for his aggressive response to any suggestion of interaction between a black man and a white woman. Moller, on the other hand, argues that it was to some extent the sexual insecurity of the white woman combined with fears of unknown worlds of inter-racial sexuality which sharpened the phenomenon of racial repugnance among certain sections of white colonists in North America.

Herbert Moller had added female hypogamy as another casual factor behind white repugnance and emotions of disgust over the phenomenon of inter-racial relations. The argument here is that women as a rule refrain from matrimonial and social relations with men of a lower social class or strata than their own. The majority of women persist in this attitude even if the price is life as an old maid and complete celibacy. In the history of Europe whenever there was a surplus of women in the upper or middle classes fathers had to confront the issue of how best to provide for their unmarried daughters.

Significant here is the tendency of women to identify themselves completely with their husbands or lovers, while men do not share this urge to any comparable degree. Hypogamy as marriage beneath one's station is considered with greater aversion by women than by men.

"Whereas in Europe this feminine attitude prevented women from marrying beneath their social status, it worked in America against their marrying into culturally socially inferior races. Moreover, through their enhanced influence on family and community life, women became more or less unintentionally the foremost agents in the establishment of racial barriers. Thus the development of aversion to racial miscegenation in the thirteen colonies can be traced to the invasion of feminine sentiments into colonial society."[21]

Valuable as McLeod's and Moller's contributions to theories of race relations might be, they both overemphasize white attitudes to the relations between men and women and did not pay enough attention to white attitudes to the *offspring* of mixed mating. It is true that disapproval of mixed marriage is a profound conditioning factor on subsequent attitudes to the children produced by mixed marriages. But that very attitude to the children is itself a changing phenomenon and has to some extent to be treated as an important additional variable in its own right.

It may be true that traders are more tolerant of mixed marriages than settled agriculturalists. It may also be true that much of the initial success of mixed marriages between Arabs and black Africans was partly attributable to the fact that the Arabs were structurally nomadic in the sense of being engaged in trade in eastern Africa and the Sudan. Yet this is not the whole story. Many Arabs settled in Zanzibar permanently, and still intermingled biologically with the black societies among whom they had established residence.

Similarly, in the Sudan, migrations of Arab tribesmen often resulted in Arab settlements, and involvement in trades and agriculture, rather than commerce as such. There was a significant process of migration with whole populations settling in new areas. Fadl Hasan has even suggested that until the end of the fifteenth century the processes of Arabization and Islamization were "almost entirely accomplished by tribal migration". Inhabitants of the Sudan became arabized and assimilated into the Arab tribal system.

> " . . . the dominance of Arabic culture suggests, among other factors, that the Arab invaders arrived in large numbers and came to exercise a considerable influence over the life of the local population. Indeed, when Bruce travelled the country of the Ja'aliyyin towards the end of the eighteenth century, he saw no distinction between the indigenous population, who were already Arabized, and the Arabs (probably meaning nomads), except that the former continued to live in mud houses beside the river bank, while the latter lived in tents."[22]

Not all those who claimed Arab descent, or who included themselves more specifically in a particular tribal genealogy, did in fact have Arab blood flowing in their veins. The fluidity of genealogies and tribal affiliations exaggerated the degree of biological arabization. What is clear is that the distinction which McLeod and Moller made between attitudes to miscegenation among agriculturalist settlers and such attitudes among traders was much less vindicated in the field of Afro-Arab relations than it might have been in North America.

An important differentiating characteristic is the much stronger patrilineal principle in Islam and Arab culture as contrasted with the culture of the Germanic peoples. The idea that the father determined the tribal affiliation of the descendants was the critical difference between the Afro-Arab model of ascending miscegenation and that first model we discussed of the North American tendency to regard the offspring of mixed marriages as belonging to the race of the under-privileged — i.e. descending miscegenation.

BLACK SLAVES AND WHITE MASTERS

Critical in the comparative histories of the two models is the attitude to the offspring of slave girls mated by their masters. In the case of the American experience the law in the slave states asserted that if one of the parents was a slave, the offspring would follow the status of the mother rather than the father. The American historian Herbert Aptheker adds a footnote in the following vein:

> "Generally, of course, where the parents were slaves and free, the mother was a slave and the father was a white man, often a slave owner, who, thus in accordance with the law had both pleasure and profit."[23]

In his book, *Black Reconstruction in America*, W. E. B. DuBois refers, in parenthesis, to the consequences of that law in more vivid terms:

"The law declares that the children of slaves are to follow the fortunes of their mother. Hence the practice of planters selling and bequeathing their own children."[24]

Perhaps because they knew of this rigid prejudice against miscegenation in the Germanic section of the New World under our first model, black Americans who went to Africa were impressed by the Afro-Arab racial continuum. In the United States the divide was dichotomous — it was between white men and negroes. And a person could not pass as "white" if he was mixed enough to be "brown". In Africa, however, the division was between Arabs and black Africans — and yet there were many Arabs who were as black as black Africans. And so W. E. B. DuBois could make the following observation:

"Anyone who has travelled in the Sudan knows that most of the 'Arabs' he has met are dark-skinned, sometimes practically black, often have negroid features, and hair that may be almost Negro in quality. It is then obvious that in Africa the term 'Arab' . . . is often misleading. The Arabs were too nearly akin to Negroes to draw an absolute colour line."[25]

Slavery was a factor behind the mixed populations in the Sudan, Zanzibar, South Africa, Latin America as well as the United States. But again there was a fundamental difference between the mating of black slaves by white masters, and the mating of black slaves by Arab masters.

Within our first model of descending miscegenation based on experience in North America, we have already discussed the phenomenon of white masters making love to their slave girls, partly with a view to improving the quality of the offspring so that their own children may later be sold at a higher price. After all, lighter coloured slaves often fetched a better price than very black ones.

Experience in Latin America, with special reference to Brazil, was somewhat less straightforward. It varied to some extent historically, depending partly upon the decrees of the Government of the day. There were times and families which accepted the offspring derived from the mating of slave girls by white masters into the very body of the family, to be brought up as members thereof. But there was always an important section of opinion, sometimes triumphant in the legal process, which regarded the practice of accepting mixed children as members of white families as something which eroded the essential basis of the caste society. In the words of Florestan Fernandes:

"The incorporation of the element of colour in the legal nucleus of a great family would bring with it a form of recognition of social equality between the *white man* and the *Negro* or *mulatto*. In order to avoid this, petitions were drawn up opposing inter-marriage and subordinating marital relations to endogamic standards . . . The prohibitions did not affect sexual relations but only marital relations. Not only were the slave sex partners not elevated to the social position of the masters, but children born of these unions remained in the same condition as their mothers."[26]

Through much of the colonial period of Brazil the Crown disapproved of concubinage, and the Brazilian Church declared itself against such practices. Yet concubinage in Brazil remained alive for a long time, and was practised not only by masters but sometimes even by priests. Also widespread was a situation whereby children born of such unions assumed the status of their bonded mothers. For as long as slavery continued there was a strong tendency in Latin America, as in North America, towards *descending* miscegenation.

In this respect, the experience of South Africa was similar. A slave woman who won the favours of her master in bed and produced fair-skinned children, could indeed quite often improve her own status and the status of her children. But this would be an improvement within the slave system, becoming relieved of some chores, enjoying extra privileges, and perhaps even supervisory power over other slaves. The children also perhaps became better fed than the children produced of unions of slave with slave. But the persistent pattern in South Africa as elsewhere in the world of white slave-ownership, was to regard children of slave girls as being themselves slaves, regardless of whether the father was free or not. Descending miscegenation continued to be the rule in conditions of slave-ownership. As Van den Berghe put it in relation to South Africa's experience:

"The close symbiosis of masters and slaves, and the total subordination of the female slave to her male owners made for extensive intermixture. Other incentives accelerated the process. Through miscegenation the female slave could improve her condition and the status of her children. The White Master, on his side, had, apart from sexual gratification, an economic interest in increasing and 'improving' his human stock by producing highly priced mulatto slaves."[27]

Later on, when slavery was abolished, the idea of Coloured People in South Africa being a group apart both from Whites and Blacks began to consolidate itself. Divergent miscegenation became the new pattern. But in the background was the whole experience of regarding children born of a union between a master and a slave girl as being themselves slaves.

BLACK SLAVES AND ARAB MASTERS

The difference between this phenomenon of slavery in the white world and the phenomenon of slavery in the Arab world has had important consequences for the status of children of mixed mating. In Islam any child born to a slave girl by her master is legitimate; the legitimacy in this case confers upon the child descent from his father, including the status of a free-born and rights of inheritance; and this descent confers upon the child links with the father's tribe. In slave conditions Islam insists on ascending miscegenation. If the father is Arab the child is Arab, regardless of whether the mother is a wife or concubine, and regardless of the nationality of the mother.

If a similar system of descent had been operable in the United States, the majority of those who are now called "Blacks" would, in fact, have belonged to the "White" community. They would have acquired this paternal descent simply because most of the children of mixed unions in the United States have involved white fathers and black mothers. If the Germanic and Anglo-Saxon cultures had had as sharp a principle of paternal descent as the Arabs, the population of under-privileged black people in the United States today would have been much smaller. The bulk would have been assimilated *upwards* into the dominant and privileged community.

In South Africa, the application of the Arab principle that the father's tribe determines the child's tribe would have tilted the balance of population as between English-speaking whites and Afrikaans-speaking whites, as well as affecting attitudes to gradation of colours within the system as a whole.

"The racial prejudice of the Whites is solely responsible for the social existence of a distinct Cape Coloured group, a fact recognized by many 'moderate' Afrikaners today, and indeed by some Hertzogites as early as the twenties. Except for the concern with colour of South African 'Whites' (many of whom have themselves 'Coloured blood'), Afrikanerdom would be nearly twice as large as it is today, and would outnumber the English-speaking Whites by well over two to one. For every six White Afrikaners there are approximately five Coloured Afrikaners and four English-speaking Whites. In the entire population there are four non-Whites to one White, if colour is the criterion; but, if mother tongue is taken as the criterion, there are only two non-Europeans to one European."[28]

In the Latin American model of racial mixture the application of the Arab principle of paternity would have made another kind of difference — it would have obliterated to some extent the categories of mestizo and mulatto as significant ones. Given that the child follows the father in tribal or racial affiliation, the so-called white population would have become more varied in skin colour; and conceivably also the non-white would also have had a variety of colours. But the balance between the groups — white, black, Indian would have had a different basis. Variation in colours would still have been significant but the relative populations of the different groups would be substantially changed, reducing in the process the number of those who were relatively under-privileged.

But in Islam the colour of the offspring is certainly no reason for denying its paternity and descent, even in a situation where the mother is a fair skinned Arab and so is the father. Reuben Levy, a Cambridge professor, draws our attention to the following hadith:

> "The extreme case is quoted, or invented, of a Bedouin Arab who came to the Prophet declaring that his wife had given birth to a negro child, and hinting that he wished to repudiate it. Muhammad, however, refused him permission to do so . . ."[29]

Levy also draws our attention both to the legitimacy of children born in concubinage and to the concern of the tribe as a whole in ascertaining the paternal link with the tribe.

> "In Islam it is sufficient for the father to acknowledge cohabitation with his wife or slave to establish the legitimacy of the child . . . Seeing that concubinage is lawful in Islam, it is not necessary for the mother of a child to be married to its father in order for it to be declared legitimate.
>
> The powers of the father over his children are very great, [but] he cannot sell them into slavery . . . Normally, indeed, the legitimacy of a boy is a matter of some concern to the father's family or tribe."[30]

Arab patrilinealism in Zanzibar, reinforced by Islamic prescriptions, resulted on the one hand in the cultural assimilation of the Africans into Islam, and on the other into the biological Africanization of the Arab immigrants. The local indigenous populations imbibed imported culture to a considerable extent, while the future composition of the Arab population in the Island absorbed important African strains biologically.

But when, in addition, the racial intermingling led to the emergence and consolidation of the Swahili language as the national language of Zanzibar, problems of differentiating Arab from non-Arab became compounded. The result was considerable ethnic fluidity.

We know that social mobility is the capacity of a person to move from one class to another; but Zanzibar had in addition racial mobility in the sense of capacity of a person or even whole sub-groups to move from one racial category into another.

Before the revolution, the Arab minority in Zanzibar was described as "Sub-Saharan Africa's second largest alien oligarchic minority" — following in proportional size only the white community of South Africa. But if the South African method of descent had been applied to Zanzibar, and the Zanzibari method of descent had been applied to South Africa, South Africa's proportion of Whites would have been greater than it is today — and Zanzibar's proportion of Arabs would have been much smaller than it was at the time of the revolution.

The substantial issue to be borne in mind is precisely the ethnic fluidity which was characteristic of Zanzibar's racial situation. In the 1930s and 1940s the Arab population in Zanzibar shot up significantly, not because new immigrants had arrived from the Persian Gulf, nor because the Arabs' natural rate of reproduction had suddenly taken a sharp turn upwards. In 1924 the Arabs as a percentage of the total population of Zanzibar consisted of 8.7%. By 1948 the Arabs were up to 16.9%.

> "A small fraction of this increase was doubtless Arab. But the vast bulk of the increase in the Arab population had to come from within Zanzibar society, from among segments of the population which had previously opted for categories of self description other than Arab. Between 1924 and 1931 large numbers of former non-Arabs changed their minds, as it were, about the ethnic category most suited to their own descent and decided to 'join' the Arab community."[31]

On the coast of Kenya during the colonial period similar shifts in racial categorization took place. The Arab population of the coast of Kenya was barely twenty thousand by the 1948 census. The population rose by a few thousand in the early 1950s simply because groups of Arabized coastal tribes, previously designated as non-Arab were at last given recognition by the British Colonial authorities as Arabs. They had themselves been pressing for such recognition from the British Colonial authorities, though their credentials were challenged by those who were already recognized as Arabs. The British Colonial authorities, perhaps partly influenced by the bewildering fluidity of intermingling between Arabs and Africans, decided to confer the more prestigious title of Arab upon the new claimants from the coast.

The advantages which Kenya coastal Arabs enjoyed as against Kenya coastal Africans were sometime more substantial than

F

prestige. Terms of service for jobs were, during the period, categorized into European terms of service, Asian terms of service, and African terms of service. The Arab sector, by its racial ambivalence, was sometimes eligible for the Asian terms of service, and sometimes not. Certain banks in Mombasa classified all Arabs as Africans, and paid them accordingly. East African Railways and Harbours also classified many Arabs as Africans and paid them accordingly. And yet in much of the civil service within Kenya, Arab civil servants were often regarded as being eligible for Asian terms of service. The pigmentational and racial ambivalence of the Arabs converted them into marginal men.

In the entertainment world there were also differentials in privileges among the groups. A symbolic differential concerned films which were given the grade of X by the censors in colonial Kenya. X-films in Kenya meant "Not to be shown to Africans and children under sixteen." The term "African" at the initial introduction of the censorship law encompassed Arabs, and so they too for a while were kept out of film shows bearing the title X. It took a demonstration organized by a prominent Mombasa Arab, Shariff Abdulla Salim, to force the "Majestic" cinema in Mombasa to admit a group of militantly defiant local Arabs. Once the breach was made at the "Majestic" cinema, gradually the term X as a category of censored film implied only Africans and children under sixteen, and no longer Africans, Arabs and children under sixteen.

This resulted in conferring significant powers of racial categorization on the gatekeepers and ticket-sellers at the cinemas. An African could indeed acquire the privilege of seeing an exciting sex film, or a film involving violence, if he could convince the booking-office clerk or the gatekeeper at the "Regal" cinema that he was an Arab and not an African. On the other hand, a black Arab might have to argue his way, or even bribe his way into the cinema, if the clerk insisted in regarding him as an African.

In the Sudan, ethnic fluidity has also been a persistent feature of the whole process of acculturation. It is true that the initial impetus of Arabization did include the coming of large numbers of Arabs. It is also true that Arab immigration continued in varying volumes over many years. But Sudanese Arabs themselves often grossly exaggerate the numbers of Arabs who came in. Much of the population of northern Sudan is a population of Arabized Africans, rather than Arabs as such. Whole groups began to identify with particular Arab tribal names, and genealogies grew up, of varying authenticity, establishing the Arabness of the different groups.

"Unfortunately we know remarkably little of the way in which

Arabization was accomplished. The whole of our knowledge is derived from two different types of sources: the first, a limited number of contemporary medieval Arabic writings and the second, a large body of Sudanese genealogical traditions which in their present form were compiled at a much later date."[32]

Fadl Hasan warns us that the genealogical traditions which are at the moment current in the northern Sudan indicate a high degree of Arabization. The adoption of Arab genealogies by the inhabitants of the Sudan is very widespread. The fact that there is a preference for adopting such genealogies indicates at the minimum a high degree of cultural Arabization.

"However, any conclusions that are drawn from these genealogies as to tribal origin, must be accepted with some reserve."[33]

The sheer fluidity of ethnic affiliations, and the cultural pull of the dominant identity, have resulted in a high degree of integration in northern Sudan. Denominational differences in religion assumed a greater political significance in the Sudan than the racial categories of the northern population. Disputes as to whether such and such a family is really Arab by descent or not, and evaluations of family prestige partly in terms of lighter shades of colour, have all remained an important part of the texture of Sudanese life in the north. Prejudices based on colour have by no means disappeared. There are black Arabs, deeply black, whose credentials are fully respected in relation to their Arab genealogies. There are others who may be a shade lighter, and yet have their Arab credentials disputed by at least some families. The political sociology of shades of colour remains a part of the Sudanese scene. But the phenomenon of inter-marriage and miscegenation, on the basis of patrilineal descent, have resulted in a more integrated model of racial mixture than that afforded by either the North American experience, the Latin American experience or the experience of South Africa.

SOUTHERN SUDAN: TOWARDS A BIO-CULTURAL SOLUTION?

Is the policy of inter-marriage relevant for the problem of southern Sudan? Will the Arab model of descent, practised in terms of racial mixture, provide one long-term solution to the southern problem?

There have been signs in the Sudanese scene indicating a groping for the utilization of racial mixture as an integrative device. Official circles to Khartoum have sometimes been reported to have encouraged a more relaxed attitude in the north to the idea of Arab girls being married to black southerners.

Arab attitudes to inter-marriage have been asymmetrical. When the Arab man marries into a different community no special stigma is attached to the union, and the children, in any case, become Arab. But, when an Arab woman is married to a non-Arab man, a different set of suppositions arise. The logic of patrilineal descent necessarily entails that there should be disapproval of an Arab girl marrying a non-Arab (be the bridegroom an African or a European). After all, the children of such a union would not themselves be Arab. It is the relaxation of this resistance to give away Arab daughters to non-Arabs that the Khartoum Government has sometimes cautiously recommended.

But here an additional complicating factor enters the scene. Islam recognizes no racial distinctions in regard to marriage; but it emphatically recognizes religious distinctions. Racially mixed marriages among Muslims are fully valid in Islam; but religiously mixed marriages are more complex. The Muslim man may marry either a Jewess or a Christian woman without necessarily converting her. Islam in India extended this to the idea of marrying a Hindu woman without necessarily converting her. But a marriage between a non-Muslim man and a Muslim woman is not valid in *orthodox* Islam. There are Muslim jurists who argue that the marriage of a Muslim woman to a non-Muslim man is irregular rather than void. There are supporters of this interpretation in some parts of the Muslim world, including Pakistan and the Sudan itself. But the dominant feeling among Muslim jurists is that the marriage of a Muslim woman to a non-Muslim man is, according to *Sharia*, null and void.

Ameer Ali, the Indo-Pakistani Islamic jurist, recommended a flexible interpretation of this prohibition. And D. F. Mulla more recently has reaffirmed the proposed distinction between an irregular marriage and a void marriage. Asaf Fyzee, yet a third Islamic jurist, accepts the distinction, but insists that in the case of a marriage between a Muslim woman and a non-Muslim man, the marriage is not merely irregular but it is void.

"The present position appears to be that the *Nikah* of a Muslim man with an idolator or fire-worshipper is irregular and not void. Mulla goes on to say, however, that the marriage of a Muslim woman with a non-Muslim is only irregular, not void. This is, it is submitted, an inaccurate statement of the law. The marriage of a Muslim woman with a non-Muslim is declared by the Koran to be *batil*, void and not merely irregular. Thus it would seem that reform, in consonance with the view of Ameer Ali, can only be introduced by legislation."[34]

Discussion in the Sudan has also been conducted on the distinction between an irregular marriage and a void marriage. The reformers and modernizers, particularly those sympathetic to the marriage of northern girls to Christian southerners (preferably highly educated), have encouraged a more liberal interpretation of the *Sharia*. But, on the whole, northern Sudanese parents have tended to be orthodox in such matters. Southern suitors for northern girls have been confronted with stipulations from some parents that they should be practising Muslims for a period of at least two years before they could be regarded as eligible husbands for Muslim girls. Problems of circumcision have also sometimes intruded. The majority of non-Muslim southerners are not circumcised, and this influences questions of eligibility for marriage to northern girls.

Islam is clear in its prescription that the Muslim male ought to be circumcised. Circumcision in Islam does not command quite the degree of sacred covenant as it does in Judaism. This is partly because the Jews, in their isolation as a minority in other parts of the world, gradually converted the circumcision rite into an over-powering symbol of their separate identity. Nevertheless, circumcision in Islam is important enough to be practised among Muslims all over the world, regardless of other differences. It is certainly a powerful influence in Arab Islam and is often regarded as a prerequisite for masculine eligibility in matrimony.

The reported policy of the Khartoum Government to encourage flexibility on marriage customs between northerners and southerners aroused a good deal of suspicion among the more nationalistic southerners. That the policy was motivated by the ambition of bio-cultural assimilation was something which the more politically conscious southerners immediately grasped. The official encourage-ment of such flexibility was, to some extent, counter-productive. It created resistance among the more politically conscious southerners, and exposed those who married northern girls to the risk of ridicule and political disapprobation.

Southern nationalists might have been more tempted to encourage the marriage of northern girls if there was a feeling that such an enterprise was officially disapproved of. In such circumstances, the marriage of a northern girl by a southern man would become a kind of defiant assertion of parity of esteem with the north. It would have been similar to situations in North America where black desires for white mistresses were sometimes motivated by political ambitions to assert parity of dignity with the white community — taking white girls to bed became a symbolic political protest.

But in the Sudan the actual official encouragement of inter-marriage made the phenomenon more suspect, and might therefore have been counter-productive.

Nevertheless, from the main perspective of Arabs marrying others, the theses of this paper remain basically secure. The union of an Arab male with a non-Arab Sudanese woman, where it is legitimate, produces more Arabs rather than half-castes. The dominant group increases in size. It becomes possible to envisage a situation when more and more Sudanese become, linguistically and by claimed descent, Arab Sudanese.

The civil war itself has had consequences relevant to this whole process of inter-marriage. Arab soldiers in the south have taken mistresses, or married southern girls. Where the offspring is illegitimate, it could either remain with the mother, as is often the case, or later be claimed by the father for Arabization and Islamization in the north. The Sudanese, both Arab and black African, are, on the whole, strongly patrilineal. This has tended to encourage fathers to claim their children, particularly if they are boys, for inclusion into their original family. The Dinka seem to be at least as patrilineal as the Arabs. In general, it would seem that if the father is Dinka the child is almost certainly also Dinka, especially if it is a boy.

A more distinct example is that of the Dinka of north-western Sudan, who have close contacts with Baggare Arabs who come down annually in search of water and good pastures. During the Miriam wars with the Dinka, the Dinka captured Arab girls and some young Arab men. Many of these were integrated to some extent with the society which had captured them. In the villages of Jorbioc and Akuang Akuet, there are Arab Dinkas with names such as Ngong. In appearance many betray their mixture, but they are Dinka by language and culture.[35]

But, in the final analysis, inter-marriage between Arab and southerner in the south is still in its initial stages, and cannot yet be regarded as a substantial contribution to the integration of the country as a whole. Nevertheless, the issue of biological intermingling when coupled with cultural assimilation has to be regarded as an important dimension in the slow process of nation-building.

One facilitating factor for the biological approach to national integration in the Sudan is the fact that regionalism and race are beginning to be cross-cutting. Arabized southerners are already part of the scene, and groups like the Dinka have relatives in the north. Some calculations of Dinka in the north put them at nearly half-a-million. Inter-marriage between Arabs and Dinka has taken place both in the north and in the south.

Estimates of the population of the Dinka in the Sudan as a whole are varied. The Nuer are sometimes included as a sub-section of the Dinka, partly because the languages are mutually intelligible. When the Nuer are included, the population of the Dinka may be up to nearly four million. This makes the group the largest single tribe in the Sudan as a whole, both north and south. It also allows for the possibility of significant Dinka influence in the Sudanese nation should the present composition of the Sudan survive the civil war and other pulls to which it is subjected. If one out of every five Sudanese is a Dinka, and if the tradition of inter-marriage between the Dinka and the Arabs is increasing, the possibilities of nationally significant racial integration are indeed real.[36]

CONCLUSION

Much of what is going on in the Sudan today is in part a repetition of what went on in Egypt earlier, the gradual conversion of a country to Arabism and its culture. The Sudanese process appears noticeable partly because the majority of Arabs in the world are fairer than black Africans. What is often overlooked is that when Egypt was conquered by the Arabs, the Arabs from the deserts of the peninsula were darker than the Egyptians they were subjecting. The Arabs from the peninsula were also darker than the Syrians whom they converted to Islam in that first wave of conquest. The Fertile Crescent and Egypt, partly because of their diplomatic prominence over the centuries, began to be identified with the leadership of the Arab world. Because they were fair, it was assumed that the very origins of Arabness implied light Mediterranean skin.

But the purest Arabs come from further south in the Arabian pensinsula, and these are darker. Moreover, the Arabs of the peninsula proper have intermingled more with racially dark-skinned people than have the Arabs of the Fertile Crescent to the north.

If the Sudanese Arabs are dark, so are many of the inhabitants of Mecca and Medina. They may not be as dark as the Sudanese, though some of them are. The Arabs of Mecca and Medina are a blend of Asia and Africa, while the Lebanese and Syrians, for example, are a blend of Europe and Asia.

In their expansionism the Arabs have insisted on asymmetry both in culture and in miscegenation. This is certainly true also with regard to the Arab impact on the Sudan. Arabic is a conquering language, sometimes absorbing a little of the local languages, but in its very pride tending towards ultimate triumph. Patrilinealism, as we shall indicate, operates in terms of permitting and even encouraging Arab men to marry women from other communities, but forbidding or discouraging Arab women from marrying others.

The example of Zanzibar, on the other hand, is distinct. The Arabs in Zanzibar stood for asymmetrical miscegenation, but they also stood for symmetrical acculturation. The Arabic language was not an irresistible conqueror, flattening out local linguistic opponents. On the contrary, many Arabs of Zanzibar actually ceased to be Arabic speakers — and became native speakers of the basically Bantu language of Swahili. The Arabs of Zanzibar had allowed themselves to become *less* "Arab" than the Egyptians and Sudanese had done — and yet at the time of the revolution the Zanzibar Arabs were regarded as less native to their part of Africa than northern Sudanese were deemed to be in theirs.

The passionate hatred of the Arabs at the time of the revolution within Zanzibar was, in some ways, one of the most remarkable anomalies in contemporary African history. There seems to have been more passionate hatred of the Arabs in Zanzibar than there was hatred of the white man in Tanganyika. It is true that there were differences in situations. Some of the worst brutalities committed by white people against local Tanganyikans were committed by the Germans before the British assumed control following World War I. The British, the new rulers, turned out to be also exclusive in their social habits. But they were not as arrogant or as cruel as the Germans in the history of Tanganyika. Neverthless, there is no escaping the fact that the British were a small minority of people, conferring privileges on local Indians and local Europeans, exercising considerable hegemony over Africans, and clearly demanding separate treatment.

The Arab oligarchy in Zanzibar, on the other hand, mixed socially with the Africans, called many Africans uncle or nephew or cousin, shared the same religion with them, prayed shoulder to shoulder in mosques, appreciated the same jokes, sometimes frequented the same brothels.

Yet, by 1958, it was already clear that a deep anti-Arab animosity in large sectors of the African population in Zanzibar, had consolidated itself. When racial riots erupted in 1961, there was no doubt that all the years of mixed marriages and reciprocal acculturation had not resulted in minimizing hostility. The question which arises is whether that hostility may have been partly due to the very interpenetration between the groups which had taken place. Had the British, by keeping themselves completely apart, averted in the short run those depths of feeling? It is true that in Kenya there was sufficient anti-British hostility to erupt into a Mau Mau insurrection, but again, was it significant that the Mau Mau movement took place among the Kikuyu, the most acculturated of Kenya's peoples at the time, partly because of their very nearness to the British authorities? Elsewhere in Kenya resentment of the white man was there, but with nothing of the depth illustrated on that tragic island of Zanzibar in January 1964 against the Arabs. The problem which this raises is whether tension and hostility increases rather than diminishes when the dominant group narrows the cultural gap between itself and the under-privileged group.

According to this thesis, the Arabs of Zanzibar expedited their vulnerability to African challenge as they themselves became more culturally African. The adoption of the Swahili language as the dominant language of Zanzibar, and the decline of Arabic except in a section of the Arab population, was, in some ways, an establishment of cultural parity between Arabian culture and the Bantu linguistic cultures. But did this bring the revolution nearer? Are there occasions when economic imbalance is indeed stabilized precisely by cultural compartmentalization? Where a dominant group looks and speaks differently, and displays a very different way of life, it may perhaps have to face less of a challenge than if it mixes more fully with the population and reduces the social and cultural distance.

In the latter situation where the cultural differences are fading, the economic imbalance becomes more conspicuous. By becoming almost the only residual difference between the privileged and the under-privileged, the economic disparity becomes the more exposed.

It might, therefore, be said that those who worked out the philosophy of apartheid were basing their experiment, at least in the short run, on sound sociological grounds. If the economic imbalance between the whites and the non-whites was to be stabilized for a while, it made sense to attempt to keep the cultures apart.

And yet such stability can only be a short-term achievement. It is true that Zanzibar remains a tragic case of bio-cultural assimilation. The population was becoming a relatively homogeneous Swahili-speaking people, sharing the same religion as well as the same language. It may also be true that the situation became revolutionary precisely because an economic imbalance based largely on land-ownership persisted in spite of cultural homogenization.

But the tragedy of Zanzibar may have been the tragedy of a premature racial revolution. Sudan may remain unsure as to whether it is part of the Arab world or of black Africa. But independent Zanzibar could not have sustained its Arab identity for much longer. The mixture of the population internally, the retreat of the Arabic language, the emergence of a Swahili culture, and the links which this forged between the island and the black East African mainland, were almost bound to accelerate the de-Arabization of Zanzibar rather sharply. Indeed, the anti-colonial movement itself had already divided the Arab community between those who continued to take pride in their Arab descent and those who were emphasizing their Zanzibari identity. By the year of independence it was the latter who were winning. Independent Zanzibar would have been the most culturally integrated of all countries south of the Sahara, with the possible exception of Swaziland and Somalia. Just as many Africans in colonial Zanzibar had found it expedient to claim Arab descent, so many Arabs after independence would have found it expedient to emphasize their African descent.

It should not be forgotten that the "minority" government which was overthrown in January 1964 had obtained 46% of the popular vote only a few months earlier — by no means a "small" minority. In an election seven years before that (in 1957) the school of thought represented by this minority government — "Ours is Zanzibar nationalism" — won less than a quarter of this support. In other words, support for this concept of the *Zanzibar nation* was growing rather than diminishing when the revolution took place. But these trends were never tested under conditions of independence. The Zanzibar revolution took place within less than four weeks of attainment of independence.

But what if Arabism had remained strong in Zanzibar in spite of independence? In such a case the long-term solution would have had to lie in the *ascending* nature of Afro-Arab miscegenation. Let us assume that the Arabs had remained dominant, had continued to inter-marry, and had still recognized all children with Arab fathers as Arabs. In such circumstances, and given no sharp differences in fertility between Arabs and Africans, the proportion of local Arabs to local Africans would have continued to increase. It had certainly been increasing for the previous three generations, both because of ascending miscegenation and because the racial composition of Zanzibar was fluid enough to make it possible for some unmixed Africans to claim Arab descent. Again, as Michael Lofchie has pointed out, the Arabs were 8.7% of the population in 1924, and had risen to 16.9% of the population of Zanzibar by 1948.[37]

It is precisely this principle of ascending miscegenation which makes a fundamental difference between prospects for racial mixture in the Sudan today as against such prospects in Southern Africa. Claims that Sudan and Southern Africa are similar racial situations are, at best, naive, or more likely, propagandist.

The Portuguese territories in Southern Africa are an imperfect illustration of the *ambivalent miscegenation* of Brazil, but with greater discouragement of mixed unions than is now characteristic of Brazil.[38]

Rhodesia, with its Anglo-Saxon background, started with *descending miscegenation*. A population of Eurafricans had been growing. They were the offspring of European fathers and African mothers. In the villages they were accepted in the communal way of life and brought up according to the custom and language of the mother. But the disintegration of village life, and the drift towards the cities, have brought to the surface the problem of these racially mixed people.

While fellow Africans in the villages had readily assimilated the "half-castes", the Africans in the cities have shown greater distrust of these lighter-coloured lumpenproletariat.

The Eurafrican has also had problems with European employers. As one observer put it some years ago:

"He goes to a prospective employer, but owing to his light skin the white man expects him to know English (as all 'Coloureds' do) and generally be more sophisticated than an African straight from the kraal, which is all he feels himself to be. He is again rejected."[39]

But how many Eurafricans are there in Rhodesia? The exact numbers are as obscure as they were when the following observation was made:

" . . . the total Eurafricans in the Native Reserves can scarcely be less than 10,000; it might be even ten times that number. Nobody knows. But it is growing faster than ever."[40]

But even at that stage the situation showed signs of future transformation from descending miscegenation (as in North America) to *divergent miscegenation* (of the South African "Coloured" Model). Eurafricans in Salisbury had begun to appeal to the Government for recognition as a distinct community, and for compulsory registration as such, and for rights of compulsory education.[41]

Since U.D.I. the chances have increased for Rhodesia to drift towards the South African system of apartheid, complete with divergent miscegenation. Ian Smith's own views about Africans displayed early symptoms of sexual repugnance and racial stereotyping. He told two hundred journalists at a news conference in London way back on the eve of U.D.I. that he had regular confidential reports of the "sordid happenings" in some countries in Africa with black Governments. In some places, Mr. Smith asserted, European parents dared not let their daughters go to school without escorts. "This is the kind of conduct which Rhodesia is resisting"!

When asked if Africans in Rhodesia should be denied universal franchise because one Minister in a black African state had tried to seduce a stenographer, Mr. Smith retorted angrily: "It was not a case of seduction. It was attempted rape. How would you feel if that had happened to your wife or daughter?"[42]

It seems doubtful that Rhodesia would succeed in working out an apartheid system which would go to the extent of creating Bantustans. What is more likely is that Rhodesia is evolving a system intermediate between the old American model of descending racial mixture and the current South African model of more rigid compartmentalization.

This contrasts sharply with the problem of Southern Sudan. The war in the south flared up precisely because the Khartoum Government was *opposed* to the idea of maintaining the south as a separate Bantustan.

For as long as the south was kept separate, and assumed that it would remain separate, tension was minimized. But the very attainment of independence in the Sudan created in the south fears that southerners would no longer be left alone, and subsequent policies of deliberate cultural assimilation increased these anxieties. Again, precisely because the Sudan does not practise apartheid, the danger of tensions between groups comes sooner. Converting the south into a Bantustan, as the missionaries and British Colonial authorities had done, had for quite a while delayed the outbreak of hostility, though memories of prior interaction and slave raiding remained potent.

On independence, it was open to the Sudanese government to assure the south that it would be a Bantustan, left to its own cultural ways under the paternal guidance of Italian missionaries. But it was partly the rejection of apartheid in the Sudan which opened the way for tensions. And as the Sudanese now inter-marry, and as Arabic acculturation gathers momentum, the price which will be paid will be in terms of increased social tension, at least for a while.

It is unlikely that asymmetrical miscegenation in the Sudan will ever come to an end. The Sudanese, as well as the black Africans like the Dinka, are too patrilineal to evolve a system where both men and women may marry as they wish across racial boundaries without incurring certain social reservations. But the system of *ascending miscegenation* guarantees a form of upward mobility which has no equivalent in any other type of racial mixture.

As for symmetry in acculturation, this is more feasible in the Sudan than elsewhere in the Arab world, and has, to some extent, already taken place. The recency of culture contact has produced varieties of Arabic in the Sudan which bear the strong imprint of non-Arabic African languages. The cultural symmetry in the Sudan is not quite of the level attained in Zanzibar or Persia where the local subjugated group profoundly influenced the conqueror culturally, as well as permitted itself to be influenced thereby. Nevertheless, the degree of reciprocity in the Sudan is greater than further down the Nile, or elsewhere in the Arab world now that Zanzibar is no longer part of it.

But the most stable of all interactions is a combination of cultural symmetry and economic balance. Where the groups learn from each other as well as teach each other, without creating a society of vast disproportion in economic advantages, the possibilities of a stable society are there.

The emergence of socialistic ideas in the Sudan may reinforce the levelling tendencies of race mixture. The Sudanese Communist Party is certainly the largest in independent Africa and one of the oldest south of the Mediterranean African countries. The Party's political fortunes have varied from regime to regime, but it has played a part in disseminating more moderate socialistic values to other groups in the Sudan which are less explicitly Marxist.

The triumph of an egalitarian ethic seems likely in the Sudan in the long run. Northern Sudanese intellectuals are disproportionately left of centre, however anti-communist some of them may be.

If the country survives, the Sudan may be the first modern nation in Africa to have creatively used a combination of socialism and sex for national integration.

REFERENCES

1 R. C. Stevenson, "Some Aspects of the Spread of Islam in the Nuba Mountains (Kordofan Province, Republic of the Sudan)", in *Islam in Tropical Africa*, I. M. Lewis (ed.), (London, 1966), p. 209.

2 Consult, for example, H. Bamford-Parkes, *Gods and Men: The Origins of Western Culture* (New York, 1959), Section 3; William H. McNeill, *The Rise of the West* (Chicago and London, 1963), especially Chapter VI.

3 In this paper we use the word "miscegenation" in the full realization that its origins are racialistic. The whole concept implied by it is based on a disapproval of racial mixture. Our own use of it is, in spite of the origins of the word, intended to be value free. By miscegenation we mean mating between different races, in or out of wedlock, resulting in children of mixed parentage.

4 *Casa Grande E. Senzala* (Rio de Janeiro, 1958), 9th edition, pp. 12-13. Cited by José Honorio Rodrigues, *Brazil and Africa*, translated by Richard Mazzara and Sam Heilman (Berkeley and Los Angeles, 1965), p. 55.

5 This sort of answer was given by a Nigerian and by an Afro-American resident in Ghana in discussions in September 1964.

6 For quite a while, the United States' Supreme Court had avoided a direct ruling on the constitutionality of laws which forbade mixed marriage. But those laws began to disappear in the 1960s in spite of the Supreme

Court's inhibition. Enough changes were emerging from the political scene to make reforms in this direction inevitable. For a useful background article see Arthur Krock, "Miscegenation Debate", *The New York Times* (Review of the Week) September 8th, 1963. See also the article by Charlotte G. Moulton, published in *The Nationalist* (Dar es Salaam), November 11th, 1964.

7   This distinction between race prejudice based on colour and race prejudice based on purity of blood is also discussed in Mazrui, "Political Sex", *Transition*, Volume IV, No. 17, 1964. The article is reprinted as Chapter 15 in Mazrui, *Violence and Thought: Essays on Social Tensions in Africa* (London, 1969), pp. 306-18.

8   See José Honorio Rodrigues, *Brazil and Africa* (Berkeley and Los Angeles, 1965), translated by Richard Mazzara and Sam Heilman, p. 64.

9   Ibid., p. 75.

10 Rodrigues, *Brazil and Africa*, op. cit. p. 75. Consult also Donald Pierson, *Brancos e Pretos ma Bahia* (Sao Paulo, 1945), pp. 186, 188-9.

11 See Pierre van den Berghe, *South Africa: A study in Conflict* (Berkeley and Los Angeles, 1967), pp. 39-40.

12 Muddathir 'Abd Al-Rahim, *Imperialism and Nationalism in the Sudan: A Study in Constitutional and Political Development, 1899-1956* (Oxford, 1969), pp. 4-5. See also The Republic of the Sudan, Ministry for Social Welfare, *First Population Census of the Sudan: Twenty-one Facts about the Sudanese (1958)*, pp. 13, 23.

13 This point is discussed in similar terms in Mazrui, *Towards a Pax Africana: A study of Ideology and Ambition* (London and Chicago, 1967) p. 113. See also Yusuf Fadl Hasn, *The Arabs and the Sudan: From the Seventh to the Early Sixteenth Century* (Edinburgh, 1967), especially Chapter 5, pp. 135-76.

14 Blyden, *Christianity, Islam and the Negro Race* (London, 1887), reprinted in the African Heritage Books, edited by George Shepperson and Christopher Fyfe (Edinburgh, 1967), pp. 24-5.

15 Ibid., p. 19.

16 Dean Stanley, *Eastern Church*, p. 34. Cited by Blyden, ibid., pp. 19-20.

17 McLeod, *The American Indian Frontier* (New York, 1928), pp. 60-61.

18 Ibid.

19 Ibid., pp. 359-60.

20 Herbert Moller, "Sex Composition and Correlated Culture Patterns of Colonial America", *The William and Mary College Quarterly*, Vol. II, April 1945, pp. 131-3; 136-7.

21 Ibid., p. 137.

22 Fadl Hasan, *The Arabs and the Sudan*, op. cit., p. 175.

23 Herbert Aptheker (ed.), *One Continual Cry: David Walker's Appeal to the Coloured Citizens of the World, 1829-1830* (New York, 1965), p. 41.

24 *Black Reconstruction in America, 1860-1880* (1935; reprinted Cleveland and New York, 1962), p. 35.

25 DuBois, *The World and Africa* (1946; enlarged edition New York, 1965), p. 184.

26 See Ordenacoes Filipinas, Book 5, Titles XXIII to XXX. Cited by Rodrigues, op. cit., p. 61.

27 *South Africa: A Study in Conflict*, op. cit., p. 41.

28 Van den Berghe, *South Africa: A Study in Conflict*, op. cit., p. 42.

29 Levy, *The Social Structure of Islam* (Cambridge, 1962), p. 137.

30 Levy, ibid., pp. 136, 143 and 138. Consult also Asaf A. A. Fyzee,

Outlines of Muhammadan Law (London, 1964 edition), especially Chapters 2 and 5.

31 Michael F. Lofchie, *Zanzibar: Background to Revolution* (Princeton and London, 1965), pp. 73-5.

32 Fadl Hasan, *The Arabs and the Sudan*, op. cit., p. 135.

33 Ibid.

34 Fyzee, *Outlines of Muhammadan Law*, op. cit., pp. 95-6. See also Syed Ameer Ali, *Mahommedan Law* (Tagore Law Lectures, 1884), Vol. I, 4th ed., Calcutta 1912. Also Vol. II, 5th ed., Calcutta 1929. Consult also Dinshah Fardungi Mulla, *Principles of Mahommedan Law*, 15th ed., Calcutta 1961.

35 I am grateful for much of this information to Southern Sudanese informants in Kampala.

36 The estimates here are at their most generous, made usually by educated Dinka in exile. The official estimates made twenty years ago are much more modest, placing the Dinka cluster in terms of one-and-a-half million or two million rather than four. Consult *Census*, op. cit. Consult also George Peter Murdock, *Africa: Its Peoples and their Culture History* (New York, 1959), especially Chapter 43. The more selective and restricted 1962 estimates made in the Sudan reportedly placed the Dinka at about three million.

37 Lofchie, *Zanzibar: Background to Revolution*, op. cit., Table 3, p. 74.

38 For a general historical background see C. R. Boxer, *Race Relations in the Portuguese Colonial Empire* (Oxford, 1963). See also Rodrigues, "Influence of Africa on Brazil", *Journal of African History*, Vol. III, No. 1, 1962; Institute of Race Relations, *Angola: A Symposium* (Oxford).

39 See *Manchester Guardian*, April 28th, 1956.

40 Ibid.

41 *Africa Digest*, Vol. III, No. 8, May-June, 1956, pp. 38-9.

42 *East Africa and Rhodesia* (London), October 14th, 1965, p. 95. Disapproval of mixed *marriages* in Rhodesia is even stronger than disapproval of casual mating between the races. A distinguished United Nations official was once denied a job at the University College in Salisbury because he had a white wife. The man was himself a black Rhodesian.

5

ON ECONOMICS AND REGIONAL AUTONOMY

Joseph U. Garang

This seminar is very important.* It is for the first time focusing attention on what many people consider the core of the Southern problem, namely the question of the economic and social development of this region.

For many years politicians have raved, cried, shouted and threatened about inequalities between North and South. But they never understood that these inequalities cannot be overcome except by the economic and social development of the Southern Provinces and the lifting of the Southern masses out of centuries of backwardness and superstition. These leaders drew up plans which would satisfy the interests of the small intellectual elite but not once did they demand social change.

It is said in the world press and elsewhere that the core of the Southern problem is the slave trade or that it is religious strife between Christianity and Islam.

But the slave trade came to an end more than seventy years ago. How can it be the cause of a movement that began recently? As for religion, any attempt to introduce it into politics has always met with decisive opposition by both the Northern and Southern masses.

The Southern problem is a manifestation of *the national question* in the conditions of transition through which Africa is now passing, and where questions of social change, and the new democracy which must necessarily accompany it, are on the agenda of the day.

In Western Europe, the national question featured most manifestly in the period roughly beginning with the French Revolution in 1789 and ending in 1871 with the Franco-Prussian war and German unification. Rising capitalism and, therefore, the need for extensive commodity production required, as against feudal particularism,

---

* The first draft of this article was read to the Sudan Erkowit Seminar held in Juba, Southern Sudan in late 1970.

G

politically united territories or states of people speaking the same language. Language is the most important means of human intercourse and therefore the development of language and culture create the best conditions for the rapid extension of trade and thus of commodity production. In Sudan the need for trade is and was the main vehicle for the spread of Arabic as the *lingua franca* in the Southern towns. It is the merchants who have been keen to learn the local Southern languages.

The tendency of every national movement has been the establishment of a national state. Hence the appearance of French, German, Italian and other national states in Western Europe.

You will remember that feudal absolutism, for various historical reasons, had established large multi-national states in the East, such as the Russian and Austrian empires, in which one or more privileged nations dominated and oppressed the others.

But capitalism also began to develop in Eastern Europe, including among the oppressed nations. In the period 1905 to 1919 these nations — such as the Poles, Ukrainians, Serbs, Croats, Czechs, Armenians, Georgians, also raised the slogan of self-determination and in time set up national states, independently or in federation with others.

Relying on this European experience, some of our friends among the intelligentsia in the South have raised the slogan of self-determination, claiming that since the North is of Arab stock the Southern negroids have the right to an independent state or federation. Northern nationalists have answered from positions of mere sentimentalism about the "unity of the fatherland", resisting the views of those "half-educated Southern imperialist stooges".

The approach of both sides is unscientific and wide of the mark. To arrive at the correct approach it is necessary to proceed from a study of our concrete conditions in Africa and in the Sudan in particular.

Certain features of African states must be observed. First, at the time of the European scramble for Africa in the second half of the last century, most African peoples lived in conditions of natural economy which could not give rise to a political system higher than tribalism. This situation has been more or less preserved by colonialism. Therefore while national groupings such as the Dinka, the Baganda, the Bakongo, the Yoruba and the Ibos exist in Africa, they all speak distinct languages and inhabit definite territories. They have not developed into nationalities because their primitive conditions do not provide for a social division of labour and development of the language and culture. They have remained imprisoned within the political structure that we know as tribalism. In such pre-capitalist conditions a national movement proper cannot arise.

Second, the boundaries of most African states are artificial in the sense that they do not represent the aspirations of some homogeneous cultural or linguistic group to achieve statehood, as was the case in Europe. They were drawn up by colonialists on the basis of mere varying convenience and therefore the population of these states is heterogeneous, being composed of national groupings at various stages of development.

Thirdly, within these territories economic development has been uneven. In any given colony imperialism was interested in exploiting only limited areas in order to extract a given raw material. In other colonies some territories were, for historical and geographical reasons, more suitable than others for exploitation as a market. In consequence the areas where colonialism concentrated its exploitation became more developed than others and the national grouping or groups in the selected areas achieved more progress over their neighbours and developed cities, trade, a working class, an intelligentsia and national capital. The picture has not been exactly uniform but it was generally the case. We may cite the cases of Southern Ghana, Southern Nigeria, Buganda, the Northern Sudan, Southern Chad.

Fourthly, while the first period of capitalist development was marked by national particularism and the growth of national states, our era is marked by the international unity of capital and its expansion into imperialism, exploiting and oppressing all and every class within the colonies.

Consequently, the national movement arose not as a movement for the establishment of a national state but as an anti-colonial movement embracing all or most national groupings in varying degrees of participation. The slogan of self-determination was raised not in the interests of a given national grouping but in the interests of all. Alongside purely political slogans, the masses also raised slogans of fundamental social change in the direction of socialism.

Naturally, the movement for independence was led by the national groupings in the more advanced areas of the colony and, within them, by intellectuals representing the interests of national capital or the petty-bourgeois in town and country. Having thrown out the colonial power it was they who got the benefit of independence in the form of state power, high posts in the state, government contracts, etc.

Because of its class composition and orientation, the new leadership invariably fails to solve the problems of social change, particularly the problem of *uneven* development of the country. On the contrary, they take the road of capitalist development, and consequently the gap between the more developed areas and the backward areas continually widens. Experiments with liberal democracy lead to corrupt institutions not expressing the interest of the people. A bitter struggle ensues between the people and the ruling strata. To the people of the national grouping or groupings from whom the rulers come, the problem appears in its true light as a class struggle. But to the people of the national groupings in the backward areas, who are excluded from power, the problem appears as one of a struggle between their people on the one hand and the whole national grouping in power on the other.

The struggle is led by the intellectual petty bourgeoisie who rally their people behind them. Naturally these petty bourgeois intellectuals mistake their own aspirations to power and prestige as the interest of the masses of their national grouping. It is not surprising, therefore, that this petty bourgeois leadership does not raise the issue of economic and social development of their area nor problems of raising the standard of living of their people. They raise only the problem of their own share in power and in the state apparatus.

Attacked on grounds of racism or national oppression, the ruling classes or strata of the dominant national grouping reply with suppression, and to justify this suppression, appeal to the national sentiments of the masses of their grouping, seeking to rally them against the complaining national grouping as "separatists" or "imperialist stooges". It is a known fact that the petty bourgeoisie, by reason of its economic position in society, is the most patriotic and most easily affected by narrow nationalism. Consequently, in answer to the call of his ruling classes, the petty bourgeois official of the dominant national grouping or groupings goes out in earnest to suppress the peoples of the complaining national grouping or groupings.

Thus, in consequence of this struggle, the real issue of social progress is lost sight of. The forces of the masses in the country are effectively divided. And the problem of social progress is substituted by the problem of rivalry between national groupings.

The position is further complicated by the intervention of neo-colonialism which seeks to exploit the position in its interest by encouraging these divisive movements.

Thus Africa is presenting a new type of national struggle arising out of her peculiar economic and social conditions. In answer to this new challenge the call for self-determination is out of the question and therefore irrelevant.

The paramount question is that of the unity of all the masses in the entire country for the purpose of liquidating the remnants of colonialism in all fields — economic, social, political and cultural —

and the advance to progress and socialism. The golden test, therefore, is — Does the movement of a given people advance or retard the cause of social change? If the answer is positive then progressives should support that movement. If not they should oppose. The national question is secondary to the question of progress.

Consequently, Nkrumah was right in opposing the separation of Ashanti. Led by feudal princes, the Ashanti movement aimed at preserving backward conditions in the area and the retardation of general progress of Ghana. So also were the claims of Northern Nigerian chieftains correctly opposed by the nationalist leaders of Southern Nigeria. The concessions subsequently made by the Nigerian nationalist leadership in creating a federal system has proved to have been unwise. The result was the domination of Nigeria by Northern and allied reaction leading to all the complications that followed. It is obvious that the Biafran leaders and their imperialist American and French allies capitalized upon the situation created by the more classical Nigerian reaction allied to Britain. The Buganda example is of more interest because the Buganda area is more advanced than the rest of Uganda. The main separatist role was played by the Buganda feudal aristocracy, of course, seeking to preserve its dominance in the area against social change. But as a more advanced area, should Buganda not have furnished social forces interested in the unity of the whole of Uganda? The problem is that Buganda did not have commercial capital which is the force usually vocal on questions of unity. Buganda capital was in land and produced raw materials which had no market in the other regions. Commercial capital was, and remains, in the hands of Indians. The slogans of unity and social progress were therefore left to be raised by the petty bourgeois intellectuals of the more outlying regions of the North who correctly and decisively combated the pretensions of Buganda.

In Katanga and Kasai the movement had no genuine social roots. It was artificially created by the stooges of British and Belgian capital who feared Lumumba's nationalist movement. Later the whole thing became a struggle between the pawns of Belgian and British capital on the one hand and American capital on the other, ending in the victory of the more powerful American capital.

This general analysis applies to our country as well. It is a country with artificial boundaries like all other African states. Our population is heterogeneous. We have the Beja national groupings in the East, the Nuba in the centre and about fifty negroid national groupings in the south. This is to mention only a few of the variegated population of our country.

But to turn to the question in hand, namely the relations between the South and what we loosely term the North. Because of her great distance from the sea, her being sealed off by swamps, her difficult jungles and woodland and the low cultural standard of her people which did not create the demand for manufactured goods, British capitalism considered the South too expensive for exploitation. It was not willing to risk huge investments for uncertain returns. Nothing was therefore done in the South by way of the exploitation of her natural resources. She was to be reserved for pressing times in the future.

The North, or to be more exact, the territories of the Arab tribes, were for them more suitable for exploitation. They were nearer the sea; the Nile tributaries provided cheap transport for bringing in goods and taking out raw materials; the cultural standard of the people was higher and they would thus consume more manufactured goods; a huge plain gently sloping to one side and conveniently near the two Niles offered ideal conditions for cheap gravitational irrigation; with Egypt, the main supplier of long-staple cotton, making troubles which might end in the expulsion of Britain from Egypt and the loss of Egyptian cotton, the Gezira plain offered a good alternative. In the West, trees bearing the best gum-arabic in the world awaited exploitation at minimum cost. It is this combination of circumstances that encouraged British capitalism to concentrate its exploitation on the territories of the Arab nationality.

Hence railways were built, trading centres opened, and schools turned out cheap office workers. In short, the North developed in a way. Modern social classes appeared on the scene. Within fifty years the North was far ahead of the other outlying areas.

Worth mentioning also is the role of the rivalry between Egypt and Britain. Anxious to build a large pro-Egyptian intellectual stratum in the Sudan, Egypt opened the doors of her schools and colleges to hundreds of the Northern youth. Not to be left behind, Britain did the same, not only in England but also by educational expansion in the North. In this way a large number of Northern intelligentsia appeared on the schene.

The rest you know well. The colonial liberation movement was naturally led by the North and power fell into the hands of the Northern intellectuals representing the interests of national capital and semi-feudalism. The Northern intelligentsia occupied nearly all posts in the service. Southerners had neither national capital nor trained intelligentsia. They were left out in the cold. There followed the familiar story of incompetent and unconcerned leaders, and corrupt parliaments, which could not and did not take an interest in problems of progress or the redress of the uneven development between the North and the outlying regions of the country.

It is essentially these problems, problems of uneven development, that constitute the objective roots of the Southern movement.

It is true that neo-colonialism has stepped in to exploit the situation with the general object of either weakening Sudanese governments and forcing them into compromises with imperialism or, where those governments, like the present, are progressive, of overthrowing them by causing a drain on resources and frustrations in the army. It is true also that many of the Southern intelligentsia have failed to recognize the essence of the question and to date consider regional autonomy to be a marriage of convenience rather than a scientific solution.

But despite all this the objective essence of the problem is there — that the Southern movement is a movement reflecting the need for social progress in the area, for a redress of the condition of uneven development.

Thus this regime's programme rightly emphasizes problems of development of the Southern Provinces. But it has not stopped at that. It recognizes the right to regional autonomy and "the right" of the Southern people to "develop their respective cultures and traditions".

Why regional autonomy? Why this right to develop cultures and traditions?

It has to be repeated that there is no real national entity in the South, and for this reason alone the principle of self-determination cannot apply. But there are national groupings in the South, each inhabiting a definite territory, speaking a definite language (not a dialect as is generally supposed, for a dialect is a local variety of a bigger language), and with its distinct customs and traditions.

What is the future of these groupings? Will they merge with the rest of the country to form one Sudanese nation? It seems obvious that the majority of Southern national groupings will disappear or merge into others if only because of their weak numerical strength. It will not be profitable for them to cling to their languages, traditions or other peculiarities. Even this will take a very long time, as national sentiments die hard and people cling to the lands inhabited by their forefathers. The case of the Nubians of Halfa is in point. Despite centuries of foreign physical and cultural invasions and occupations, they still cling to their respective languages to-day.

However, the main point at issue is that of the large national groupings such as the 2 million Dinka, the 500,000 Nuer, the 200,000 Bari, the 250,000 Zande in the Sudan alone, and the 150,000 Shilluk. In the old days some of the more powerful groups would subjugate the others and absorb them, as the Azande have absorbed many other tribes. Such methods are now inconceivable and the bulk of the population will remain peaceful in their territories.

The merger of these peoples with others in the North to form one Sudanese nation has become impossible. More than fifty years of relative development through which the Arab tribes have passed have had their effect. A real Sudanese Arab nationality has appeared with its distinct traditions, culture and sentiments. It has left tribalism behind in view of the clear appearance of its social classes and division of labour. Since independence it has made great strides forward. There is no longer any probability of other national groupings entering this closed ring.

Thus, given democratic conditions, the large Southern national groupings might develop into nations within the Sudan. At any rate it is impossible to forecast today how things will look after the next fifty years.

A revolutionary democrat would therefore do best by not closing the door before these peoples. What is needed is such democratic conditions as would enable the Southern national groupings to develop in freedom, preserving or developing their languages, cultures, and traditions as they think best. History will decide their fate as national groupings. To do otherwise would be to introduce national oppression.

It is for this reason, among others, that the revolution stands for regional autonomy and observes the right of the Southern people to develop their cultures and traditions. Another important reason is that regional autonomy will tend to unite the Southern and Northern masses. At present the Southern petty bourgeoisie are able to rally the Southern masses behind them by appeal to national sentiment. But with the application of the democratic solution the wind will be taken out of the sails of Southern chauvinism and the way will then be open for the broadest unity of the progressive forces in the South and the North. This is important, because revolution must reach the Southern masses in the countryside as soon as possible. If we have to wait, they will come to know Arabic and we shall probably have to wait for fifty years or even more. The need for social change and mass mobilization requires that we reach these millions soon. The only way to do this is to start developing the major languages on a mass scale so that we can reach the people through the written word.

As to the constitutional form of autonomy, it should be left for study by such specialized committees as the government may deem proper to appoint. It is better not to state a pre-emptive view at this stage and thereby fetter the committees' initiative.

It must be said, however, that since its inception, the Southern movement has always cut across provincial and ethnic lines and it would be unusual if such specialized committees treated the South otherwise than as one region. Moreover, the need for economy in cadres and expense as well as for development speak against the fragmentation of the South into several regions.

Another area of legitimate concern is the creation of those modern classes who will have a real interest in the unity of the country and in progress. The government has given this matter great weight. Its blueprint says that "the building of a broad socialist oriented democratic movement in the South, forming part of the revolutionary structure in the North and capable of assuming the reins of power in that region and rebuffing imperialist penetration and infiltration from the rear is an essential pre-requisite for the practical and healthy application of regional autonomy".

It is not for small reason that the joint session of the Revolutionary Council and Council of Ministers emphasized this point. A study of the past of the Southern movement shows that right wing leaders have been dominant on the scene. At critical moments in the national struggle for independence or social progress the traditional leaders of the Southern movement have invariably stood side by side with Northern reaction against the forces of progress.

You will remember the struggle around the Stanley Baker Constitutional Committee of 1952; the events of August, 1955 just on the threshold of independence; the struggle around the American aid in May, 1958; the conflict over the October government on February 18th, 1965; the deadlock at the Round Table Conference; and the general offensive by Anyanya in the same year, are salutary examples of this stranglehold.

Since, with a socialist-oriented regime holding the reins of power, the danger of a secessionist movement is on the increase and will increase to a much greater extent the more this regime goes left, the building of a broad democratic movement is a must. Reliance on pacts of convenience with forces which today appear to be in greater command of Southern public opinion can have treacherous results. One must rely on the objective forces of progress which although they appear to be weak today, are nevertheless growing by the very nature of things.

Economic and social progress in the South will definitely lead to an increase in the strength of the democratic movement.

Finally, a few words about some practical problems. In the South we are faced with two economic and social tasks. There is the problem of development in the South as part of the Sudan as a whole and with the object of solving problems facing the whole country. Hence in the Five-Year Plan, we have made allocations for projects to produce sugar, kenaf fibre, coffee, canned fruit, rice, and so on.

Here our object is import substitution.

But we have not as yet provided for the urgent needs of the South such as reconstruction, resettlement, job-creating projects. With the conditions of peace now improving and hundreds of people pouring into towns and villages from abroad and the bush, these urgent tasks must be met with.

The view of the Planning and Co-ordinating Council for the Southern region is that we must have two development budgets for the South: one, like the Five-Year Plan, to cater for the national needs of the Sudanese economy, and the other to be a special budget for reconstruction and resettlement; in short, to care for the urgent social needs of the area. The latter budget should be at the disposal of the Committee.

Another matter which requires elaboration is the question of the development of our domestic animal wealth. Two-thirds of the population of the South depend on animal wealth. Strange as it may seem we have nothing in the Five-Year Plan for the development of this large wealth and, therefore, for two-thirds of the Southern population we have not much in store for the next five years.

6

CAN SECESSION BE JUSTIFIED?
THE CASE OF THE SOUTHERN SUDAN*

Peter Russell and Storrs McCall

I. INTRODUCTION

To examine the reasons which might be given as justification for a secessionist movement may seem like an irrelevant exercise. The combatants in secessionist struggles do not normally rest their case on a careful weighing of the pros and cons of the situation. The secessionists, once they have reached the stage of armed struggle, assert their right to self-determination while their antagonists, the national government, insist on the sanctity of national unity. Neither side is much concerned with looking for reasons to justify its position. A secessionist struggle is precisely one of those situations of political conflict where the possibility of resolving differences through the rational exchange of ideas has vanished.

While this may be conceded, there nevertheless remains a strong case for attempting to examine the merits of secession in the cool light of reason. Nowadays, whether we like it or not, no political struggle which leads to armed conflict is merely domestic. The national era, in which the "internal" affairs of a nation could on no account be considered the business of anyone outside the nation, is, if not quite dead, at least moribund today. The international community has seen too much of the havoc which the internal politics of a state can inflict on the world beyond its borders, and too much of the inhumanity which may be perpetrated within its borders under the aegis of national sovereignty, to regard all situations of internal conflict as beyond its ken. Today international organizations like the United Nations and the Organization of African Unity cannot ignore such internal conflicts, especially when they result, as in the case of the Sudan, in the death of hundreds of thousands of

* Revised version of a paper read at Makerere University, Kampala on December 2nd, 1970.

people. As the Biafra war surely demonstrated, even if the representatives of these international agencies wish to do nothing more than mitigate the loss of life and provide humanitarian relief, they have a certain obligation to involve themselves in these situations. Members of international organizations are likely to find that they must act, and they can choose to do so either with or without reflecting on the merits of the opposing claims. Our own choice would be clearly the former.

But it is not just the outsider working with an international organization who may see the importance of such an inquiry. Before a secessionist movement takes the plunge into military action there must surely be a place for rational judgment on the merits of such a course. And also when the movement is well under way and its cost in human life becomes clear, there will be some individuals on both sides who will wish to re-examine their positions to see if the carnage is not too dear a price to pay for their principles.

What are these principles? That is the question which this article investigates, in the context of the Southern Sudan. The investigation proceeds on the assumption that two absolute principles are unacceptable: absolute sovereignty or absolute territorial self-determination. The first of these is the theory that whatever goes on within the borders of a national state is wholly the business of the legal government of that state, and that this government has exclusive jurisdiction over, and the right to impose its will upon, all the citizens of that state. The second is the view that any group of people inhabiting an area of the globe's surface, no matter how small, has the right to run its own affairs and to decide which, if any, other national bodies it wishes to be associated with. Both these positions are untenable. Firstly, there are situations in which one must refuse to equate legal sovereignty with political or moral legitimacy. Imperialist white "sovereigns" who in the nineteenth and early twentieth centuries imposed their will on African majorities, or sovereign authority within Hitler's Third Reich are, surely, examples. On the other hand a willingness to regard as legitimate the claim of any group to withdraw its territory from a state so that it can govern itself would seem to be an invitation to anarchy. If neither state sovereignty nor territorial self-government can be treated as absolute rights, we must see by what considerations they are properly limited.

Our enquiry, then, has two dimensions. In the first place, we try to set out the considerations which should count in weighing the merits of any group's demands to secede from a sovereign state. Secondly, we shall apply these considerations to the facts of the Sudanese "situation" as we perceive it, to see whether in the light of these considerations the secessionist goals of the Southern Sudanese are justified. We hope our readers will appreciate these two dimensions of our paper, for as is the case with the application of any general principles it may be possible to agree with our exposition of them without accepting their application to a particular case.

II. THE BASIC CONSIDERATIONS

In our view the considerations which come into play in assessing the merits of secession fall into five categories: (i) questions of democracy and democratic rights, (ii) racial and ethnic equality, (iii) the viability of the post-secessionist states, (iv) the effects on other nations and world order, and (v) alternatives to secession. We shall take these up one at a time, applying them as we go to the Sudan. In the concluding section of the paper we shall try to pull our deliberations under these separate heads together and attempt a final assessment of Southern Sudanese secession.

(i) Democracy

It is difficult these days to find a definition of democracy that is acceptable to all "democrats". Still it would seem that even democrats who are as far apart as Maoist revolutionaries and American liberals might agree with the proposition that unless political authority is based more on the consent of the governed than on coercion its legitimacy may be called into question, even though they may disagree widely on the institutions through which such consent is expressed. This concept of "democracy", while too vague to establish a blueprint of *good* government, may at least establish a rough measure of *illegitimate* government.

In our view, if a large proportion of the population of a state is denied the opportunity both to participate in the decision to form the state and to establish its mode of government, as well as the opportunity to participate effectively in that government after the state is formed, then this would constitute a very strong argument in favour of secession. But it must be noted that the democracy test is a double-edged sword. It should be applied not only to the state as a whole but to the secessionist movement itself. For if within the population which the secessionists claim to represent there are significant segments which have not manifested a will to attach themselves to the movement and are deliberately excluded from its leadership, this would seriously undermine the justice of the secessionist cause.

In terms of fundamental rights and freedoms, this basic democratic right to participate in the authority by which you are governed must take precedence over other basic human rights such as those mentioned in the United Nations Declaration of Human Rights. No doubt every state fails to extend all of these rights to all of its citizens — for example, the right to an education, the right to a job.

But such failures hardly constitute grounds for questioning the legitimacy of such states if the bulk of its citizens can participate on fairly equal terms in governmental decisions. Thus in terms of the inherent justice or fundamental human rights involved in a secessionist struggle, we would regard democratic rights as the litmus test of legitimacy. How by this test do the Sudanese state and the Southern secessionists measure up? Let us begin with the Sudan.

The first matter to be discussed concerns the circumstances which surrounded the formation of the Sudanese nation-state. During the period 1947-1956 which culminated in the country's independence, did anything approximating a reasonable "social contract" take place? Did Southerners participate fully in the discussions and decisions which led up to independence, so that one might say that the birth of the Republic of the Sudan had their consent and support? The answers to these questions are of paramount importance in assessing the extent to which Southerners have succeeded in securing their democratic rights.

The first move to consult the South about its future occurred in June 1947, when the Juba Conference was convened by the Civil Secretary of the Condominium Government, Sir James Robertson. The background to the decision to hold the conference was as follows. Since 1930 the policy of the British in the Sudan had been to develop the three Southern provinces of Upper Nile, Bahr el Ghazal and Equatoria along distinctively negroid and "African" lines, and to exclude Northern, Islamic influences as much as possible. This "Southern Policy" was summed up by the Governor-General in 1945 as follows:

> "The approved policy is 'to act upon the fact that the people of the Southern Sudan are distinctly African and Negroid, and that our obvious duty to them is therefore to push ahead as fast as we can with their economic and educational development on African and Negroid lines, and not upon the Middle Eastern and Arab lines of progress which are suitable for the Northern Sudan. It is only by economic and educational development that these people can be equipped to stand up for themselves in the future, whether their future lot be eventually cast with the Northern Sudan or with East Africa (or partly with each)."[1]

In 1946, however, the British entirely reversed their "Southern Policy". The reasons for this were many: (i) strong pressure was being exerted by educated Northerners in Khartoum for self-rule and eventual independence of the *whole* of the Sudan, including the South; (ii) there were signs that the exclusion of Northerners from economic projects in the South was hindering its development rather than helping it; (iii) Egypt was pressing Britain not to separate the

South from the North, in the hope that one day the whole country might be united with Egypt; (iv) British East Africa was apparently not interested in closer links with Southern Sudan. Hence the British did a rapid about-face and in 1946 stated their new policy in this way:

"The policy of the Sudan Government regarding the Southern Sudan is to act upon the facts that the peoples of the Southern Sudan are distinctly African and Negroid, but that geography and economics combine (as far as can be foreseen at the present time) to render them inextricably bound for future development to the middle-eastern and arabicized Northern Sudan: and therefore to ensure that they shall, by educational and economic development, be equipped to stand up for themselves in the future as socially and economically the equals of their partners of the Northern Sudan in the Sudan of the future."[2]

In the course of the abandonment of Southern Policy, no Southerner was apparently consulted by the Khartoum Government. When this fact was pointed out by several British D.C.s serving in the South, and when the question arose of forming a Legislative Assembly for the Sudan, the Civil Secretary convened the Juba Conference in June 1947. At this conference the decision was taken to send Southern representatives (appointed by the Governor of the Southern provinces) direct to the Legislative Assembly in Khartoum. This was done, despite the fact that the Southern representatives had had no previous experience in administration or legislative councils and formed a minority of only 13 out of 95 members.[3] One wonders why the South consented to send representatives to a central legislative council in Khartoum rather than to a local Southern administrative or advisory council at such an early stage in their political development. The answer seems to lie in a change of heart on the part of certain Southerners which took place between the two days of the Juba Conference. During the first day the Southern delegates favoured sending representatives to the Khartoum Legislative Assembly only as observers who would report back to a Southern Advisory Council. On the second day many of them favoured sending full representatives and abandoned the idea of an Advisory Council altogether.[4] Asked why he had changed his mind, James Tembura said that Judge Shingeiti (a Northern delegate) had told him during the recess that if they did not do so they would have no say in the future government of the Sudan. Furthermore, it seems that the question of raising rates of pay for Southern Government officials to the standard of those in the North was made by the Northerners to appear conditional upon full participation in the Khartoum Assembly.

Although the Juba Conference is often pointed to as providing a charter for the future relationship of South and North,[5] it is difficult to see how such a charter could legitimately be regarded as having been laid down by the well-meaning but politically very inexperienced Southerners who attended it.

The next important steps on the path to independence were the visits to Cairo of representatives of Northern political parties in late 1952 and early 1953, which resulted in the Anglo-Egyptian Agreement of February 1953. As we shall see, the South played no part in these visits, nor in the negotiations which led to the agreement.

For years Egypt, insisting on unity of the Sudan and Egypt under the Egyptian crown, had opposed any moves toward Sudanese independence. But with the overthrow of King Farouk and the coming to power in July 1952 of General Neguib, himself half-Sudanese by birth, the whole situation changed. Neguib signed agreements with all the Northern political parties providing for self-determination, free elections and the evacuation of all British officials and administrators within three years. In February 1953 the British also signed. But no Southerner was invited to Cairo, and there is no record of their ever being consulted on the agreement which was to shape the future of their country.[6] From the beginning, Southerners had hoped for a long period of economic and educational growth before independence, accompanied by the attainment of political maturity. These hopes were not to be realized. With the signing of the Anglo-Egyptian Agreement the way was clear for independence, and Southerners found themselves caught up in a rush of political events which they were unable to alter or direct.

Although power to control things had by now passed out of the hands of the Southerners, their frustrations and fears culminated in a last outburst before independence. In August 1955 the Southern Corps of the army mutinied, and before it was put down the mutiny had grown into a popular uprising in which 261 Northerners living in the South were killed.[7] The exact causes of the mutiny are still being debated, but the Report states one of the major contributing factors to have been the results of "Sudanizing" the Civil Service in 1954, in which 800 expatriates were replaced by 794 Northerners and only 6 Southerners.[8]

By October 1955 the uprising in the South had been brought under control, and only one thing remained before the Sudan could become a fully independent sovereign state. This was the support of the 22 Southern members of parliament (out of a total of 97) who had been elected in December 1953. Since the end of the mutiny these M.P.s had been demanding that a plebiscite be held in the South under the auspices of the United Nations. The British replied that this was undesirable, as it "would almost certainly revive and strengthen the movement for some sort of self-rule in the South".[9] To gain the support of the Southerners for a motion for immediate independence, the first clause of the independence motion in the Sudanese parliament stated that the Southern claim for a federal system of government would be given "full consideration" in the forthcoming constituent assembly. On this condition, and because it was the first time the Northerners had given recognition to the idea of a federation, the Southern M.P.s voted for the motion on December 19th, and the Sudan became independent on January 1st, 1956.

Looking back on this course of events, one could hardly say that the South had given its full consent and support to the birth of the Sudanese nation-state. Here the situation in the Sudan contrasts unfavourably with that in Uganda or Kenya, where great care was taken by the colonial power to ensure that all ethnic and tribal groups were consulted and represented in the discussions leading to independence. Let us now turn to the post-independence years.

The first significant event concerns the promise to give the idea of federal government "full consideration" in the forthcoming constitutional deliberations. A 46-man Constitution Committee was set up in December 1956, but since the South was allotted only 3 of the 46 seats and since decisions were taken on a simple majority basis the idea of federation made no headway, and in 1958 Mr. Mohammed Mahgoub announced in Parliament that the committee "had given the Southern claim for federation very serious consideration, and found that it could not work in this country".[10]

However, the idea of federation was not dead, and further attempts to advance it were made during the life of the Parliament which was elected in March 1958. In these elections, the South was given 46 seats out of a total of 173. Forty of the 46 formed the Southern Bloc, a well co-ordinated group dedicated to federation. The Southern Bloc made contact with a number of indigenous "African" (as opposed to "Arab") groups in the Northern Sudan whose problems and interests were not dissimilar to the Southerners'. The response from some of the groups — the Beja, Fur, Nuba, and Funj — was favourable, and a meeting was held in one of the provincial capitals of the North (Port Sudan) at which the idea of the various regions managing their own affairs was enthusiastically received.[11] However, the growing demand for federation was silenced in November 1958 by the handing-over of the government by Prime Minister Abdallah Khalil to the army. Various reasons have been adduced for this hand-over, but the strongest seems to be the fear of the Khartoum politicians that the popular demand from the provinces for local autonomy would seriously weaken the power of the central government. It is significant that on November 17th, the very day the army took over, a large Fur conference was due to be held at which it was expected that the idea of federation would be endorsed. In any case, with the army take-over all political parties and all talk of federation were banned. In the words of Ali Baldo, the Governor of Equatoria:

"We thank God that by the marvellous efforts of the Revolutionary Government, the country will remain forever united. You should turn a deaf ear to any talk which comes from politicians, as you well know what has become of them in the past few years and you certainly don't want bloodshed again in the South. You are aware that anybody who interferes with public peace and tranquility will be dealt with severely and at once. During the days of Parliament, the Southern Parliamentary members advocated a federal government for the South. Such ideas are gone with politicians."[12]

With the abolition of the 1958 parliament went the Southerners' hope of furthering their demands by legitimate means. It also ended the only period in which the South has had reasonably full and competent representation in a Sudanese parliament. Later, when parliamentary government was restored in 1965, conditions in the South were too unsettled for elections. When these were held in 1967 and 1968, many of the most able Southerners had given up hope of achieving anything by legal means and were fighting in the bush. It is doubtful whether a group of legislators comparable to those of 1958 will ever again be assembled.

In March 1965 there occurred an event which raised hopes of settling the differences between South and North in a just and reasonable way. This was the Round Table Conference on the South, held in Khartoum under the auspices of the caretaker government which succeeded the army regime in October 1964. In addition to Northern and Southern delegates, the conference was attended by observers from Algeria, Ghana, Kenya, Nigeria, Tanzania, U.A.R., and Uganda. The Southern delegation was initially divided on the issue of whether to propose federation, or to propose something stronger and then accept federation as a compromise. These differences were eventually resolved and two unified Southern proposals were made, the first calling for self-determination by the peoples of the South through a plebiscite, and the second proposing a system of government which boiled down to a confederation rather than federation.[13] The Northern proposal was a scheme of regional government which placed such matters as elementary education and the organization of co-operatives in the hands of the regions.

Compromise between these two positions proved to be impossible, and the conference adjourned with the promise to meet again in three months. No second meeting, however, has yet taken place.

Not much more remains to bring the story of the South's democratic representation up to date. As stated earlier, elections occurred in 1967 and 1968. But both these elections were flawed by the unsettled conditions prevailing in the South, and are marked by extremely low numbers of votes cast.[14] More seriously still, the leader of the Sudan African National Union (SANU), William Deng, was shot dead by the army shortly after the announcement of his election in Tonj Central Constituency.[15] In these conditions one cannot say that a people's democratic rights are being exercised. As far as the South is concerned, it was no great loss when Major-General Jaafar el-Nimeiry ended the Sudan's second period of parliamentary rule on May 25th, 1969, and announced the formation of a new military government. The policy of this government towards the South does not so far seem to be very different from that of previous ones. On the one hand the government proposes a scheme of Southern "regional autonomy", the details of which have yet to be specified, and on the other it attempts to suppress the Southern independence movement by military force. No fresh approach to the problem is represented by this policy.

If the new regime in Khartoum is to make any headway towards reconciliation in the South it must grant the minimum democratic rights of the Southerners. This means, at the very least, that the future status of the South within the Sudan must be discussed with political leaders who represent opinion in the South. To exclude Southerners from such discussions either because they have been "rebels", or because they are not "socialists",[16] would in effect be to exclude any representative Southern leadership from participating in the determination of the South's future.

As was observed earlier, the question of democracy is a double-edged one. We have applied the test of democratic rights to the case of Southerners within the Republic of the Sudan. But what of Southerners within the secessionist movement? Does the leadership of the movement represent in at least some degree the will of the people? Does the movement have broad popular support? Are its leaders selected in a roughly democratic way? To these questions we must now turn.

To begin with, the difficulties of having public discussion of issues, political campaigning, and elections within an illegal movement are very great. The movement owes the formal start of its existence to three men, Father Saturnino, William Deng and Joseph Oduho, who founded SANU in February 1962 in Leopoldville. In early times it was kept going by the personal efforts of these three: in November 1964 it held its first general convention in Kampala and elected Aggrey Jaden as president with a new slate of officers. In those days, when the headquarters of the movement were in exile, the holding of meetings and conventions was fairly easy. But in 1965 the decision was taken to move inside Southern Sudan, and although this put the movement in closer touch with the people it made communications and the calling of meetings extremely difficult.[17] The last big convention was in Angudri in August 1967, which involved elections and the replacement of the earlier liberation parties and fronts by the Southern Sudan Provisional Government (SSPG). However, the SSPG did not have the support of all areas of the South: Eastern Equatoria, Zande and Moru-land did not participate. In early 1969 it broke up and was replaced by smaller splinters such as the Nile Provisional Government (NPG) and Anyidi. Threatened by the Northern army from without and factional rivalries from within, the movement stood in danger of collapse. But in mid-1969 a new Anya-Nya military government was formed in Eastern Equatoria under Joseph Lagu, which in April and July 1970 absorbed Anyidi and the NPG respectively. The whole of the South is now united under one leadership which, though not democratic in the sense that it was elected by popular vote, has been accepted by the movement as providing the best chance of withstanding the increased military pressure from Khartoum.

More important than the internal structure of the present secessionist government is the degree of support it receives from the ordinary people of the South. This is difficult to gauge exactly, but a rough start can be made by estimating the relative proportions of the population who live under the control of the Khartoum administration and of the Anya-Nya. In Equatoria, and in most parts of Bahr el Ghazal and Upper Nile, these proportions are given by the numbers living in towns and countryside respectively. In these areas the government writ extends only to the towns and "peace-camps" in which the administration encourages people to settle. A mile or two outside the towns the country is under the more or less nominal control of the Anya-Nya. Now the people who continue to live in the countryside do so of their own free will, and in defiance of the government's instructions that people should settle in "peace-camps". Hence they may be said to have "voted with their feet" in favour of the protection of the Anya-Nya rather than that of the government. The same could be said of the refugees in neighbouring countries, who remain in spite of numerous inducements to return. Subtracting the rural people and the refugees from the total population leaves at most 25% living in restricted areas under the control of the government. By this measure (and the authors know of no other at present) the popular support of the secessionist movement would seem to be at least 75%.

There are two factors which, it must be acknowledged, may seriously upset these figures. The first concerns the military balance of power. As long as the Anya-Nya are able to provide a protective screen of security around the rural areas where people live, then the people will stay there, paying their taxes and their allegiance to the provisional administration set up by Lagu's government. This administration provides a system of justice through chief's courts, with auxiliary police and prison services, primary schooling, and rudimentary medical services. But if the protective screen is broken, and security deteriorates, then people may be forced into towns or into exile. Hence military security is an extremely important factor in the popular support which Lagu's government received. If it declines, his support declines. Secondly, it is fairly clear that the people who, despite great hardships, continue to live in the country-side, do so of their own free will. But it is not clear that the same applies to the people living in towns and "peace-camps". Given their choice, many of these people might well prefer to flee to the countryside but be unable to do so because of the army. Because of these factors which are extremely difficult to assess, our figure for the popular support of the liberation movement in the South must be regarded as provisional only. Note however, that we have used "voting with the feet" as the criterion of support. If one allowed feeling and emotional identification to be the criterion, then support for Southern self-determination would probably run over 99%.

One final question of democracy should be raised. Let us suppose that, by some miracle, a democratic political system were to be established in the Sudan, with opportunities for all parties to have their voice heard and to participate in the process of government. Would the system be workable? This is not a trivial question. It is not difficult to think of political groupings of people for whom a single system of democratic decision-making might be totally unworkable (think of the black and white South Africans, for example). What are the conditions which lead to democratic unworkability of this kind? Robert Dahl has indicated that one of them is a population amongst whom the distribution of opinion on issues of vital importance is at a point "where each side is large and each regards the victory of the other as a fundamental threat to some very highly ranked values".[18] Under these circumstances a system of majority rule is likely to produce a government which is totally unacceptable to the losing side in an election. In the Republic of the Sudan it may be that, on the basic question of how the country is to be governed and of what "national character" is to be, this point has now been reached.

On the matter of how the country is to be governed the positions adopted by North and South at the Round Table Conference have not changed fundamentally. As mentioned above, the South proposed a plebiscite with the following choices: (i) Federation, (ii) Unity with the North, (iii) Separation. The North proposed a system of regional government. The two sides still appear to stand by their proposals, and no compromise is currently in sight.[19] On this point the distribution of opinion between North and South seems to satisfy Dahl's condition of an impasse. On the matter of what "national character" the Sudan should adopt, and of what its national aspirations and loyalties should be, there is no agreement either. The basic point of contention is whether the Sudan should identify with the Arab countries or with Black Africa, and although the noblest and best course would perhaps be to act as a bridge between the two, Southerners have so far shown little enthusiasm for this alternative.[20] As an extreme example of the Northern attitude the words of Ali Abdel Rahman, then Minister of the Interior, may be quoted:

"The Sudan is an integral part of the Arab world. . . . Anybody dissenting from this view must quit the country."[21]

On the other side, the decision taken by the bush schools under Anya-Nya protection to drop Arabic and to follow the East African pattern of education may be cited.[22]

To sum up, it would seem that North and South are already so far apart that a democratic system of majority decision-making might be unworkable. However, this point in itself would not necessarily justify the break-up of a state. Opinion in America on the eve of the Civil War was probably divided in this way, yet one would scarcely regard this as justifying the secession of the Southern States. Or one can conceive of a situation where similar distribution of opinion might be found between an intransigent bourgeois class of property owners and a socialist working class. In both this and the American Civil War case one might be more inclined to opt for a civil war or revolution, with a view to reforming the state so as to abolish slavery or capitalist exploitation. But these examples indicate how important it is to investigate the source of the cleavage in opinion or attitude which threatens to make democracy unworkable. What is the main political division of opinion is on racial or ethnic lines and concerns attitudes of racial superiority? This leads to our second consideration.

(ii) Racial and Ethnic Equality

Even if some racially or ethnically distinct section of a state's population were given reasonable legal rights to participate in its government, if the members of this group were consistently regarded as inferior and treated as inferiors in the day-to-day social intercourse of the nation, the value of any democratic rights they might enjoy would be gravely diminished. If they were regarded as inferior *and* denied their democratic rights this would constitute an even stronger argument against submitting to the government of those who claimed to be their "natural" superiors. In the African context this consideration is particularly important, for while it may be conceded that ethnic self-determination has not figured prominently in the philosophy of African Nationalism, a belief in racial self-determination has.[23]

Now what is the situation in the Sudan with regard to racial equality? It is difficult to avoid the conclusion that the balance is fairly heavily weighted on the Northern side. The following statement gives evidence of the attitude which certain Northerners adopt toward Southerners.

"It is unfortunately true that many Northern Sudanese, especially from among the uneducated class, regard the Southerners as of an inferior race, and the Gallaba (Northern traders) in Southern Sudan form no exception to this, as the majority of them are uneducated. The traders refer to the Southerners, and often call them 'Abeed' (slaves). This practice of calling Southerners 'Abeed' is widespread throughout the three Southern provinces. It is certainly a contemptuous term, and is a constant reminder to the Southerners of the old days of the slave trade."[24]

On the other side, many Southerners would seem to be contemptuous of Northerners, as is shown by the terms "Mundukuru" and "Minga" which they occasionally use to refer to them. Racial attitudes, however, are notoriously difficult to assess,[25] and we should look elsewhere for more concrete means of determining the relationship between the two groups. Indications of how the wind blows in this respect are provided by three tables in Albino's book, which we reproduce below:

TABLE I

GOVERNMENT SECONDARY SCHOOLS FOR BOYS IN SUDAN— SHOWING EXPANSIONS[26]

Period	No. of schools in North	No. of streams in North	No. of schools in South	No. of streams in South
Before Independence	4	14	2	3
Added after Independence	18	45	nil*	3
Total	22	59	2	6

* Malakal Secondary School, which bears the name of a town in the South which was opened in Omdurman in 1962, has now been absorbed into Wadi Seidna Secondary School.

TABLE II

INTAKE TO THE SUDAN POLICE COLLEGE[27]

Years*	No. of Northerners	No. of Southerners	Total
1950	10	3	13
1951	14	4	18
1953	13	7	20
1957	27	3	30
1960	29	nil	29
1961	36	1	37
1963	26	1	27
1964	35	2	37
Total	190	21	211

* There was no intake in 1952, 1954, 1955, 1956, 1958 or 1959.

TABLE III

OFFICERS COMMISSIONED IN THE SUDANESE ARMY[28]

Date Commissioned	No. of Southerners	No. of Northerners	Total
27.7.1954	1	19	20
1.8.1955	3	45	48
1.4.1956	3	35	38
1.7.1957	3	40	43
1.5.1958	2	58	60
1.5.1959	1	56	57
1.5.1960	2	58	60
1.1.1962	nil	64	64
1.1.1963	1	56	57
1.1.1964	nil	71	71
1.1.1965	4	67	71
Total as at 1.1.1965	20	569	589

The figures in these tables are unfortunately not up-to-date, but for the period they cover they indicate that government policy has certainly been favouring the Northern side. Under these conditions it is difficult to say that a state of racial equality prevails in the Sudan. We must however be careful about the use of the word "racial" here. The "racial" cleavage we are dealing with may be more subjective than objective, more cultural than biological. But subjective racism, however much it may rest on a mistaken conception of real racial differences, can be as potent a source of discord and inequality as objective differences of race. In Canada, for instance, until recently the French and English were always referred to as Canada's "two founding races",[29] and this tendency of Canadians to perceive their division in racial terms undoubtedly deepened the tensions between the two groups. Although in the Sudan there is a more objective basis for the racial cleavage than is the case in Canada, the line between "Arab" and non-Arab is often a very tenuous one, especially in such heterogeneous areas as Kordofan and Darfur provinces. But the point is that Northerners and Southerners tend to regard one another and treat one another as if they belonged to racially distinct groups. Besides, there are pronounced social and cultural differences between North and South, in large measure due to the fact that the South is 99% Christian or pagan while the North is 99% Moslem. These differences are also accentuated by the much higher level of "modernization" achieved in the towns of the North. When all are added to the (subjective and objective) racial differences the result is a fairly clear-cut line of division. This point is brought out in a somewhat extreme form in the following quotation from Aggrey Jaden, at the time president of SANU:

> "The Sudan falls sharply into two distinct areas, both in geographical area, ethnic groups and cultural systems. The Northern Sudan is occupied by a hybrid race who are united by their common language, common culture, and common religion; and they look to the Arab world for their cultural and political inspiration. The people of the Southern Sudan, on the other hand, belong to the African ethnic group of East Africa. They do not only differ from the hybrid Arab race in origin, arrangement and basic systems, but in all conceivable purposes ... There is nothing in common between the various sections of the community; no body of shared beliefs, no identity of interests, no local signs of unity and above all, the Sudan has failed to compose a single community."[30]

The authors would estimate that the vast majority of problems connected with the dispute between North and South in the Sudan have an underlying "racial" basis, where the word "racial" carries with it the social and cultural implications just mentioned. This point is sharpened by the fact that the express policy of the North seems to be to "assimilate" the Southerners in the sense of replacing their various indigenous tribal cultures by a single Islamic and Arabic one. Southerners, however, have shown little enthusiasm for this, and it seems plain that if such assimilation takes place, it will be against their will. This point is an important one when the question of secession is being considered, since the majority of nationalist and secessionist movements in history have appealed to the preservation of their cultural identity as one of the strongest justifications for their stand. (Consider the Quebeckers in Canada, the Scots and Welsh in Britain, the Kurds in Iran, the Basques in Spain, etc.) As far as the rights and wrongs of the matter go, the authors take the view that a threat to cultural identity counts as a consideration in favour of secession only if the threatened assimilation is forced, i.e. against the will of the people. Thus a minority group within a country whose government is tolerant of their cultural and ethnic traditions will have less justification for attempting to secede than a group facing a government whose policy is enforced assimilation. On this count, in the opinion of the authors, the Southerners have some justice on their side. Note incidentally that social *assimilation* is a very different matter from social *modernization*. As far as is known, Southern Sudanese have no objection to schools, roads, health services and communications; they merely want such modernization to be along the lines of their own choosing rather than in a pattern imposed by Khartoum.

In sum, the division between North and South in the Sudan more closely resembles that in South Africa or in the Portuguese African territories than in a country where opinion is divided on social or economic policy. As long as the political conflict is articulated primarily in racial terms, it is not easy to see how the differences can be satisfactorily reconciled within a unified state. Either the ruling group which denies equality must change its beliefs, or be ousted from power by the oppressed group. Or if this is unlikely, as seems to be the case in the Sudan, they, the oppressed, will as a matter of principle have a strong case for secession.

(iii) Viability of the Post-Secession States

The justification of important political acts, like secession, can not be entirely confined to deontological considerations of justice. Most of those who assess the merits of secession will wish to attach some importance to the consequences for the well-being of those affected, both within and without the state, by secession. In the next section we shall consider the external consequences of secession. Here we shall focus on the way it is likely to affect the population within the state — both in the part that secedes or threatens to secede, and in the part that remains.

Certainly one of the strongest arguments used against secessionist movements in the past has been that they would divide the state into two fragments, one or both of which would be severely crippled economically and scarcely able to survive as a viable nation. Here the possibilities should be appraised along two time intervals. It is important to consider how much better or worse off the two sections of the fragmented state would be immediately after the secession; it is equally, if not more, important to consider how the long-term economic prospects of the region would be altered by secession.

In the Sudan it would seem to be clearly the case that if a successful secession took place now in the short term the majority of people in both parts of the Sudan would be economically better off. This may be demonstrated as follows:

a)   The North is spending large amounts on the war in the South, without any economic return. The most recent estimate of these expenditures the authors have seen is between S£12 and S£20 million per year,[31] which is a lot for a government whose total annual revenue in 1968 was S£98 million.[32] Besides these expenditures by the Sudan Government, additional contributions are made in the form of military aid by such countries as Russia and Egypt,[33] and although these costs are not directly borne by the Sudan Government it is unlikely that some long-term arrangement has not been made for their repayment.

b)   Active fighting in the South began in 1963 and has grown steadily worse, with a peak in 1965 and a considerable increase in 1970. During this time large numbers of Southerners living in the countryside have not been able to grow enough food to feed themselves let alone provide money for clothes, salt, soap, medical treatment, etc. Because of the fighting, they have had to move their homes deeper and deeper into the forest. Meanwhile those living in towns such as Juba, Wau and Yei, who are isolated from those in the countryside by a double cordon of Northern troops and Anya-Nya, have seen the price of food increase out of all proportion.[34] There is no doubt that secession would improve the immediate economic condition of the majority of Southerners enormously.

But short-term economic factors are one thing; long-term conditions are another. It is the long-term prospects for development which would be most severely jeopardized by the break-up of the Sudan. The North with the modernized skills and technology of the urbanized segment of its population has much to offer the South, while the South in turn with its fertile land and water resources has much to contribute to the North. There can be no doubt that the long-term economic outlook for both parts of the country would be brighter when linked together in a common national economy. To take one example; it was proposed in 1946, as a result of studies conducted by the Jonglei Investigation Team, that a canal be built on the White Nile from Jonglei to near Malakal to by-pass the area of the *sudd* and thereby avoid the very large loss of water by evaporation in the swamps. Although the main beneficiaries of the plan, through the provision of increased amounts of Nile water for irrigation purposes would be the Northern part of the Sudan and Egypt, the studies provide for agricultural projects in Southern Sudan which, although they would involve radical changes in the present way of life of the pastoralist Dinka, Nuer and Shilluk peoples, would doubtless be of overall economic benefit.[35] It is clear, however, that the implementation of the scheme would be very much more difficult were Northern and Southern Sudan to separate.

This being said, that the eventual economic consequences of separation would in theory be less attractive than those of staying together, the practical point must be made that up to now the conflict in the Sudan has stultified economic activity in the South. Given the present political deadlock, development of the immense agricultural and other resources of the South is impossible. In fact, the situation has regressed since 1956. Four examples will illustrate this.

a) During the period of the premiership of Abdallah Khalil (1956-58), Messrs. Boxall and Co. applied to undertake sugar production in the South, and drew up plans for a sugar factory at Mongalla. The government, however, suggested that the factory be built in the North and the sugar cane transported from the South for processing. When the company rejected this idea as too expensive, the plan was cancelled. The Mongalla sugar project was eventually moved to Gineir and Kashm el Girba in the North to give livelihood to persons displaced from Wadi Halfa by the Aswan Dam.[36]

b) In 1959-61 a German firm applied to utilize the papyrus of the *sudd* region for paper production. Although the company wished to build the factory near the source of raw material at Malakal, the government insisted on a site in the North and the project was abandoned. After a time the government opened its own paper factory at Aroma in the North, using cotton stalks as raw material.[37]

c) By far the most successful enterprise in the South was the Zande Scheme, which started in 1947 and grew rapidly to a flourishing industry, employing many tens of thousands of Azande in the growing, spinning and weaving of cotton. But the civil war brought production to a stop in 1965, and today nothing remains of the Zande Scheme except empty fields and deserted houses, the people having all retreated into the forest out of the reach of the Northern soldiers.[38]

d)   The last example is of a different kind, though illustrating the same theme of progressive economic impoverishment. For centuries, copper has been mined in small quantities at Hofrat en Nahas in western Bahr el Ghazal, although no large-scale commercial development of the deposits was undertaken. In about 1963, however, Hofrat en Nahas and a small area surrounding it were quietly transferred to Darfur Province in the North, and it appears that the deposits are now being mined by modern methods.

In conclusion, then, we may say that the economic resources of North and South are complementary, and would supplement each other nicely in a unified economy. But their exploitation presupposes co-operation between Northerners and Southerners. As long as the present political deadlock continues, the economic viability of a united Sudan will be less than that of its two component parts taken separately.

One other important point remains to be considered under the heading "Viability of the post-secession states". This is the question of whether more ethnic and minority problems (as distinct from economic ones) may not be created in the post-secession states than were present in the original one. To take an illustration of what we mean, one of the arguments against the secession of Biafra was that this would create a "stranded minority" — the non-Ibo residents of Biafra — with potentially the same problems that Ibos originally faced. Would the separation of North and South in the Sudan create new problems analogous to this?

To take the South first, at the moment there are a number of Northern ("Arab") traders there, whose position following secession would be roughly analogous to that of the Asian shopkeepers in East Africa. Ironclad guarantees would have to be provided that those who wished to return to the North would not endure financial loss in the process. On the side of the North, the problem is more difficult, As mentioned earlier, there are groups of indigenous "African" peoples in the North (Beja, Fur, Nuba, Funj, etc.) whose position *vis-à-vis* the so-called "Arabs" (see comment above on the mis-use of this term) might be much worse after secession than before. According to the 1956 census, the population of the Sudan was divided as follows:[39]

Arabs	39%
Southerners	30%
Non-Arab Northerners	28%
Others	3%
	100%

If the South separated, the indigenous Africans in the North would cease to belong to a 58% African majority as in the present Sudan, and would find themselves comprising a 40% minority in a new Northern Sudan. This does not seem *a priori* to be a very happy solution. In another twenty years it could result in a fresh African secessionist movement in the North analogous to that of the South today. A few words might be said about the development of political consciousness among the African peoples of Northern Sudan at this point.

It was mentioned earlier that in 1959 the Southern members of parliament made contact with certain regional groups in the North who supported the idea of federation. These groups were not the first to represent Black African ideas in the North. The first was an association known as the "Black Block" (Arab *kutla soda*) which was founded as a social organization in Khartoum as early as 1938 and which was prevented from becoming a political organization by the British because of its radically anti-Arab views. The Black Block had no representation either in the legislative assembly of 1948 or the parliament of 1953, and seems to have died out around 1955. Its ideas lived on, however, in such groups as the Social Organization of the Nuba mountains (founded 1954) and the Beja Congress. In 1964 the Nuba organization changed its name to GUN (General Union of the Nuba Mountains) and adopted a constitution which included clauses against the buying of Nuba land by non-Nubas, against the sending to Parliament of non-indigenous "Arabs" to represent the Nuba and Fur people, and against the paying of poll-tax to the Khartoum government. In the 1965 elections GUN elected 8 M.P.s and the Beja Congress 11. Despite invitations to join the NUP and Umma parties, they refused, and continued to serve as independent spokesmen of indigenous Africans in the North. In the 1969 elections, they suffered severe losses in parliament, only 5 GUN and no Beja Congress candidates being elected. The movement started to go underground, with groups such as Suni in Darfur and the Free Negro Organization[40] infiltrating the army and police. In 1969 these groups united under the name of the United Sudanese African Liberation Front (USALF)[41] and attempted a coup against the government: they were forestalled by the successful army coup which brought General Nimeiry to power. Today they are the principal vehicles for the channelling and diffusion of political consciousness among the Negro peoples of Northern Sudan.

To return to the question of what sort of post-secession states would result from the separation of North and South, it is the impression of the authors that the indigenous Africans of the North would be unhappy at the prospect of becoming a 40% minority in a new Northern nation. The state of their political self-awareness is still no doubt less "black" and less "African" than that of their Southern compatriots, but the day may come when they feel themselves in roughly the same position as the Southerners do now. If the rights and the sentiments of this segment of the Sudanese population are to be respected, then either (i) separation may have to be rejected as a solution, or (ii) the line of separation may have to be drawn farther north, as so to include them in the southern part.

(iv) Effects on Other Nations and World Order

As we have already argued no violent political struggle in today's world can be regarded as a matter of purely internal concern. Secession in the Sudan, the largest state in Africa, could not but have a significant impact on the world beyond the Sudan's borders. Of particular concern, in so far as we are considering points which might count against a secessionist movement in the Sudan, would be its influence on centrifugal forces within other African states and its possible effect on African unity.

On the first point it cannot be denied that a successful secessionist movement anywhere in Africa would give some encouragement to those separationist tribes which are so prominent a feature of political life in the newly independent states of sub-Saharan Africa. Certainly, one of the greatest practical obstacles to the success of the Southern Sudanese secessionists is the unwillingness, thus far, of any other African nation to support their cause. And it must be remembered that this bias in favour of preserving national integrity is not confined to Africa. The United Nations itself is, after all, an association of *nations* with a firm commitment in its charter to the principle of national sovereignty. Recently the politics of some of the world's more developed nations such as Canada, Britain and even France have been enlivened by ethnically-based separatist movements. Granted that most of these are not such serious threats to national existence as the Southern Sudan, the fact remains that the nations of the world, especially those of Africa, believe they have an interest in keeping existing states intact.

These considerations must be borne in mind in examining the case *against* Southern Sudanese secession. But there are at least two points which may diminish the weight of these arguments in the Sudanese context. The first is that the Sudanese secessionist movement is not tribal but racial. The sense in which it is racial and the extent to which social and cultural factors contribute to the differences between North and South have already been discussed. It suffices to point out here that the racial character of the dispute makes the Sudanese situation more like that of Mozambique, Angola or Guinea than that of Katanga or Biafra. We shall return to this point later.

Secondly, and more importantly, the general normative issue must be raised: is national sovereignty to be regarded as absolute? We have already argued that this position is unacceptable. Where a large, fairly homogeneous group within a nation is consistently denied its democratic rights and treated as racially inferior, the principle of inviolability of national unity or sovereignty is, surely, no longer tenable. However, it might be contended that the new states of Africa constitute a special case in this respect. It might be argued that in these states, beset as they are by particularist loyalties, many of which were deliberately nurtured by their former imperialist rulers, the sanctity of existing borders should be accepted as an unbreakable first principle. Is this argument of sufficient force to off-set Southern Sudanese claims to the right to secede?

Certainly it is one of the strongest against secession. But one might ask how far it can be pushed. Could the argument justify *any* degree of maltreatment of an ethnic or racial group by the government of an African state? The authors feel that their answer to this question must be a negative one, and would argue that the most ardent African nationalist should give some weight to the points raised above under the headings of democracy and racial equality. A double standard of national decency is incipient racism. In fact, it is the worst kind of neo-colonialism to argue that African states cannot live up to the same standards of humanity and justice that are applied to other nations. This was precisely the argument colonialists used to oppose granting independence to African people. As Abu Mayanja put it, in a different context, "If we say that the conditions in which we can have civilized, decent, responsible or responsive government, do not obtain . . . we shall have betrayed the principles upon which our freedom and our sovereignty is founded, we shall have betrayed the cause of African democracy. We would be assisting those racialists who believe that the African . . . is incompetent, is incapable, is not ready."[42]

This having been said, the fact remains that a commitment to African unity has always been a distinctive feature of African nationalism, giving it a more universalist, less parochial quality than the nationalism of either European or Asian countries. As Abu-Lughod has pointed out:

"African nationalism developed along more comprehensive lines than had earlier types; it became a more inclusive movement than any of the Asian varieties. It conceived of the inhabitants of Africa as brothers . . . We may cite Black Africa's support of North African independence and its willingness, after the attainment of independence by all, to incorporate North Africa within the African context."[43]

This Pan-African sentiment is extremely significant both in the struggle against colonialism and neo-colonialism on the African continent and in the African cultural renaissance and quest for identity. The Sudan as an intermediate link between Arab North Africa and sub-Saharan Africa has been seen as epitomizing within itself the essentially dual character of African unity:

> "The enclosure of these two ethnic personalities (Negro and Arab) within a single territorial entity is itself an approximation to the concept of Afro-Arab marginality for the Sudan. Whether we take the Sudan as a dichotomous duality, . . . or . . . as an ethnic continuum, or as an inter-racial mixture, the country still emerges as a paradigm case of an Afro-Arab dual identity."[44]

Viewed in this way, the separation of North and South in the Sudan might seem a blow struck at the very principle on which African unity is based. But although in theory the Sudan may be a bridge between Northern and Sub-Saharan Africa, and although her fascination may lie in what Mazrui calls her "profound inter-mediacy", in practice she may not play this linking or intermediate role very well. On the contrary, if the racial animosities within the Sudan intensify, they are likely to spill over into other parts of the continent and embitter relations between Arabs and Negroes elsewhere. It is not even clear that the Sudan government genuinely desires the role of serving as a link between the two parts of Africa. Her current foreign policy of identifying more and more closely with her fellow Arab states, and in particular her recent federal union with Libya and Egypt, seem hardly calculated to increase her effectiveness in this role. Hence (in practice as opposed to theory), the secession of the Southern Sudan may not be such a severe blow to African unity as might appear, and could perhaps remove a source of friction between Arabs and Negroes that might one day prove harmful.

One other "external effect" must be mentioned: the danger of outside intervention. Katanga and Biafra demonstrate how quickly and with what disastrous consequences African civil wars can involve non-African powers from both the East and the West. If outside powers play a major role in precipitating the secessionist struggle, as was surely the case in the Congo, the secessionist movement's legitimacy is seriously undermined. This was certainly not the case in the Southern Sudan. But there are indications that the Southerners have recently received some support from at least one other country, and have also been helped by a White mercenary.[45] At the same time, as we have already noted, the amount of military assistance Khartoum receives from Egypt, Russia and now possibly

I

Libya seems to have increased considerably in recent months. If the struggle in the Sudan continues indefinitely there is a possibility that the Middle East belligerents will find a new area of conflict in Southern Sudan and drag their Great Power patrons into it.

No one who cares for African independence or world order can regard this possibility with equanimity. But one can hardly place the onus of responsibility for avoiding such a possibility entirely on the secessionists. Southerners who are attacked by Egyptian soldiers in Russian helicopters are going to seek arms of a comparable technological level wherever they can find them and that will most likely be from their enemies' enemies. More than anything else the gravity of such a possibility points to the need for the intervention of an agency such as the OAU. before the conflict escalates to the point where large-scale participation by outside powers is inevitable.

(v) Alternatives to Secession

Even if in terms of justice and internal and external consequences, a reasonable case for secession may be made out, one might still feel justified in asking whether the secessionists could gain their legitimate ends by some other means. In most contexts, and certainly in the Sudanese case, a secessionist struggle will entail dislocation, a great deal of bloodshed and loss of life. The cost in human suffering compels us to ask two questions: is it worth it, and is there any alternative?

The first question is impossibly difficult to answer. How does one measure the struggle for justice, freedom or democratic rights against physical hardship and death? Perhaps all we can say is that if we achieve our goal, with the majority of our people still alive, then it was worth it, and if we do not then it was not — we should have tried another way. To ask the question of the Southern Sudanese is to ask the same question of the freedom fighters in southern Africa or of the Palestinian guerillas. To the extent that it can be answered, we have done so already in the sections on democratic rights and racial equality.

The second question, whether there is any alternative to attempting secession through armed conflict, is a much more fruitful one. We could begin by laying down the general principle that no such conflict could possibly be justified until every legitimate means to the same end has been explored and exhausted. Was this the case in the Sudan? A sketch of an answer to this question has already been given in the section on democratic rights, and we can review the main points here.

In 1953 the Anglo-Egyptian Agreement for the independence of the Sudan was signed, on which the Southerners were not consulted.

Their representatives in Parliament voted for independence in December 1955 on the understanding that a federal system of government would be given full consideration, but the latter was voted down in a constitution committee in which the South had 3 out of 46 seats. Just as the Southern M.P.s in the 1958 parliament were beginning to interest their Northern non-Arab colleagues in the idea of federation, power was handed over to the army and all political discussion was banned for six years. In March 1965 the Round Table Conference on the South was adjourned without agreement, and has not been re-convened since. One might feel that all this does not justify the use of force. But human nature being what it is, it is at least understandable that Southerners should feel that the use of legitimate channels of protest had brought no result, and that the only alternative left to them was armed resistance.

The present situation in Southern Sudan is that a civil war is taking place in which no quarter is asked or given. But does this mean that the doors are irrevocably closed to negotiation, and that only military victory by one side or the other will bring a solution? The authors do not believe this to be so. On the contrary, since the conflict is a guerrilla one in which it is virtually impossible for one side to defeat the other decisively, the chances are that sooner or later both sides will realize that they have more to gain than to lose by negotiating. And when this time comes, it is quite possible that the Southerners may be able to realize their concrete political goals at some point which stops short of absolute separation. But it is unlikely that they would succeed in doing so were the *threat* of secession not there to force the Northerners to take them seriously. So the answer to the question "Is there any alternative to secession?" seemed to be "Yes". But the nature of the case is such that in order for there to be any genuine alternative, the Southerners must make it appear that there is none. Only in this way would it be possible for them to achieve their ends by negotiation rather than by force.

III. CONCLUSION

In this article we have attempted to present at least the major considerations which should be taken into account in assessing the right claimed by any group of people to secede from any country. We have then tried to apply these considerations to the particular case of the Southern Sudan. The difficult point has now come, at which we must try to pull together all the different considerations that we have discussed, and to make some sort of overall assessment of the Southern case.

Plainly it would seem that under categories (i) and (ii), namely democratic rights and racial equality, the Southerners have a good case. It would be difficult to say that they have ever succeeded in securing their democratic right to be heard and to be taken seriously in the decision-making councils of Khartoum. And the facts of discrimination against them on a personal level in education, in economic development, and in securing appointments in the civil service, police, army, etc., are fairly plain. So far their case is a strong one. But when we come to consider the internal and external effects of secession under categories (iii) and (iv), the position becomes less clear. As far as the viability of the Southern post-secession state is concerned, a vast amount of economic development and reconstruction would have to take place before a level of prosperity approaching that of Uganda or Ethiopia could be achieved. As for the northern post-secession state, there is the risk of creating a stranded minority among the indigenous non-Arab peoples who one day might find themselves in the same position as the Southerners. Finally, the effects of secession on African unity might be serious, although no doubt the potential divisive effects of the present conflict are also serious. As far as alternatives to secession in section (v) go, there would seem to be some, although they would seem at the same time to require that the threat of secession be present to make them appear attractive.

So what is the upshot of it all? Is Southern Sudanese secession justifiable? The authors find it difficult to give a definitive and unqualified answer, and leave the reader to make up his own mind. (He will in any case probably have done so already.) It seems to be a matter of weighing the *rights* of Southern secession against its probable *consequences*. The reader may conclude that, other methods having failed, the Southerners are justified in attempting to solve their problems by secession. Alternatively he may believe that no matter how just their cause may be, the consequences of separation would be too harmful to allow him to endorse the idea of secession. In the end it comes down to whether one places a higher value on justice, or on material well-being and international concord.

However, although the authors have refrained from drawing any *hard* conclusion, they feel entitled to make at least one or two soft points. The first is, that the development of a secessionist strategy by the Southern Sudanese has got more to be said for it and less to be said against it than other recent secessionist movements in Africa, such as those in Katanga and Biafra. These cases differ from that of Southern Sudan in having far less justice on their side (in the case of Katanga none at all), in lacking the element of racial discrimination, and of being characterized by the fact that the wealth of the seceding area was greater than that of the area being seceded from (always a suspicious feature, laying the secessionists open to the charge that they merely wish to distribute their wealth amongst fewer people).

In fact the resemblances between Southern Sudan on the one hand and Biafra and Katanga on the other are very small. If parallels are desired, they may be much more appropriately sought in the case of Angola, Mozambique and Guinea. Here we have the same history of a people who are denied their democratic rights by the government in power, the same element of racial/social discrimination, the same state of civil war in which the majority of the population are in the countryside giving active or tacit support to the secessionists, while a minority remains in the towns under the control of the government. And this is the second soft point we should like to make, namely, that the secessionist movement in Sudan is more akin to the liberation movements in Southern Africa than to any other hitherto existing African paradigm.

REFERENCES

1 Khartoum Secret Despatch No. 89, August 4th, 1945, quoted by R. O. Collins, "The Sudan: Link to the North", in S. Diamond and F. G. Burke (eds.), *The Transformation of East Africa* (New York, 1966), pp. 386-7.

2 Letter of 16th December, 1946 from the Civil Secretary to the Governors of the Southern Provinces and others, quoted in B. M. Said, *The Sudan: Crossroads of Africa* (London, 1965), pp. 164-5.

3 The South comprises about one-third of both the population and the area of the Sudan.

4 See the full report of the Juba Conference in Said, op. cit., pp. 46-71.

5 Thus Ismail el Azhari, the first Prime Minister of the Sudan: "The Sudan should be one unit on the basis of the decision arrived at during the Juba Conference in June 1947." (Quoted in the *Report of the Commission of Inquiry into the Disturbances in the Southern Sudan during August 1955* (Khartoum, 1956), p. 87.)

6 This fact has even been used to argue that since the creation of the Republic of the Sudan rests on no social contract with the people of the South, talk of Southern *secession* is inappropriate. Thus, "The Southerners reject charges of secessionism on the grounds that, since they were not party to the Cairo agreement involving Britain, Egypt and the Arab political parties of the Sudan, and providing for the country's joint independence, they are simply not bound by it." (Thomas Land in the *East African Journal*, June 1970, p. 46.) The principle employed here seems to be that one cannot secede from that to which one has never belonged.

7 See the previously mentioned *Report of the Commission of Inquiry*, p. 80.

8 *Report*, pp. 111, 114.

9 The Marquess of Reading, speaking for the British Government, quoted in J. Oduho and W. Deng, *The Problems of the Southern Sudan* (London, 1963), pp. 32-3.

10 O. Albino, *The Sudan: A Southern Viewpoint* (London, 1970), p. 41. It might be worth noting here that alone among all the countries of Africa, the Sudan still has no constitution.

11 Albino, p. 42.

12 *Morning News*, Khartoum, March 29th, 1961, quoted in Albino, pp. 45-6.

13 For the main proposals and the resolutions of the Conference see M. O. Beshir, *The Southern Sudan* (London, 1968), pp. 88-97 and Appendices 16-19.

14 According to Albino, p. 72, the winning candidate in one of the Torit Constituencies obtained 30 votes, and in Kajo-Kaji 95.

15 Albino, p. 74. The assertion that Deng was shot by the Army is, however, denied by official sources who accused the Anya-nya.

16 There may be very few Southerners who are "socialists" in terms of the Nimiery Government's version of socialism. But many Southern leaders would probably subscribe to the conception of "African Socialism" as defined by President Nyerere of Tanzania.

17 For example, it takes the movement a minimum of 45 days to send a message from Yei in Equatoria to Renk in Upper Nile.

18 Robert Dahl, *A Preface to Democratic Theory* (Chicago, 1956), p. 98.

19 The Twelve-Man Committee which attemped to carry on the work of the Round Table Conference produced a report in September 1966 which recommends a more decentralized system of regional government. However, it is unlikely to be decentralized enough to meet Southern demands, and in any case the report is now a dead letter. See Albino, pp. 123-31.

20 For the bridge concept see Ali Mazrui, "The Multiple Marginality of the Sudan," in *Violence and Thought* (London, 1969), pp. 163-83.

21 *Parliamentary Proceedings: Second Sitting of the first session of Parliament*, 1958, p. 3. Quoted in Albino, p. 6.

22 There are more than 150 such schools in Juba and Yei districts alone. Languages used are English and the vernacular.

23 See, for instance, Ali Mazrui's discussion of the Principles of Racial Sovereignty in Chapter 3 of his *Towards a Pax Africana* (Chicago, 1967).

24 *Report of the Commission of Inquiry*, pp. 123-24.

25 For an interesting historical survey of racial attitudes adopted by Arabs towards Africans over the past fourteen centuries, see Bernard Lewis, "Race and Colour in Islam", *Encounter*, August 1970, pp. 18-36.

26 Albino, p. 100.

27 Albino, p. 104.

28 Albino, p. 105.

29 For an example of this subjective racism in Canada see Peter H. Russell (ed.), *Nationalism in Canada* (Toronto, 1965), esp. Ch. I.

30 Aggrey Jaden's speech to the Round Table Conference, March 1965. Cited by George W. Shepherd, Jr., "National Integration and the Southern Sudan", *The Journal of Modern African Studies*, 4, 1966, pp. 195-6, and by Ali Mazrui in "The Multiple Marginality of the Sudan", loc. cit., p. 168.

31 Ruth First in *The Standard*, Tanzania, March 12th, 1970, p. 6.

32 *United Nations Statistical Yearbook*, 1969, p. 602.

33 For example, it is reported that Russia has recently supplied the Sudan with 60 MIG 21 jets based at Juba (*The Evening Standard*, London, November 3rd, 1970). This information would require additional confirmation.

34 A visitor to Juba in September 1969 reported that unground *dura* (a Sudanese staple grain slightly larger than millet was selling for 80-90 piastres per kilo — about 16-18 Ugandan shillings.

35 Although this may not be the place to voice them, the authors confess that they have certain misgivings about the premises on which the Jonglei project is based. Granted that enormous evaporation takes place in the *sudd* region, it is difficult to conclude that this water is "lost", since presumably it falls again as rain somewhere else. Winds in the area are frequently from the Southwest, hence it is possible that a fair percentage of the "lost" water falls as rain in the Ethiopian highlands. But these highlands feed the Sobat, the Blue Nile and the Atbara, which eventually flow back into the Nile, so that the Jonglei project may in the end be only a means of robbing Peter to pay Paul.

36 Albino, p. 90.

37 Albino, pp. 90-91.

38 Albino, pp. 95-96.

39 *Morning News*, Khartoum, January 18th, 1958, cited in Oduho and Deng, op. cit., p. 8.

40 The latter group is referred to in a speech by Mr. Awadallah, the then Sudanese Prime Minister, which is quoted in the *Uganda Argus* of July 31st, 1969.

41 See the letter by Tia Gita Tutu of USALF in *The Economist*, August 29th, 1970, p. 4. The author gives a clear picture of the feelings of the non-Arab peoples of Northern Sudan.

42 *Uganda Parliamentary Debates*, 2nd Series, Vol. 73, July 6th, 1967, p. 632.

43 Ibrahim Abu-Lughod, "Nationalism in a New Perspective: The African Case", in Herbert Spiro (ed.), *Patterns of African Development* (Englewood Cliffs, New Jersey, 1967), p. 43.

44 Ali A. Mazrui, "The Multiple Marginality of the Sudan", op. cit., p. 169.

45 See Antony Terry in *The Sunday Times*, London, March 1st, 1970, p. 6, and also the *Uganda Argus*, November 11th, 1970, p. 1.

7

THE BORDER IMPLICATIONS OF THE SUDAN CIVIL WAR: POSSIBILITIES FOR INTERVENTION

A. G. G. Gingyera-Pinycwa

To grasp fully the border implications of the Sudan civil war, we propose to construe the word *border* as meaning other frontiers besides physical or geographical boundaries. We choose to do this because there are many non-physical or non-geographical boundaries that, at least potentially, have implications for the Sudan civil war. Such are borders determined by the human make-up of the Sudan, by its religious make-up, as well as by the role the Sudan has carved out for herself in international affairs. All these factors supplement geography to give the Sudan a multiple system of borders the implications of which could be as consequential to the conduct of the civil war as those of geographical borders.

But the implications of borders can be equally multiple. Hence we propose right at the outset to define the scope of our discussion with regard to these as well. Of the many possible implications, two are basic and may be reasonably expected to characterize any civil war. The first of this is the likelihood of across-the-border or outside intervention in the dispute. The second likely consequence is also across-the-border, but flows in the opposite direction, taking the form of refugees fleeing into neighbouring countries. Of these two basic processes associated with the border in a situation of civil war, we will in this paper concentrate on the first, namely, the possibilities for intervention in the Sudan civil war.

According to a now well-known thesis, internal strife of the type now current in the Sudan can hardly help having international implications.[1] Such strife, according to this thesis, will tend to draw in outsiders. This may come about in the following manner. The weaker side in the conflict might seek to strengthen itself by looking outward beyond the borders of the given state for assistance both material and non-material. Whether such assistance comes or not, an external factor is introduced into the initially limited struggle.

This is the first channel for the internationalization of a civil war like that of the Sudan. But no sooner does the weaker side thus look outward than its behaviour is followed by the stronger side, too, which must now on the one hand confront the outsider intending to help, and on the other seek help in its own turn from outside in order to counter any advantage gained by the weaker side. The Nigerian civil war, for example, demonstrated these developments very clearly. Biafra's resort for help to such countries as France and Portugal was countered by Nigeria's hostility toward these countries, as well as by her own quest for external assistance from such countries as Britain and the Soviet Union.

Viewed in this perspective, the Sudan civil war could have a complex system of border implications, all arising from what one student has described as the "multiple marginality" of the Sudan.[2] In several respects that could be pertinent to the conduct of the civil war, the Sudan is either a crucial *borderland* or has *inside it* borders that are crucial. We designate the borderland character of the Sudan or the borders inside it as crucial because they are such that it is possible for the principle antagonists, namely the North and the South and their sympathizers, to range themselves on opposite sides of these divides. The Sudan has the misfortune of having so many of these that much of what we shall attempt to say about the border implications of its civil war is not common but unique to it. We will now proceed to examine the intervention possibilities in the Sudan civil war in terms of these multiple dividing lines.

We might perhaps start by looking at the Sudan in its African setting. The Sudan, like other North African countries that call themselves Arabic, regards itself as an African country belonging to the African world of which, as one Sudanese scholar put it, the Sudan is a "microcosm", reproducing all its physical, racial and cultural diversities.[3] The country has, therefore, side by side with such other Arab countries as Egypt, Libya, Algeria, Morocco, and Mauritania, effectively established its identity as an African country at the diplomatic level. It was thus one of the countries to attend the first Conference of Independent African States held in Accra in 1958. Similarly, it was one of the original signatories to the OAU. Charter, the foundation document for that organization. Further, the "Africanness" of the Sudan appears so unchallengeable diplomatically, that the country can even risk taking very active and controversial roles in such purely African problems as the Congo Rebellion of 1964-65, and the crisis over the recognition of the Amin regime that came into power in Uganda in January 1971. There have been times when some black Africans were hesitant about accepting these Arab countries into the African fold and, indeed, when the Arabs themselves were doubtful of their role in Africa. But such times are now past or are fast passing away.

Nevertheless, the Sudan, because it is the point where black African meets brown or white African, must go through an ordeal which no other Arab countries seem to be subjected to. This is the ordeal of having the "Africanness' of some of its citizens challenged. Right through the Sudan runs a border that separates the South from the North more decisively than geography alone could have done. Ethnically and culturally, the Southern is negro, Sudan with affiliations tending southward to Uganda, Congo and Kenya rather than northward. This is the portion inhabited by the Nilotic peoples such as the Dinka, Nuer, Shilluk, Anuak, and Jo-luo; the Nilo-Hamitic peoples such as the Bari, Latuko, Toposa, and Murle; and the Sudanic peoples such as the Madi, Moro, Belanda and Azande. To the North of the zone inhabited by these peoples, one finds the brown or even black people who either style themselves Arabs or accept Arab culture and who ethnically and culturally are therefore apart from the Southerners.

Until quite recently this border, which significantly coincides with the front line of the present civil war, was taken for granted, with little being done to iron it down. The Northerners looked to the North and revelled in the glories of Islam and Arabism, of which they deemed themselves a part.[4] The Southerners wandered about, indifferent to the frontier, in search of a livelihood. It was not until the emergence of nationalism in the years after World War I that the Sudanese nationalists awoke to the realization of the implications of this border. For years, since the establishment of Condominium rule in 1899, the British (who were supposed to govern with Egypt but actually governed alone) had been following a "Southern Policy" which according to one, not exactly disinterested, scholar

"was aimed at the elimination, by administrative means, of all traces of Muslim-Arabic culture in the South and the Substitution of tribal customs, Christianity and the English Language, with the ultimate objective of giving the three Southern provinces a character and outlook different from that of the country as a whole and even, possibly, separating them from the main body of the Sudan and lumping them together with other 'possessions' further south, in order to form a great East African Federation under British control."[5]

This policy was one of the most important targets of Sudanese nationalism and had to be terminated in 1946. But it was in fact already too late. The damage had been done. Over twenty years of separate administration and separate acculturation had awakened

the Southerner to the question of his identity. He now came to see
himself as being distinct from the Arabs, from whom he came to
expect very little consideration. That, of course, is what has been at
the heart of the civil war. There are perhaps two important points to
note here. First, the genuineness of the Southern contention. There
can be no honest doubt that when they say that they are not Arabs
either ethnically or culturally, the Southern Sudanese are correct.
A line of division certainly does exist; denying it may be necessary
for the Sudan's politicians who are attempting to erase it; but it is
not in line with the truth. The second point follows from the first.
If the Southerners are non-Arab in ethnicity and culture, they share
close affinity in these two respects with a large portion of the
Negro-African world. Thus the Sudanese are both in the Sudan on
the one hand and in the Congo and Uganda on the other; the
Nilotics are in the Sudan on the one hand, and in Uganda on the
other; while the Nilo-Hamites are on the one hand in the Sudan and
on the other in Uganda and Kenya. With so many differences between them and the Northerners to whom they are opposed, and so
many similarities between them and the peoples of neighbouring
countries, the Southerners have a good chance of drawing in their
Southern neighbours to intervene in their favour against the
Northerners, from whom they are both ethnically and culturally
cut off. Why this has so far not happened we shall attempt to explain
later.

If we press on with our exploration of the Sudan in its African
setting we encounter yet another crucial line of division that could
play an important role in determining the pattern of external
intervention in the present civil war. This time it is a border that is
determined denominationally. The pattern of religious affiliation in
the Sudan presents that country with a second crucial internal
boundary. This is the boundary between Islam, on the one hand,
and Christianity and paganism, as it is sometimes called, on the
other. To be sure, the Sudan in this respect is akin to the so-called
"Sudanic" states whose belt runs across the continent from the Horn
of Africa and the Red Sea in the East to the Atlantic Ocean in the
West and whose distinctive common feature is the bond of Islam.[6]
It is further correct that even going southward one finds in Uganda,
Kenya, and Ethiopia substantial Muslim elements. But all these
links are external, as it were. The regimentation of Muslims versus
non-Muslims that the Sudan escapes on its international borders is
tragically and too obviously present within the country itself. While
there are sprinklings of Muslims in the Southern Sudan, the basic
picture with regard to denominational ecology within the country is
clearly that of a Muslim North confronting a Christian-cum-animist

South. Thus, here too, the Sudan has a sensitive internal border which, because it unfortunately coincides with the line dividing the combatants in the civil war, could easily be exploited by outside denominational sympathizers. In this regard, the call of the Holy Jihad against infidels may not yet have been heard in the fifteen or so years of the civil war, either because that method of conflict resolution has become outmoded in modern times, or because the Muslim North is the stronger side. But the frequent allegations by the Khartoum Government that some European Christian missionaries were attempting to arouse in the Southerners an attitude hostile to Islam, should help to indicate the potentials of the problem of intervention along the Muslim/non-Muslim border.

Viewed in yet another and broader setting, the Sudan still cannot escape its haunting marginality. This is the Middle Eastern setting in which the Sudan, by virtue of its claim to be an Arab country, also belongs. Together with Islam, Arabism was for long one of the two principal bases of self-identification in this section of the Sudan that has since become dominant in the independent regime. They provided the bases for national glory and pride.[7] Although nationalism has since provided additional bases, the identification with Arabism and with the Arab World remains very strong. Thus the Sudan is a member of the Arab League, a participant in Arab summit meetings and other get-togethers, and, most recently, was for some time a participant in the federation talks that culminated for Egypt, Libya and Syria in the agreement to federate. Because of this close association between it and the Arab World, the Sudan has been charged with bearing out the Southerners' claim that their wishes are not taken into consideration. Numbering well over four million out of a population of about twelve million, the Southerners, who are not keen for membership of the Arab World, feel they are being dragged willy-nilly into that orbit. However, the point that is pertinent for us is the fact that the claim of the Sudan to be an Arab country is not only significant as a racial line dividing black Africans from Arab Africans, but because it puts the country on one side of yet another frontier that has a consequence for the civil war. This very claim to belong to the Arab World appends the Sudan to the Middle East and hence makes the Sudan an actor in the very difficult international politics of the Middle East.

In this Middle Eastern arena the dominating feature is, of course, the Arab-Israeli war that has been going on since 1948. By virtue of its membership of the Arab World, the Sudan finds itself ranged against Israel, and is thus affected on yet another crucial frontier — a frontier most amenable to Israeli penetration in order to fish in the troubled waters of the Sudan civil war. In this respect, it is perhaps fortunate for the Sudan that it has not so far involved herself whole-heartedly in the Arab-Israeli conflict. Had this not been the case, no one perhaps would be able to imagine the path that the civil war in the Sudan would have taken. As it is, it appears that Israel has been taking a line similar to that which one finds in recent American thinking on nuclear strategy—a line of measured action or retaliation not going too far beyond what the enemy dares to do or has ventured to do. Reports of Israeli assistance to the Southerners are heard from time to time and it is difficult to say whether or not they are false.[8] But our interest lies in the danger potential of that border in Middle Eastern international politics which separates the Arab countries, including the Sudan, on the one hand, and Israel on the other.

It is clear that across-the-border foraging for support for their respective causes could be mutually rewarding for both the Israelis and the Southern Sudanese. By intervening in the Sudan civil war, Israel could at the minimum divert some of the massive Arab forces away from her own frontiers; while for the Southern Sudanese, association with Israel implies not only better military training and the possibility of military equipment, but also a chance of having the Southern Sudan problem taken more seriously both by the Sudan itself and by the world at large. In the latter respect, it might be suggested that the best chance the Southerners have of improving their prospects in the civil war is by baiting Israel to greater intervention. More than that of the neighbouring and ethnically similar African countries, Israeli intervention would not only be based on more meaningful power but, as we shall next proceed to show, would draw in some other powers who up to now have shown no interest in the Southern cause. This kind of conclusion from the pan-Africanist point of view may be deemed traitorous; but looked at from the point of view of the Southerners who are under pressure, it is unavoidable.

Let us next proceed to look at the Sudan in yet another setting which creates a border that could be crucially important in the course of the civil war. This is the global context. The relevance of this context follows in the first place from the previous one to which we said the Sudan belongs, namely the Middle East. Whilst the Arab-Israeli conflict, which is the dominant feature of international politics in the Middle East, does take place in a limited area of the globe; it is nevertheless of global importance. In the main this has been the case because of its strong "suction-effect" on the two super-powers, the United States and the Soviet Union. Since the concert and cooperation of these two giants on one side of the Arab-Israeli conflict in the crisis of 1956, they have drifted farther and farther apart. The overall result of this has been such that the Israelis, to put it mildly, tend to have the balance of American sympathy and material support on their side, while the Arabs tend to have the balance of Soviet sympathy and material support on theirs. But what is more, in the event of a Middle East flare-up, each of these super-powers would feel as concerned as if they were actually combatants, despite such attempts at mediation as they usually put up. In the global context, therefore, we encounter yet another area where the "Arabness" of the Sudan cuts it off from the rest of the world in such a significant manner that the division could be a crucial point of external intervention in the civil war. The border of alignments in world politics, in so far as it impinges on the Middle East, coincides with the Arab-Israeli border. Accordingly, we may conclude that should an Arab-Israeli conflagration be wide enough it would reach the Sudan and with it would come the rival sympathies of the super-powers. That eventuality would place the civil war in a wider setting, with consequences that would no doubt increase the temperature of the situation considerably.

But viewing the Sudan in its global context, intervention on the part of the super-powers in her civil war could also come about without relation to the Arab Israeli conflict. Let us explore this by looking at the practice of intervention of one of the super-powers. According to one scholar who has studied the patterns of American intervention in local conflicts of this kind, American thought in recent decades has passed through two phases. In the first, covering the 1950s and the early 1960s, Americans had a picture of what the general lines of U.S. policy were and would probably continue to be, based on the following assumptions:

> "Instability in the developing world had a kind of fixed significance for both Moscow and Washington. Each seemed destined to play a fore-ordained role, one fomenting conflict, the other counter-attacking."[9]

The fomenter of the conflict was allegedly the Soviet Union, whilst the U.S. assigned herself the role of counter-attacker. This simplistic assumption, which guided American foreign policy for about two decades after the war, has since been replaced by a more sophisticated conception of how conflicts arise and of the circumstances under which the U.S. might intervene. The new or revised conception is closely tied to the American national interest, which, according to Bloomfield, ought to be seen in respect to local conflicts as a function of considerations such as the following:[10]

1. Explicit treaty obligations between the U.S. and another.
2. Communist profit with its bandwagon effect from a given outcome.

3. Available U.S. forces.
4. Distance.

If we now return with these bases (the old and the revised) for American intervention to the specific case of the Sudan civil war, it becomes clear that although no treaty obligation exists between the U.S.A. and the Sudanese; although the Sudan is remote from the U.S.A.; and although U.S. forces may not be readily available, American involvement could come about if the Sudan, even without any view to the Israeli-Arab struggle, carried that contemporary Arab alignment with the Soviet Union too far. Should the Soviet Union or the Chinese appear to be making undue penetration into the Sudan, a possibility would be created where the U.S., both under its old and revised assumptions about local conflicts, might be tempted to consider intervention.

It will be seen, therefore, that there are many possible borders or frontiers that are pertinent in any full discussion of intervention in the Sudan civil war. Within the African context, the Sudanese of the North and those of the South, the combatants in the civil war, belong to different groups whose emotions or sympathies, if incited, could lead to their seeking intervention. In the Middle Eastern context we encounter a similar potential for intervention in the civil war; as also when we consider the Sudan civil war in its global setting.

Yet, despite the multiplicity of borders dividing the Northern and Southern Sudanese, the history of the Sudan civil war does not conform to the thesis we noted at the begining of our essay: that of the likelihood of external intervention in civil strife. It is true that Egypt, Libya and Algeria have all at one time or another been accused of intervention on the side of the Arab Northerners. It is true that the Soviet Union has been similarly suspect. On the other hand, we find Israel, West Germany and the United States accused of training the Southerners and of supplying them with equipment. Finally, European missionaries have also been accused of meddling in the affairs of the Sudan. But the over-all picture remains, on balance, that of a civil war in which the combatants have been left alone by the rest of the world to settle their differences as best as they can. The Negro-Africans of the continent have kept aloof, and Christianity has not been a force strong enough to goad the Christian world into intervention in favour of the non-Muslim Southerners. From across the Arab-Israeli frontier, Israel has not been sufficiently pressed in the Arab-Israeli conflict to undertake whole-heartedly a diversionary tactic in the Southern Sudan. Lastly, even the super-powers, whose presence in global affairs is near ubiquitous, have not found a sufficient urge to intervene seriously. How is one to explain this unique aspect of the Sudan civil war?

We have, in passing, drawn attention to what appear to us to be some of the major reasons for the relative non-intervention by important factors within the Middle Eastern and global arenas. It will be recalled that we suggested in relation to the former arena that the most likely intervener, Israel, has not yet been sufficiently pressed by the calculus of the Arab-Israeli conflict to undertake a very active diversionary adventure in the Sudan on the side of the non-Arab Southerners. Secondly, we suggested that partly because of this and partly because of the absence of a serious clash of interests in the Sudan among the two super-powers, the latter have themselves found so far little temptation to involve themselves seriously in the civil war. But how is one to explain the relative aloofness from the civil war on the part of countries within the African arena, where such high potentials for intervention are to be found?

The answer seems to lie partly in that mixture of idealism and realism that has guided the international relations of independent Africa since 1957, and partly in the failure of the Southern Sudanese. Let us start by examining the notion of idealism in African international relations. Here the reference to the year 1957, the year of Ghana's independence, is significant, for many of the ideas that form part of the idealism we wish to understand emanated from Kwame Nkrumah of Ghana. Nkrumah led the way in articulating certain ideas pertaining to African inter-state relations which may not have been practised, but which had the effect of creating an atmosphere of camaraderie among African states and leaders. Such were, for example, his pan-Africanist ideas associated with the notion of African unity that he preached so fervently. The idea of African personality was another. His notion of a continental solidarity embracing both Negro and Arab Africans was a further important addition to the corpus of the idealism.[11]

Nkrumah, of course, had his opponents in the continent. His uneasy relationships with francophone Africa is a case in point. Thus, apart from being incensed by his taunts that they were not really independent of France, the francophone states were less than warm to his idea of solidarity with the Arabs.[12] Even in anglophone Africa his notions were not universally welcomed. The Nigerians never liked his leadership,[13] and his quarrel with Nyerere, another leader of African thought, over the very idea of African unity, is another well-known instance of the controversial nature of the man and his ideas.[14] Finally, and apart from such opposition by fellow African politicians, some of his pet notions about African inter-state relations and solidarity with the Arabs went counter to such ideas as that of *negritude*; so did the notion that Professor Ali Mazrui has

K

described as racial sovereignty, with its evident emphasis on colour as a basis for political arrangements.[15] But despite all of these facts, for many years after Ghana's independence, an atmosphere prevailed, in which to a large extent relations were guided by the ideals which Kwame Nkrumah enunciated, namely, ideals extolling the unity and brotherhood of all Africans, "Africans" being defined as including all the people of the continent except the whites in Southern Africa.

The reality of this phase of idealism in African inter-state relations was well evidenced, for example, by Uganda's foreign policy toward the Sudan in the Obote era, as the following case will show. Early in 1966, there came up for debate in the Uganda National Assembly a motion to "note with the deepest regret the silence of the Uganda Government over the frequent violations by Sudanese troops of our territorial integrity".[16] In his contribution to the debate, the Minister of State for Foreign Affairs explained that their decisions as regards the Sudan

"would not be influenced in the least by the fact that the North was Muslim while the South was Christian. Nor would they be influenced by the feeling that the Southerners are black and the other are 'mere Arabs who should be rounded up'."[17]

This idealistic phase of African international relations is now evaporating, as witnessed by such inter-state quarrels, even among the purely black African states, as that between Malawi and her neighbours, or the issue of the seating of Uganda at the OAU Foreign Ministers Conference at Addis Ababa earlier in 1971. But during the period when it prevailed, it constituted a tide far too strong for the counter-current to which the Southern Sudanese opened the gates by their unwillingness to co-exist in one polity with the Arabs. The prevalent philosophy emphasized the unity and brotherhood of all Africans, Arabs included. But that of the Southern Sudanese emphasized the differences among Africans.

As we have said, this ideal of the one-ness of Africans has begun to evaporate. Will the future bring a better African appreciation of the problems of the Southern Sudanese? The answer to this question time alone will determine. But already signs are beginning to appear that unless the problem is solved soon, the Southerners may, in proportion to the erosion of the idealism we have described, gain sympathy from some African states. Opportunities like the misunderstanding between the Khartoum regime and General Amin's Second Republic in Uganda — a misunderstanding which is itself indicative of the erosion of idealism in African inter-state relations — could be heaven-sent chances for the Southern cause.

The element of realism which, together with the idealism we have just examined, we suggest has been operating against African intervention in the Sudan civil war, has to do with the problem of secession of a people from an existing polity. Now, one way to look at the phenomenon of secession is to view it as an exercise in the revision of existing boundaries, and it is in terms of this alternative that we wish to define realism in African inter-state relations.

This realism has found expression in what we might term the principle of the "sacrosanctity" of the existing African boundaries. Generally speaking, there has been little, if any, inclination among the African states to tinker with the existing boundaries.[18] As is well known, the majority of the African states owe their existence to the haphazard boundary demarcation made by the European imperial powers, in the process of which ethnic homogeneity was never taken into account. Single ethnic entitles that had hitherto lived independently were brought together within the folds of the newly carved-out-countries. In other cases, single ethnic entities were split up between two or more countries. As long as the European imperial powers remained in control of the situation they had thus created, Africans took no serious account of the potential problems inherent in such boundaries. But in the post-independence period it was difficult not to take cognizance of the situation. Were these boundaries and the ethnic heterogeneity they caused to be revised or left intact?

It soon became quite obvious that if ethnic homogeneity within a territory was to be taken seriously after independence, then there would not only be no end to the chaos of adjustment it would occasion, but that the task of adjustment itself would be herculean. Accordingly, these states chose to disregard the problem and to keep intact the colonially demarcated boundaries and the territories they enclosed.[18] This, therefore, was the line taken at the first conference of the independent states of Black Africa held at Sanniquellie in Liberia in July 1959, when it was decided that each state should retain its national identity and its constitutional structure; and, further, that no state was to interfere in the internal affairs of any of the other states.[19] This same decision was re-affirmed two years later, again in Liberia at the Conference of Monrovia, when the twenty participating independent African states adopted a resolution on the following principles which were to govern the relationships between African states:[20]

1. Absolute equality;
2. non-interference;
3. respect for the Sovereignty of each state and its inalienable right to exist and develop its personality; and
4. strict condemnation of the setting up in one state of subversion centres directed against other states.

Lastly, it was this inclination to regard as sacrosanct the existing boundaries that inspired articles III and VI of the OAU. Charter Article III commits members of the organization to the following principles:

1. The sovereign equality of all states;
2. non-interference in the internal affairs of states;
3. respect for the sovereignty and territorial integrity of each state and for its inalienable right to independent existence.

Article VI stipulates that member states pledge themselves to observe scrupulously the principles enumerated in Article III.

Now, as we know only too well, international resolutions and laws of this kind can, of course, quite easily be disregarded. But the Sudan has been very lucky so far. As we have seen, none of her neighbours has shown any inclination to infringe these rules at the expense of her territorial integrity.

The contrast between her experience in this regard and that of other states which have been ravaged by civil wars, such as Nigeria in 1967-70 and the Congo in 1964-65, leads us to yet another explanation of why other African states (and, indeed, countries involved in the two other arenas in which we have been viewing the Sudan), have not cared to intervene in her civil war. This is owing to the failure of the Southern Sudanese themselves. Whether or not outsiders will intervene is to an important degree determined by at least two factors which, in the circumstances of the Sudan, appear not to have been operative.

The first of these is the quality of the propaganda put out by the side which requires outside intervention to bolster its weak position. Propaganda is essential both to publicize the issue in question, and to incite outsiders to intervention. The Biafrans did a very high quality job in this regard, but our opinion is that the Southerners have not quite made their mark as yet. The state of affairs in the Sudan is barely known even in the countries as close as Uganda, Kenya and the Congo.

The second factor conducive to outside intervention is the possibility of victory for the weaker side. The weaker side must be seen to be making some headway toward its goal. The establishment of a viable government with recognized jurisdiction among the people on the weaker side, a firm grip on some territory and the possession of a centre of administration, are some useful indicators to outsiders that, if victory is not certain, it is at least possible. In these respects, too, the Southern Sudanese appear so far not to have done as well as other secessionists or other insurgents.

But the misfortune of the Southerners is the good fortune of the Northerners. Thus, if intervention would help the Southerners, non-intervention helps the Northerners who, at present, are the stronger. The result of the absence of any meaningful intervention from outside has been that the Khartoum government, equipped with all the paraphernalia of a state, has had a very clear advantage over the Southerners. But this advantage has had some negative effects also, to which we shall draw attention before closing our analysis.

The very clear advantage enjoyed by the Khartoum government seems to have introduced a factor of undue intransigence in the civil war on their part. One sees this, for example, in the reported attempt to Arabize and to Islamize the South, where the substitution of Friday for Sunday as a holiday is evidence of the attempt. One sees it, too, in the attempt on the part of the Sudan to rivet itself to the politics and sentiments of the Arab world; for understandable as the inclinations of the Sudan towards Arabism are, considering its ethnic and religious make-up, a more considerate formula for association with the Arab world would seem to be needed if the Negro Southerners are to be given the serious consideration which they merit.[21] Finally, and perhaps most disturbingly, one sees this intransigence in the complacency of the Khartoum government towards the civil war, and in the failure of that government to consider seriously the Southerners' demand for autonomy or federation. For while few will chastise the Khartoum government for opposing secession, very few perhaps will see any strong reason why autonomy or federation should be opposed, given the reasonable grounds for the latter. We thus end our analysis on a note of optimism, in the hope that the Khartoum government will, as General Nimeiry intimated when he assumed power, become more magnanimous and less intransigent toward the Southerners, and apply itself to meeting those demands of the South which require less than outright secession.

REFERENCES

1 The thesis is discussed at much greater length in J. N. Rosenau (ed.), *International Aspects of Civil Strife* (Princeton, N.J., 1964).
2 A. A. Mazrui, *Violence and Thought* (London, 1969), Chapter 8.
3 M. A. Al-Rahmin, "Arabism, Africanism and Self-Identification in the Sudan", *The Journal of Modern African Studies*, C, 2 (1970), p. 233.
4 Ibid., pp. 244-5.
5 Ibid., p. 242.
6 Ibid., p. 233.
7 Ibid., p. 244.
8 See, for example, *Newsweek*, May, 10th, 1971, p. 10.

9   L. P. Bloomfield, "Patterns of American Intervention" in W. C. Olson and F. A. Sonderman, *The Theory and Practice of International Relations* (Englewood Cliffs, N.J., 1970).

10 Ibid., p. 328.

11 See A. A. Mazrui, *Towards a Pax Africana* (London, 1967), especially Chapter 4 for a fuller discussion along this line.

12 Ibid., Chapter 4.

13 Ibid., Chapter 4.

14 See, for example, A. Mohiddin, "Nyerere and Nkrumah on African Unity", Paper presented to the University (of East Africa) Social Sciences Conference at Makerere, Kampala, in December, 1968.

15 Mazrui, op. cit., Chapter 2.

16 Hansard (of the Uganda National Assembly) January 17th, 1966.

17 Ibid. The phrase "mere Arabs", etc., was a quotation from the speech of one of the members of the national Assembly who was in favour of action against the Arab Northern Sudan Government.

18 See D. Thiam, *The Foreign Policy of African States* (London, 1965), especially Chapter 1, where the matter is treated more fully.

19 Ibid., pp. 43-4.

20 Ibid., pp. 45-6.

21 See *Uganda Argus* of January 16th, 1970, where Mr. John Logic chastises the Sudan Northerners for this.

8

THE EDUCATION OF SOUTHERN SUDANESE REFUGEES

Donald Denoon

The education of Southern Sudanese refugees raises a series of problems which may be considered as educational, financial, administrative, and, unfortunately, political. These problems presented themselves most acutely in Uganda, where the number of refugees, the number of school-age children, and the educational opportunities were all rather greater than elsewhere in the Sudanese diaspora. It is therefore the Uganda situation which may be regarded as the most important in this context.

Education in the Sudan before independence was characterized by dualism, whereby most of the education available in the South was rather different from that available in the rest of the country. This dualism is scarcely surprising in light of the approach of the British administrators to most of the Sudan's problems. In effect Southerners were exposed to a greater use of English as the medium of instruction, Christianity as the ideology of educational institutions, and Europeans as instructors, than was the case elsewhere. The other relevant feature of education in the South was that it was extremely selective: the primary school leavers competed for secondary school places at Rumbek, whose educational calibre was therefore extremely impressive. Outside Rumbek educational opportunities were very limited indeed.

Southern refugees who were anxious to continue their education had at first a very limited range of opportunities and yet a very considerable capacity to benefit from them. They sought places in schools where English was the medium of instruction and where the curriculum and the ethos closely resembled that of the Southern Sudan. These requirements could be fulfilled almost exclusively in African Commonwealth countries and, to a limited extent, in Ethiopia. For reasons of contiguity, Uganda was the first resort for most refugees and therefore for most refugees anxious to continue their education. Having received a kind of education comparable to that of Ugandans, and being the products of a slightly more competitive and exclusive educational pyramid, they were eligible academically for admission into Uganda schools and colleges. In principle the burden could have been spread over the whole of Commonwealth Africa. In practice Zambia and Malawi at first had few school places at all, and later had refugees from Southern Africa to cope with. The same was true of Tanzania, while the Kenya government adopted a somewhat restrictive approach towards refugee students. The country of first asylum therefore was normally the country in which education was sought and found. These numbers were later swollen by an influx of refugees from Rwanda and Congo-Kinshasa during the 1960s.

A problem also arose from the educational virtues of the Sudanese refugees. Had they been ineducable, there would obviously have been no problem: since they were well able to compete with Ugandan students and in terms of ability deserved school places, they could not be ignored.

Since the late 1950s the character of the educational problems has changed considerably. The number of refugees who have received any education in the Sudan has declined. Presumably the Islamization of the Sudanese educational system, the greater use of Arabic, and the continued warfare in the South contribute to this change. Meanwhile primary education facilities have been made available for refugees living in refugee camps and settlements in Uganda. Since these educational opportunities are almost identical to those available to Ugandan children, Sudanese refugees have become indistinguishable from Ugandan scholars in terms of educational background. The number of secondary and tertiary refugee students has also tended to increase steadily. With the passage of time, therefore, the scale of the educational problem has increased. The increase in scale has forced educational and refugee authorities in Uganda to consider the kind of education appropriate to the students, whereas this problem did not seem acute when the number of scholars was in any case small. These choices will be considered later in the present chapter.

The financial problem, though severe, has not proved insuperable. Primary education, as provided throughout East and Central Africa, is a relatively cheap enterprise. By concentrating refugees in primary schools in the settlements, and by providing minimal teaching materials, the various authorities have cheaply provided primary education which could probably stand comparison with that of most rural areas of Uganda. If it is imperfect, at least it is equivalent to that provided for most non-refugees. Secondary education is naturally more expensive. Nevertheless, refugee officials in 1969 believed that every refugee who was academically eligible for a place in a government secondary school had adequate scholarship support. That opinion may have been a trifle optimistic, but at the worst the number of eligible students unable to find scholarship support must have been very small indeed. In addition, a small number of refugees were supported in private secondary schools when they were believed to deserve government secondary school places. The net result was that refugee candidates for secondary school places were at least as likely as Ugandans to gain admission and to receive scholarship support. The position as regards tertiary education is less clear. The Uganda school system qualifies students to compete for university places throughout the world, and it is therefore difficult to form an accurate impression as to the fate of refugee (or indeed Ugandan) school leavers. The writer is not aware of any refugee applicant to Makerere University who gained admission but no scholarship support; and it seems likely that Sudanese refugee opportunities at this level were also at least comparable to those of Ugandans. This is to say that finance has not, so far, proved a serious impediment to the education of Sudanese refugees in Uganda. If Sudanese primary scholars are at a slight disadvantage, secondary scholars are at least on terms of equality, and tertiary students may be marginally better placed.

Administration has proved much more problematical. Paradoxically, this may be attributed to the fact that there are simultaneously too many and too few administrators of projects relating to the education of Sudanese refugees. The United Nations High Commission for Refugees has a suite of offices and a battery of staff in Kampala, and voluntary organizations also maintain establishments, though on a more modest scale. The Uganda Ministry of Culture and Community Development has an office devoted to refugee scholars, who are also considered by officials in the Ministry of Education, while admission to the refugee settlements requires the approval of officials in charge of internal security. The voluntary organizations are also numerous: the Church of Uganda, the Catholic Church, the Society of Friends, the International University Exchange Fund, World University Service and a variety of other organizations concern themselves with the education of refugees.

The interests and approaches of these various bodies are not necessarily identical. The Uganda government, naturally, wishes to know how many refugees are receiving education, especially as almost all are in Government school places. If the Government does have precise figures on the subject, it has a monopoly of statistical information. Voluntary organizations, on the other hand, are understandably (though perhaps unjustly) nervous about handing over sums of money to a ministry which is reluctant to reveal information regarding the names and numbers and costs of students supported. The High Commission for Refugees, by its constitution, operates on terms laid down by the host government: voluntary organizations, despite their constitutions, generally do the same. Again, the churches regard scholarships as part of a wider function, namely the cure of souls: while the secular organizations tend to demonstrate an acute lack of interest in the spiritual or other non-financial well-being of their charges. There is a further limitation on the efficiency of these administrators. It is not possible for them to meet with government representatives to form a committee (since that would derogate from the decision-making authority of the government) and therefore the co-ordination of refugee scholarship work is rather incomplete. The equalization of scholarships and of eligibility for them is necessary — yet this can be accomplished only by guess-work and hearsay. At the same time there are too few administrators capable of distinguishing between Ugandans and Sudanese, between a twenty-five year old primary student and a teenage secondary scholar, between the brother of a cabinet minister and the son of a peasant. It seems likely that there is a certain amount of wastage as a result.

A certain amount of suspicion attaches to the admission of scholars to upper-secondary forms in 1970. All upper-secondary education is provided by government schools, and the government selects entrants on the basis of public examinations. In 1970 for the first time no professed Sudanese were admitted. Since education is one of the most valuable scarce resources in the country, it seems reasonable to suppose that the Uganda government decided to restrict this resource for citizens only by means of administrative action. Among the numerous consequences of this decision is an increase in the unwillingness of private organizations to share their information with the relevant ministries. The continued existence of too many administrators is not likely to be overcome in the near future. The government undoubtedly has the right to restrict entry to its schools, and in many ways it is a remarkable testament that it has not hitherto done so. Neverthless that decision complicates relations between administrators, just as it alarms the refugee scholars themselves.

The most interesting, and least tractable, problems relate to what may be described as the political problems of educating refugee scholars and students. Most administrators (myself included) like to think of themselves as politically neutral in their dealings with refugee problems, This is, however, an impossible aspiration. Education in Africa is a scarce and expensive commodity, and in most countries the availability of educational opportunities and the nature of those opportunities involve hotly-contested political decisions. Since refugee organizations make these decisions, they are willy-nilly involved in political affairs. This is not simply a theoretical observation but a reality which affects almost every aspect of decision-making by and for refugee students, as the following illustrations may demonstrate.

To start, at random, with finance, we may consider the following equation: a given sum of money will pay the annual scholarship of one university undergraduate, or twelve secondary school students, or perhaps one hundred primary school children. By what criteria does one decide how best to allocate that money? One might apply the same criteria as the Uganda government, and thereby evade the issue by aiming at comparability. But the Uganda government does all three things, and gives no guide lines for deciding which educational expenditure is most important. One might, alternatively, apply the same criteria as the Sudanese government except that the same difficulties arise. A further difficulty presents itself in the fact that many refugees do not expect to return to the Sudan as at present constituted (or, in some cases, however, constituted). To decide that, despite the reluctance of the students, Khartoum priorities should prevail is to make a political decision, by asserting that the good of the Sudan is the same as the good of the refugee students. That decision not only intrudes upon the area of decision-making normally reserved for governments, it intrudes on the area normally reserved for God.

In practical terms, a choice is presented as between academic and technical education. Since most administrators have themselves received an academic training, it is sometimes difficult to refuse to allow refugees the same opportunity. On the other hand, the kind of technical education available in the host country may not necessarily equip refugee students to play a useful role in Uganda, in the settlement camps, in a united Sudan or in a divided Sudan. At first sight there seems to be a means of evading these issues, by providing whatever education is most suitable to the aptitude of the particular candidate. By adopting that approach, however, administrators may provide a much wider choice of options to the candidate than is available to Uganda citizens. Whatever line of policy is adopted, it is bound to have considerable repercussions on the educational calibre of the refugee community: yet a choice must be made, since to do nothing will also produce considerable repercussions. Having had political decisions thrust upon him, the administrator is not permitted to abdicate, though he will almost certainly wish to do so. Those decisions, in turn, compel the administrator to make political predictions regarding the political form and material needs of the refugee community. Prediction, in turn, may prove self-fulfilling. To make an extreme example: if scholarships are provided in such a manner as to foster the growth of a group of "new men" analogous to those who came to power in East Africa during the early 1960s, that may possibly influence the chances of a successful Southern secession. Conversely, the encouragement of the training of technical personnel in competition with similar personnel in the host country may possibly influence the graduates to seek employment with the Sudanese government. Similarly the kind of education visualized by President Nyerere for young Tanzanians might well encourage the primary school leavers to attempt to develop the agricultural potential of the settlement camps. In short, there is no escaping the making of decisions which will have political implications.

A second set of implications, which cause equally acute unease amongst administrators, arises from a comparison between the educational opportunities of refugees and young people in the host country. It has already been stated that it becomes necessary for administrators to distingush between refugees and Ugandans. That distinction is necessary because considerable numbers of educationally qualified Ugandans cannot afford school fees, and a certain number of these therefore pose as refugees in order to find scholarship support. That state of affairs reflects the fact that some Ugandans feel discriminated against in favour of refugee candidates. In principle that suspicion is based upon false premises. It is perfectly defensible to assert that refugees have no hope of paying school fees unless charitable organizations step in, whereas Ugandans all have at least a minimal opportunity of borrowing money from more affluent kinsmen. On the other hand that contrast may not hold good in every case; and in any case it is painful and invidious to turn away an able young Ugandan, interested in education and uninterested in social speculation. The problem is not made any easier by the fact that most refugee officials are from countries where education is considered a right rather than a privilege.

It seems likely that political problems will proliferate rather than decline in future. Since Uganda appears to have reached saturation point so far as educational opportunities for refugees is concerned other host countries have to be discovered. Since Francophone countries are disqualified on grounds of language, the choice is limited to Anglophone Africa. Immediately further problems present themselves. In Zambia and Malawi, educational policy aims at providing four years of secondary education leading possibly to a four-year university degree. In East Africa policy aims at a six-year secondary school system, leading possibly to a three-year degree. Sudanese policy approximates closely to that of Zambia and Malawi in this respect: refugees not unnaturally prefer the East African policy, since the qualifications are more widely accepted. Anglophone West Africa is also divided between these two policies, so that decisions are inescapable.

Nor is the end in sight. Political changes in Khartoum have produced a series of governments each of which has adumbrated proposed solutions to the troubles of the South. Each proposal has won the support of some refugees, but seldom in significant numbers. One consequence is that the refugee community as a whole has not determined to settle permanently in a host country, but is nevertheless unwilling to return to the Sudan. The contrast between Sudanese and Rwandese refugees in this respect is (to all appearances) striking. Rwandese refugees do not expect to return to Rwanda, and many have thrown their talents and energies into improving the settlement areas and (*inter alia*) building and staffing their own schools. Most Sudanese have remained refugees rather than immigrants, and correspondingly ambiguous in their commitments. It is for that reason that policy-decisions remain in the hands of a variety of officials representing fund-raising organizations, and cannot devolve upon the community most vitally concerned.

Because of the far-reaching implications of decisions made by refugee relief organizations, it is scarcely surprising that the Sudanese government is interested in their activities. The government's policy of encouraging a general return of all refugees, and refugee students in particular, encourages the Sudanese authorities to regard scholarship activities with suspicion and even occasional disfavour. They suggest that the return of the refugees would be facilitated if fewer scholarships were available, and they are undoubtedly correct. There is a long-standing offer of free places in the University of Khartoum for any refugee who is academically qualified for admission. If that were the only available opportunity for tertiary education, it would almost certainly be seized by a considerable number of Southerners. At present certain difficulties hedge the offer. Refugees appear to have to present themselves for interview prior to acceptance, and their position in Khartoum in the event of failing to secure a place would presumably be embarrassing, if not worse. Secondly the University of Khartoum accepts students on completion of the equivalent of Ordinary level, and therefore (perhaps unjustly) has a lesser international reputation than universities in East Africa. Thirdly, the University is, of course, in Khartoum, which for obvious reasons is less than a magnet for refugee students. However there are people who might be described as educational (as opposed to political) refugees, and it ought not to be the policy of scholarship bodies to finance such refugees. There again, the distinction between two categories of refugee may be logically clear, but in practice is difficult to apply, since educational deprivation is one of the factors contributing to the flight of so many thousands of Southerners.

The education of Sudanese refugees, in short, cannot be considered in isolation. It is not fundamentally an educational problem, but an aspect of a more general refugee problem, affected by and in turn affecting the political and social environment in which the refugees live. Since the refugee community is accustomed to an educational system very similar to that of Uganda, there is strictly speaking no *educational* problem at all other than those affecting Ugandan scholars and students equally. Financially and administratively, though problems continue to exist, the position of refugee scholars and students is at least much more satisfactory than it was half a dozen years ago. The "forgotten war" implied "forgotten refugees", for whose general welfare and education very little was being done. Through the voluntary fund-raising and organizational activities of a number of individuals in Uganda, interest has been aroused, funds collected, and at least some system introduced into disbursements. The collection, allocation and distribution of funds for refugee education are all capable of improvement and there is every reason to expect that they can and will be improved.

What remains is a series of essentially political decisions. A meeting of all refugee relief agencies, the Uganda government's administrators, and representatives of the refugees and of the Sudanese government might well be able to agree to a set of criteria to be adopted, and thereby relieve administrators of the burden of political decision-making. Such a meeting, once in session, might well discover a great area of common ground. Yet such a meeting is inconceivable. It could only take place if there were a basis of common assumptions shared by the Sudanese Government and the Southerners; and if those common assumptions could be discovered, there would be no refugee problem to discuss. Meanwhile the most neutral course politically lies in implementing the priorities laid down in the Organization of African Unity man-power statements, whether or not that has any relevance to the needs of Sudanese refugees. A "solution" to the problem inherent in Sudanese refugee education is not attainable without a "solution" to the civil war itself. Until then the education of refugees will continue to be in the nature of First Aid administered by the Red Cross: not necessarily ideal, and administered by organizations not directly involved in hostilities.

9

POLITICAL TRENDS IN THE SUDAN AND THE FUTURE OF THE SOUTH

Dunstan M. Wai

"It would be fallacious to view the military and politics separately. Particularly in the developing countries the militaries are part and parcel of contemporary politics and cannot be divorced from it — in theory, reality, or analysis. In Africa, for example, the sheer growth in the number of incidents directly involving the military in political affairs is astounding."

Kenneth W. Grundy,
Conflicting Images of Military in Africa

I would like to begin by emphasizing the importance of the military in Sudanese political affairs. Military rule is not particular to the Sudan — the military "ingredient" in developing political systems is found throughout Independent Africa. For the greater part of its life since independence, punctuated only briefly by short-lived civilian and parliamentary governments, the Republic of the Sudan has been ruled by the army. In any discussion of political trends in the Sudan (and also in some other areas of Africa), the significant role of the army cannot be ignored. This preface hints at the broader concerns of the chapter; in which I shall try to delineate the main political trends in the recent history of the Sudan, keeping the Southern Sudan question at the centre of my discussion. After all, the Southern Problem has persistently been one of the chief factors helping to topple regimes in Khartoum.

I. POLITICAL INTEGRATION AND LEGITIMACY

Professor A. Mazrui has noted that "the most fundamental problems confronting African countries are reducible to two crises: the crisis of national integration, and the crisis of political legitimacy".[1] The Sudan is no stranger to these problems. Although Arab culture, Islam, and the Arabic language have provided a unifying element in the Northern Sudan, and although there is a

strong feeling of "Arabness", sectarian differences exist between
the Ansar of the Western Sudan, and the Khatmiya of the Eastern
Sudan. There exist also feelings of tribalism among the Nuba and
Beja communities of African origin. The instability of politics in the
North may perhaps be attributed to the fact that "if a society is too
homogeneous over racial, linguistic and religious cleavages, then
democratic political organization is not likely to be stable".[2] That is, a
democracy must have both a minimum of social homogeneity and a
minimum of heterogeneity.

In the Southern Sudan, there is, on the other hand, a marked
absence of agreement concerning Sudanese nationhood. This
indifference to "belonging" has been correctly observed by Dr.
Richard Gray:

"Completely isolated from the North until more than a century ago,
embittered by decades of subsequent hostility, and administered
separately until the threshold of independence, the Southerner feels
himself to be an African, while the ruling Northerner is proud of his
Arab consciousness."[3]

The Southern Sudanese have often used the differences between the
North and the South as an argument for secession. This is clearly
shown in the words of Aggrey Jaden (then President of the Sudan
National Union):

"The Sudan falls sharply into two distinct areas, both in geographical
area, ethnic groups, and cultural systems. The Northern Sudan is
occupied by a hybrid Arab race who are united by their common
language, common culture and common religion; and they look to the
Arab world for their cultural and political inspiration. The people of the
Southern Sudan on the other hand, belong to the African ethnic group
of East Africa. They do not only differ from the hybrid Arab race in
origin, arrangement and basic system, but in all conceivable purposes —
there is nothing in common between the various sections of the
community; no body of shared belief, and above all, the Sudan has
failed to compose a single community."[4]

Jaden's statement reflects the deep feeling among many Southern
Sudanese against any Khartoum regime. But the fact is that most
of the Northern Sudanese are, in the words of Professor Mazrui,

"Arabised Negroes and are Arabs by acquisition rather than by
heredity."[5]

The difference between the people of the South and the North is
basically more one of culture than of race. The Southern problem

has always been mainly a political one with some cultural, historical and economic aspects and psychological manifestations.

The North and the South are not fully politically integrated and the one "people" of the South are divided into several different tribes. The South has not been fully penetrated by authorities in Khartoum. The fighting movement in the South is based on the negation of both legitimacy of any Khartoum government in the South, and legitimacy of government institutions, (i.e. strong central government, one Parliament, one Sudanese people, etc., etc.).

II. INDEPENDENCE AND THE PARLIAMENTARY REGIME 1954-1958

Parliamentary life in the Sudan 1954-58 was characterized more by factionalism, nepotism and corruption than by Party politics, and consequently its debased quality was to be used by Lieutenant General Abboud and his colleagues as a justification for their action in November when they seized power. The ruling party, the National Unionist Party (NUP) suffered a conflict of personalities. The Prime Minister, Ismael Azhari, eliminated men from his Cabinet who questioned his leadership.[6] Among these were two Southerners, Bullen Alier and Buth Diu. These two criticized the government policy towards the Southern Sudan. As Alier and others have shown in their papers, the Southern Sudanese demand for federation was ignored and policies of discrimination in the field of employment, as clearly shown in the Sudanization of posts, led to the mutiny of 1955 by the troops of the Eqautoria Corps in the South. The repression of the mutiny in the South was the beginning of the use of force as an instrument of coercion in the South by independent Northern Sudanese administrations.

The political situation was persistently unstable. The mutiny in the South was a blow to the prestige of the Prime Minister, Ismael Azhari, and a setback to his party. A dissatisfied faction of his party formed the Peoples' Democratic Party (PDP). The PDP and the Umma Party (a party banned by the Mahdi followers, the Ansars) were linked together in a temporary and opportunist coalition. The National Assembly Resolution of December 19th, 1956, which promised federation for the South was repudiated by Abdalla-Bey Khalil's ministry, which came to power after a defeat of Azhari's cabinet in a motion of no confidence in early 1956. The Umma/PDP coalition government continued to employ repression in the South and ignored advice and warnings from Southern Members of Parliament. In March 1958, the country voted in general elections.

In the new Constituent Assembly, three Southerners were appointed as Ministers. But these were not nominated by the Liberal

L

Party which represented the South as a unit. The Liberal Party reacted promptly and formed the federal bloc. It was prepared to vote with the NUP in opposition, especially on questions concerning the South. The Southern alliance with the NUP undermined the stability of the Government. The Prime Minister depended on Southern support to obtain Parliamentary ratification for an economic and technical agreement with the U.S.A. The country faced an economic crisis; for not only was the 1958 cotton crop poor, but the world demand for cotton was declining and prices were falling. A budget deficit of nearly three million Sudanese pounds was forecast for 1958. The PDP was adamantly opposed to Abdalla Khalil's policy towards the West, and so to avert a vote of no confidence Parliament adjourned until November. Before adjournment, the Southern M.P.s had boycotted several sessions of the Constituent Assembly on grounds of under-representation of the South in the Constitutional Committee (see chapters by Alier, and Russell and McCall). At this point it may be true to say that the periods of civilian governments were characterized by political manoeuvring, rivalry and intrigues, corruption, reckless squandering of national resources and continued political oppression of the Southern Sudan. The Southern demand for federation or autonomous status within a united Sudan was answered with an accelerated policy for integration of the South in a unified nation, with a single administrative cadre (predominantly Northern Sudanese), a single educational system, one national language (Arabic) and a single religion and way of life, that is Islam. As has been shown by all the other contributions in this volume, this policy has been consciously pursued by all post-independence democratic governments, with greater emphasis on religion by Abboud's military regime.

III. THE MILITARY REGIME OF ABBOUD 1958-64

In addition to economic problems, coupled with political strife between parties in the North, and the discontent and unrest in the South, the Sudan began to experience its first military rule after independence when General Abboud staged a successful coup d'état. The coup was not a transfer of power, but it is generally believed to be a political expediency on the part of the Prime Minister, Abdalla-Bey Khalil.[7] Abboud was supposed, by his agreement with Bey Khalil, to hand back the reins of power to the Prime Minister after reducing the dissenting voices to submission, but the General refused to return to his barracks until he was eventually overthrown by a civilian uprising in October 1964.

The Sudanese army under Abboud was not a homogenous political force. This is clearly demonstrated by the fact that there were three attempts at military coups against Abboud's ruling supreme Council in the armed forces.[8] Corruption flourished in the army and in the Civil Service. In his article, "The Sudan, the Revolution of October 1964", Professor Robert W. Crawford attributes the overthrow of Abboud to public disenchantment:

"General Abboud's bloodless revolution of November 17th, 1958 was accepted by most Sudanese as a necessary step in their struggle for independent political maturity. Its acceptance was a result of their increasing disenchantment with civil political rule, due to the inability of the political parties to work together constructively. It was the hope of most that the new military government would be able to make the necessary decision, and take the necessary steps, to ensure the country's progress without seriously curtailing the inherent determination to maintain individual liberty and integrity demanded by the people. But as the military regime more and more consolidated its position of authority, an increasing number of individuals became more disenchanted with what was, as well as with what was not, happening."[9]

This observation was true in the North and the October Revolution of 1964 is correctly attributed to increased disillusion with the Abboud regime. The main focal centres of opposition to the regime were the Trades Union Movement and the students and staff of the University of Khartoum. Additionally, of course, the fighting in the Southern Sudan persistently remained a headache to the government.

Abboud and his colleagues made "the basic error in judgement that the Southern Sudan problem was susceptible to a military solution",[10] and refused to accept that it is essentially a political one. In the Southern Sudan, by September 1963, the mutineers of 1955 had regrouped under the name of Anya-Nya (meaning in the Madi language "snake venom" or "incurable poison"). Increased Anya-Nya activities led to increased Sudanese army reprisals. These led to the killing of many innocent people and the burning of villages by both forces. The intensity of the situation made the army regime restless. Mass killings of both Northern soldiers and local inhabitants worried many people in the country. The army junta had denounced the rebellion as an imperialist instigation against the people of the Sudan and denied the existence of the Southern Question. The situation in the Southern Sudan could not, however, be dismissed as an imperialist intrigue. President Abboud later came to realize that all could not be attributed to Imperialists. There was a fundamental problem to be recognized, and in September 1964 he appointed a commission of inquiry composed of 19 Northern and

13 Southern Sudanese. The terms of reference of the Commission were:

a) Without infringing the present constitutional structure or the principle of a unitary government, to study the factors which hinder harmony between the Northern and Southern parts of Sudan, and to make recommendations with a view to consolidating confidence and achieving internal stability and unity.

b) The commission could consult with whom it desired and with those nationals who so wished, particularly those from the Southern Provinces.

c) The commission would submit its report to the Minister for Headquarters Affairs.

The appointment of the commission was the begining of the end of the Abboud regime. The Southern problem became an important and frequent topic of discussion at the University of Kharotum. It was, therefore, "no surprise that the original anti-government rioting began in Khartoum on the night of October 21st, 1964, when the police broke up a student meeting held in defiance of a government ban".[11] The meeting had been called to discuss the Southern Question, a topic which served as the springboard for direct criticism of the military regime. The general public in the North had also become apathetic to the military leadership. The public were helped by "splits in the army command and in the officer corps at several levels that toppled an already shaky junta".[12] On October 26th, leaders of the Free Officers (some of whom became the leaders of the May Revolution of 1969) served General Abboud with an ultimatum demanding concessions to the conditions advocated by the students of the university, They were firm and threatened to bombard the Presidential palace by October 30th. After a general strike and mass demonstrations, the military government was replaced by a transitional civilian government. The fall of Abboud was an achievement of unprecedented magnitude by the Sudanese people. Professor Ali A. Mazrui's description of this achievement deserves quotation at length:

"Abboud's fall was itself a triumph of public opinion in the North, and an index to some degree of meaningful national consensus. A series of demonstrations in Khartoum, some of which were led by University teachers, shattered the confidence of the military regime. In some ways, the fall of Abboud was the most striking manifestation yet of the democratic potential of the Sudan. It is not in every country that the military would bow to popular indignation. It is not every country in Africa that popular indignation expresses itself in spite of possible reprisals from government forces. It is true that the military's forces seemed to have been partly connected with patriotic sentiment and with a reluctance to shed too much Sudanese blood in the streets of Khartoum. One could therefore say that the fall of Abboud in October 1964, was as creditable to Abboud and the military at large as it was to demonstrators in the streets demanding a return to parliamentary politics. In the conditions of Africa today, and indeed of the Middle East, soldiers are to be given national credit when they are too inhibited to slaughter too many of their compatriots."[13]

Thus, with a concerted effort, the Sudanese people overthrew the repressive regime of Abboud and ushered civilian rule into the country.

IV. TRANSITIONAL GOVERNMENT

The overthrow of the military regime created the possibility of the development of new relations between the Northern and Southern Sudanese. The Prime Minister, Sayed Sir el Khatim el Khalifa, was widely respected by the Southerners, having himself worked in the South as Under-Secretary of Education for a number of years. He was looked upon as the most likely man to resolve the North-South conflict. He appointed two Southerners to his Cabinet: Clement Mboro as Minister of the Interior, and Ezibon Mondiri as Communications Minister. He considered the Southern Question as item number one on the agenda of issues facing his government. He invited politicians from the South in and outside the country for a Round Table Conference and relaxed the state of emergency in the South. Some political observers stated that during this period, most Northerners felt that the overthrow of the military regime was sufficient for the Southerners to recognize them as their kith and kin. But the psychology of the problem was more complicated than the Northerners had envisaged.

The Southern politicians inside and outside the country were sharply divided in their approach to the call for a Round Table Conference. The late William Deng believed in returning to the Sudan and fighting from within. The rest of his colleagues in exile were sceptical. After much pressure from within the Sudan and from neighbouring countries, most of them, however, agreed to go to the Round Table Conference at Khartoum in March 1965.

Professor Al-Nazir Dafalla, then Vice-Chancellor of the University of Khartoum, chaired the conference. The Northern politicians attributed the deterioration of relations between the North and the South to the British policy towards the South, missionary activity, wrong approaches in the past by their political parties and the ruthlessness of the military rule of Abboud. They appealed for a new approach to the problem: the renunciation of force, and the application of a peaceful solution. For them, any solution to the conflict would have to be based on a united Sudan; and they stuck to their previous tactics which ruled out federation from the start. On the other hand, the Southern Sudanese were in three groups: some advocated a decentralized system of government in the Sudan, others advocated federal status for the South and a third group demanded self-determination. In the final analysis, it could be argued that mutual mistrust, suspicion and lack of statesmanship from both sides, North and South, undermined the hope for a possible compromise. On the whole the conference was a failure: there was, however, agreement on a number of reforms, such as the "Southernization" of administrative posts, the stepping up of educational opportunities, and increased economic development in the South. A twelve-man committee was appointed to resolve the question of constitutional agreement and to implement the reforms suggested. Another significant fact was that the conference brought Northern and Southern politicians together for the first time for many years.

V. PARLIAMENTARY RULE 1965 — MAY 1969

The transitional government of Sir-el Khatim el Khalifa was soon replaced by that of Mohammed Ahmed Mahgoub, a conservative and a man widely known for his antipathy to the South. Political intrigues motivated by the struggle for power dominated political trends in the North. Mahgoub's government was a coalition of his Umma Party and the National Unionist Party of the late Ismail El Azhari. It was a shaky marriage: Azhari wanted to be the executive head of the Sudan and thought that it was for him to represent the Republic at Organization of African Unity summits and those of the Arab world. Mahgoub objected to this and argued that Azhari was the nominal head of State (President of the five-man Supreme Council) and that the head of the Government, i.e. the Prime Minister, should rightly represent the country at such meetings. This argument continued until Azhari got his way.

The Mahgoub government resorted to the use of force to solve the Southern Problem. The situation intensified. The civilian population became a target of attack: entire villages were burnt to the ground and those inhabitants who escaped vanished into the bush and many fled to the neighbouring countries. The entire village life of the Southern Sudan was disrupted and the Sudan spent over twenty million pounds per annum on the upkeep of the army in the South. Mahgoub appeared not to have learnt a lesson from the Abboud regime's approach to the Southern Question. The most ruthless of these mass killings were the Juba and Wau massacres of July 8th and 11th, 1965 respectively. In 1966, a leaflet was issued by the liberal Soldiers and Officers Front entitled "The Battle in the South is against Imperialism", which attributed these killings in Juba and Wau to the fact that the troops in the South lacked positive motives for the fighting and a spirit of despondency prevailed among them. The government refused to listen to them, refused advice from army officers in the South, ignored facts on the situation in the South and always fed public opinion in the North with blatant untruths.

Sadiq el-Mahdi instigated a successful vote of no confidence against Mahgoub within the Umma party, of which he was the President, Sadiq clashed with his uncle the Imam, El Hadi Abdal Rahman el Mahdi, over his desire to secularize the government by removing it from sectarian influences based on the rivalry between the Ansar and the Khatmiyya. Undoubtedly, this was a radical idea in the light of the Northern Sudanese political temperament, and Sadiq was accused of heresy. He failed to mobilize the radical support of the young Sudanese who entertained his political ideas and eventually he found himself overwhelmed by the forces against him. Towards the end of 1967, the old rivals — Mahdists and Mirghanists of the Ansar and the Khatmiyya sects respectively — combined to undermine Sadiq's authority. They won, but at the cost of splitting the Umma Party, and Mohammed Ahmed Mahgoub, again became Prime Minister at the head of the Umma Wing, opposed to Sadiq and supporting Abdel-Rahman El-Hadi (Mahgoub was head of the government but not of his party and never acted independently without the knowledge of El-Hadi). Before his overthrow, Sadiq had applied a little moral restraint on the use of force in the South. He replaced some laws, including those which allowed security forces to shoot people at random, to slash crops and to confiscate cattle, sheep and goats: Sadiq was pro-West in his policies and during his term of office he used some channels in the West to put pressure on the Southern Sudanese to cooperate with him. There is doubt as to whether he was genuinely interested in solving the problem of the South of whether he wanted, as all Northern politicians had done, to capitalize on the problem for political gain. But whatever the case, he eventually succeeded in winning the support of the late William Deng's Sudan African National Union (SANU).

When Mahgoub returned to power, he reimposed his former laws and introduced more sinister ones in the South. Dissatisfaction continued in the country and the security situation worsened in the South. Some of Mahgoub's Ministers were ideologically divided and because of this division and because of personality clashes the coalition in the government was unstable. Economic difficulties grew and pressures for an Islamic Constitution also grew. The government was virtually incapable of moving out of the political and economic impasse facing the country.

Early in 1969, Sadiq el-Mahdi and his uncle, the late Imam El Hadi, were reconciled in an attempt to stabilize the government. It was agreed that Sadiq was to be Prime Minister and the Imam the President elect. Mahgoub would not compromise with Azhari, whose party had the majority of members in the Assembly and thus failed to form a new coalition. Sadiq had capitulated to sectarian rule. On May 25th, 1969 the government was overthrown by the liberal wing of the armed forces. The military coup immediately installed a "progressive" regime which appeared at first socialist in its sympathies.

VI. REGIONAL AUTONOMY FOR THE SOUTH

The government of Major-General el-Nimeiry announced at its inception a bold and positive policy of regional autonomy for the South. In its long policy statement on the Southern Question, the government maintains it is a continuation of the October Revolution of 1964 which toppled the military regime of Abboud. The statement traces the history of the Southern Problem and the relations between the North and the South and then provides the crucial guidelines for government action. That the government has recognized the legitimate interest of the South is very important and that it has a new objective understanding of the historical roots and their contemporary manifestations of the Southern problem is reassuring. Perhaps most important is the fact that for the first time specific programmes and progressive steps have been outlined to deal with the problem in a concrete way.

In September 1969, I had the privilege of being a member (secretary) of a delegation from Makerere University at Kampala, Uganda, which made a Sudanese government-sponsored visit to the Sudan to assess the political situation, and came back to report to their colleagues and other interested Southerners. This assessment, which follows, may suffer (inevitably) from a personal bias, but it is the product of first-hand observation and I am at least aware of the somewhat prejudiced position I was in as a "government-sponsored" visitor.

During our three weeks' visit to the Sudan (September 6th-27th, 1969), we met Southern Sudanese from all walks of life; members of the elite, students at Khartoum University, former political leaders, government civil servants, church leaders and many people from the rural areas. In our discussions we were interested in discovering the opinion of both the Southerners and Northerners about past governments, the May 25th, Socialist Revolutionary Government, and about the policy of Regional Autonomy for the South. The Southerners we met also expressed their opinions about the Southern Sudanese leaders in exile. We had long discussions on a variety of issues in Khartoum, Malakal, Wau and Juba.

Both Southerners and Northerners whom we met expressed disgust with the former party governments. They felt that the political parties which dominated the country had been unable to grasp or perceive the real meaning of independence. To them, independence meant Sudanese flag parades, conferences and the presentation of a good image, but was not a means to transform the society economically and bring prosperity and happiness to the people. The political parties had no programme to execute, only an ambition to hold power. They acted in their own interests and neglected the interests of all the members of the Sudanese "nation". Consequently, corruption spread through all the machinery of the state and the door was open to foreign influence, through which reactionary and conservative forces infiltrated some sections of the society to give unreserved support to the political parties. The Southerners in particular were disgusted with the escalation of the war in the South and the mass, arbitrary killings. Failure by the former regimes to resolve the problem of the South aroused their condemnation. Chief Majok of Bahr el Ghazel Province is purported to have said:

"Past government were government of thieves and profiteering bandits. They have been busy enriching themselves from the National Treasury, and at the expense of the Sudanese people, who were neglected to suffer from hunger, ignorance and disease."[14]

Another prominent Southern chief of Rumbek district, echoed the same feeling when he is alleged to have said:

"The past government were really failures and could not solve the national problems, including the Southern problem. In the meantime, they busied themselves with the squabbles for leadership at Khartoum and only neglected the national problems. They considered the Southern problem as the problem of outlaws only. They went further to forget the masses (the natives) and their immediate needs; like prevention of tribal fights, hunger and so on."[15]

Such were the feelings of many Sudanese, both Northerners and Southerners, whom we met; and such feelings were understandable and could be justified. The new leaders spared no effort to accuse their predecessors not only of not having taken up the struggle against under-development, but of having led the country into bankruptcy. They argued that malpractice, fraudulent activities, and corruption emptied the coffers of the State. And according to statistics revealed, the balance of trade has steadily decreased since the October Revolution of 1964 and because of priority given to the importation of consumer goods and luxury articles, the reserves decreased from about 61 million Sudanese pounds in 1964 to 14 millions by May 1969. The foreign debt beat all records: 91 million pounds — double the amount of 1964 — and the foreign loans were used to hide the budgetary deficit caused by extravagant spending instead of financing development projects. It was reported that the civil list of the former late head of State, Ismael el Azhari, was forty times more than that of Abboud. The number of Sudanese bureaucrats also rose unnecessarily from 25,000 to the spectacular figure of 58,000 in two years. In 1968, the State enterprise registered a deficit of 31 million Sudanese pounds. The ordinary man in the country was suffering terribly under the pressure of inflation and the government, rather than take money from the rich petty bourgeoisie group, put pressure on the poor "common man". Indirect taxation brought 56 million pounds in the year 1968-69 against 8 million pounds taken from direct imports, and the volume of the internal debt, as a result of government loans from local banks, was 39 millions in June 1966 and 46 millions in June 1969! A flight of capital, mainly of foreign origin, deprived the country of some 52 million pounds, according to some estimates.

What the Sudan needs, therefore, is a radical change in the political and economic orientation. The socialists are only too happy to be in power and they seem to have some determination to transform Sudanese society on a socialist pattern and are not willing to tolerate the traditional forces. It also seems that the new leaders have some deep attachment to the idea of a genuinely independent Sudanese nationalism, although their vigilant policy towards Israel propels them to disproportionately greater attachment to Arabism. It could, however, be said that while they show some uncertainties about the methods of reaching their goal, they are much clearer about the direction in which they wish to lead the country. If they do not have the conscious purpose of guiding the Sudan to a more democratic policy, they certainly came to purify the political process of corruption and nepotism and to replace the politicians and political confusion with authority, order, discipline and rationality.

As I have indicated in the foregoing discussion of the reaction of Southern Sudanese to the policy of Regional Autonomy, there is general enthusiasm. Some government policies, however, drew scepticism from many of the Southern elite. At the time of our visit there was a talk of creation of a Democratic and Socialist Movement in the country and in particular in the South, this was interpreted by some Southerners as an attempt by the late Minister of State for Southern Affairs, Mr. Joseph Garang, to build a political base for himself in the South. This accusation against Mr. Garang was reinforced after the abortive Communist coup in July 1971 (details of this event will be discussed later). Mr. Garang had, however, explained to us that the Democratic and Socialist Movement was aimed at creating a movement of people conscious of the philosophy of the May 25th Revolution and who were able to defend it. It was also aimed at a Socialistic political education of the masses both in the North and in the South so as to create a common political awareness and thus eliminate distrust between the Northerners and Southerners. Mr. Garang further explained that the Democratic and Socialist Movement could not be launched in a suspicious atmosphere and therefore a political solution to cultivate an atmosphere conducive to its operation was a necessary forerunner. He concluded that the immediate problem for the government was to win the confidence of the Southerners by practical and visible results. Some Southerners, however, insisted that the talk of a creation of a Democratic and Socialist Movement was a Communist strategy in return for the adoption of their regional policy for solving the Southern problem.

Another confusing and disheartening problem is the government's educational policy which contradicts the June declaration of Regional Autonomy. The new educational policy has abolished village schools in the South and unified the two patterns of education in the country. Whatever merits this policy has, the fact remains that it aims at the total replacement by Arab culture of African cultural values in the South. That is not the spirit of the policy statement on Regional Autonomy.

VII. OPPOSITION TO THE NIMEIRY REGIME

Feudalism and revolutionary socialism are diametrically opposed ideals. One cannot tolerate the existence of the other. What culminated in the battle of Aba Island was not surprising in the light of the policies laid down by the Nimeiry regime at its inception. We have mentioned earlier in this chapter that Sudanese politics since the time of self-government have been dominated by feudalism, and reactionary groups revolving chiefly around the Ansar and Khatmiyya sects. The late El Hadi Abdal Rahman el Mahdi inherited the leadership of the powerful Ansar religious sect. He was proud and had a burning ambition to become a divine leader of the whole "Sudanese Nation"; hence his blessing on the idea of making the Sudan an Islamic State by law. A large number of the Ansars had been restricted to illiteracy and poverty for generations. The Mahdi family manipulated them to strengthen its political position. El Hadi used them as a political tool. They believed in him and never questioned his wisdom; their loyalty was demonstrated in their uprising against the state in March 1970. It must, however, be mentioned here that President Nimeiry is an Ansar himself and so are some of his colleagues in the Government. The battle of Aba Island was therefore ideological and political rather than religious. It was also a battle of personalities.

The Khatmiyya sect had not been as vocal in its opposition to the present regime as the Ansar group, because of the Pan-Arabist trend in the government. The sect is an ardent supporter of Arabism.

It was revealed by the government that Ansars under El Hadi Abdal Rahman and the Mahdi family began to organize themselves for subversion in February 1965, after the setback of the October Revolution. This group began to implement this ambition to hold power in the Sudan by importing war materials and raising funds by various ways and means from foreign circles. It relied "on the Moslem Brothers organization, on sectarian reserves and others".[16] Preparations to execute this plan of seizing power by any means were intensified after the May coup d'état.

The elements that oppose the Nimeiry regime are not only confined to the dissolved Umma Party. Others include the Moslem Brothers, some leaders and cadres of the Unionist Democratic Party, the supporters of Sharif El Hindi and others who hate the experiment with Socialism. There was also an attempt before the battle of Aba Island to unite the two factions of the Umma Party, the Moslem Brothers and other elements among the students, officials, workers, the various government units and the armed and security forces. Thus the opposition of March 1970 to the government was enormous.

The government ordered the siege of Aba Island and forced el Hadi el Mahdi to surrender. El Hadi was to be arrested with the minimum possible casualties. But the resistance offered to the government forces prompted retaliation, and many innocent people lost their lives in this confrontation. El Hadi Abdal Rahman el Mahdi, the leader of the Ansar sect and the titular head of the Umma Party, was killed at the Sudan-Ethiopia border in an attempt to flee the country. The battle of Aba Island effected the liquidation of a powerful conservative and neo-colonialistic group in the Sudan. The temporary loss of strength of the Ansars introduced a new element into Sudanese politics, especially with regard to North-South relations. For the first time the religious aspect of the conflict has disappeared. The Sudan was about to become a Moslem State by law at the time of the May coup d'état. Now at least the Southern problem is looked at rationally and essentially as a political issue and the question of religion is discarded. Sectarianism has been temporarily buried.

VIII. COUP AND COUNTER COUP

When Nimeiry came to power, he invited a number of civilians to take office as Ministers. They included three civilian Communists, one of whom was the late Joseph Garang. The Communists, who had been approached about the coup d'état before it took place, thought that it was not an opportune time because the mass movement in the Sudan was not gaining ground. They believed a coup should be the culmination of a growing mass struggle leading to a change of power, and not merely a device for solving contradictions within the existing political situation. The Communists, however, offered support for Nimeiry's government when he launched his coup. General Nimeiry needed their support as the Communist Party was well organized and had infiltrated the Trades Union Movement and the student organizations. Sooner or later, Nimeiry called on the Communist Party to liquidate itself voluntarily in order to make way for the formation of a political organization within which all the forces of the Revolution should be incorporated. A minority in the Central Committee of the Communist Party and some of its members who were appointed Ministers (except the late Joseph Garang) endorsed the President's call for dissolution. A special conference of the Party was convened in August 1970 and took the decision to maintain the independent existence of the Party by a vote of four to one. The Party agreed in principle to support the Nimeiry regime on specific programmes only.

The militant Communists continued to disagree with the government on many issues. They and the nationalists (as opposed to the pan-Arabists) were opposed to Nimeiry's excessive alliance with Egypt and Libya and resented Nimeiry's intention to join the Arab Federation of Libya, Egypt and Syria; they favoured a policy orientated towards Africa rather than towards the Arab world; hence they had a strong interest in finding a solution for the problem of the Southern Sudan as an essential part of their policy of winning

African friends. They also attacked the government's economic and educational policies. But serious as these differences might have been, the pivot of the crisis between Nimeiry's Revolutionary Command Council and the Communist Party was the role of the working class and the direction of the revolution in the Sudan. They were certainly external factors in influencing General Nimeiry's attempts to liquidate the Party. Possibly the alliance with Egypt and Libya might well have carried with it undertakings to suppress the Communist Party, and this view would seem to be supported when Libya hijacked the plane carrying the leaders of the short-lived coup.

It must, however, be remembered that General Nimeiry is both a pan-Arabist and a Nationalist, and that he resented the dogmatism of the militant Communists. He arrested many leading Communists, including the late Secretary General Khalid Mahgoub; and in November 1970, he dismissed two Communist sympathizers from his Revolutionary Command Council, Lt.-Colonel Babiker el-Nur and Major Hashim el-Atta, both former Assistant Prime Ministers. A third man dismissed at the same time was the powerful Minister of the Interior and the chief co-ordinator of the May coup, the late Major Farouk Osman Hamadalla, a non Communist and essentially a Nationalist. Relations between the Government and the Communists deteriorated to a low ebb.

On July 19th, 1971, Major Hashim el-Atta overthrew the Nimeiry regime. El-Atta set up a new Revolutionary Command Council of seven members under the chairmanship of Lt.-Colonel Babiker el-Nur, who together with his colleague Major Farouk Osman Hamadalla, was in London at the time of their coup. The new regime of el-Atta, however, was short-lived. A counter-coup was staged which successfully restored Nimeiry and his colleagues to power on July 22nd, 1971. During the counter-coup, many officers and men of the military lost their lives. All the principal leaders of the coup were swiftly court-martialled and executed by firing squad. Those put to death included Lt.-Colonel Babiker el-Nur, Major Hashim el-Atta, and Major Farouk Osman Hamadalla. Three prominent leaders of the banned Sudan Communist Party which was implicated with the coup, were hanged. They were Abdel Khalid Mahgoub, the Secretary General of the Party, Shafie Ahmed El Sheikh, a Trade Union leader of international standing and Joseph U. Garang, Minister of State for Southern Affairs in Nimeiry's government. The execution of the three civilians caused anger and uproar throughout the world. The tragic episode opened a new chapter in the history of the country.

After the events of July 19th-22nd, 1971, there was a quickening of the political tempo. The Revolutionary Command Council under Nimeiry was once again in full control and passed what is now known as the Republican Order No. 5, which came into effective force on August 12th, 1971. This order is to act as the transitional Constitution of the Sudan under which the country is to be ruled until a new permanent Constitution is passed. Under this order, the Sudan shall be a one-party presidential republic in which the President is both head of State and of the government.

A referendum was held between September 15th-30th, in which Nimeiry was the sole presidential candidate. He received an over-whelming majority of the votes cast. On becoming president, he dissolved the Revolutionary Command Council, appointed three Vice-Presidents, namely, Bahiker Awadalla, Abel Alier, Minister of Southern Affairs, and Major-General Khalid Abbas, Minister of Defence. He also announced many ministerial and governmental appointments and changes.

It seems that the July coup and counter-coup meant no funda-mental change in the government's declared policy of Regional Autonomy. The hanging of the late Joseph Garang, however, disheartened many Southerners and Northerners who saw in him a genuine dedication to bridging the conflict between the North and the South. His implication in the el-Atta coup has never been proved. He was a member of the Central Committee of the Communist Party, a fact which President Nimeiry knew very well and yet continued to retain him in his Cabinet until the day el-Atta launched his coup. There is, however, now a marked acceleration in President Nimiery's implementation of the policy of Regional Autonomy. There might therefore be some truth in his accusation that the late Garang retarded his policy by attempting to establish first a Communist base in the South. After the Referendum, President Nimiery appointed three Southerners as Commissioners in the South and a Deputy-Minister for Southern Affairs. He has also made some contacts with the Anya-Nya leadership with a view to calling a Round Table Conference to discuss the future of the South. He has certainly found in Abel Alier a man of integrity, respect and high credibility among Southern Sudanese; and therefore Alier's position will help the government in winning the confidence of the South, provided that it talks less and does more reconstruction.

IX. THE FUTURE OF THE SOUTH

In discussing the future of the South, I need to say something about the political leadership in the South. I shall try to discuss the Southern Sudanese leadership in two categories: the group outside the Sudan, and the group inside the country. It is my hope that such an attempt will enable us to deduce what the future holds for the Southern Sudan.

As a product of the trauma of the tragedy of the Southern Sudan, it would be unfair to the South itself if I attempted to whitewash every evil in the Southern Sudanese political leadership. The critical analysis that follows is well-intentioned, for self-criticism is an asset to any political group. It must also be recognized that just as there are different layers of comprehension and meaning so are there different forms of perception and desire.

The failure to resolve the Southern Question has had adverse consequences. It has created a situation of potential disintegration among the Southern Sudanese both inside and outside the country. However, although there were many factions among the Southern politicians both inside and outside the country, there has been a marked improvement in unity among the Southern elite in the country since the May coup d'état. We shall trace the political factions among them from 1964.

Soon after the October Revolution of 1964, the Sudan Unity Party was formed by Mr. Santino Deng, one of Abboud's Ministers. He stood for a united Sudan and is known for his ultra-conservative views. Since he became a Minister in the former Abboud regime in 1958, he has lost contact with the Southerners. Khartoum has become his permanent home. Philemon Majok, a former member of the defunct five-member supreme council formed his own party. This party, because of its reactionary views, received some support from the former sectarian groups in the Northern Sudan. The Southern Front which emerged during the October Revolution became the voice of the Southern civil servants and professionals. It stood for self-determination, but its influence was not sufficient to achieve substantial reforms for the South from the Mahgoub government, of which it was a partner. Before the dissolution of political parties in May 1970, the party had become pragmatic in its policies and claimed to be a watch dog for the South. The Sudan African National Union (SANU) of the late William Deng had the largest number of Southern Members of Parliament in the dissolved National Assembly. SANU was vacillating between secession and federation. All these parties were rivals and each claimed to represent the true interests of the Southern people. As I have already mentioned, after their dissolution most of their supporters joined the present Nimeiry government and some are personally involved in the Ministry of State for Southern Affairs.

It is perhaps important to mention that Southern politicians practising politics in the Sudan from Independence to the time the May Revolutionary Government came to power, made tactless alliances with conservative business groups such as the Umma and the National Unionist Parties which had no genuine policy for resolving the North-South conflict. Perhaps they had no alternative. This was true of the Southern Front, whose militancy subsided and ended in a coalition with Mahgoub, who had never made any political attempt to solve the Southern question. At this juncture we may mention the political role of Joseph Garang, the late Minister of State for Southern Affairs. Garang had long been a Communist, and believed in a socialist approach to the Southern Problem. The Communist policy of Regional Autonomy had been adopted. Garang was a dynamic politician of keen intellect, but his ideological inclination alienated him from the Southern elite who have no taste for Communism.

In general, we may conclude that Southern elites in the Sudan are more politically refined, more responsive to change, and have a more sincere devotion to reaching an honourable solution to the Southern Problem than Southern politicians in self-exile. The fact that they sank their differences to effect the policy of Regional Autonomy shows how responsible they are. Their cooperation on a common issue is very impressive. Their political maturity and selflessness may perhaps be attributed in part to their education. Most of the Southern political leaders now in the Sudan are graduates and their approach to politics is motivated by a desire to serve the South rather than by personal gain. The propaganda put out by some Southern politicians outside the country, which claims that Southern leaders in the Sudan who cooperate with the Nimeiry regime are traitors because they are interested in personal gain, is in my view an unfortunate and unwarranted accusation.

Incompetence and factionalism are two political evils that have plagued the Southern politicians outside the Sudan. Until the middle of 1970, five "governments" were in existence and these were namely, the Nile Republic Provisional Government, the Anyidi Revolutionary Government, the Anya-Nya National Organization, the Sudan Azania and Sue Republic. Each of these claimed to be the legitimate spokesman for the South. I shall try to give the brief background of each of these factions.

Following the return of William Deng to the Sudan in early 1965, the SANU wing of Aggrey Jaden functioned as the only Southern Party outside the Sudan. But soon after, Joseph Oduho, a former Member of Parliament, formed his Azania Liberation Front. Oduho and his group pledged to establish a "free independent African Nation in the Southern Sudan called Azania". Oduho had perhaps formed his party for reasons of personal leadership since there was no difference in policy from Jaden.

M

Towards the end of 1965, Aggrey Jaden joined Oduho as Vice-President in an attempt at unity. But not long after this, Oduho dismissed Jaden from his party because the latter was alleged to have met William Deng in Nairobi and to have discussed the Southern problem without his authority. In 1966, Jaden formed a provisional government in the forests inside the Southern Sudan. Oduho was by this time under Anya-Nya arrest in the Eastern Equatoria forests following his sharp division with the late Fr. Saturnino Lohure, one of the founders of the Southern Liberal party in the 1950s.

In September 1968, Jaden felt that he was not being respected and supported in his leadership. He began to take a cautious and reserved attitude to issues. It was alleged that there was an underground movement to depose him, championed by his Vice-President, Camillo Dhol. The situation became confused as tribalism entered the struggle for power, and Jaden abdicated his position and fled to Nairobi. There is no doubt whatsoever that Jaden is a refined, cool-headed but extremely indecisive politician. Following Jaden's flight, a convention was alleged to have been held and Gordon M. Mayen was reported to have been elected President. This was in March 1969. The convention renamed the Southern Sudan the Nile State. Although the Nile Government seemed dominated by the Dinka, it was so because most of Jaden's supporters — mainly people from Equatoria Province — refused to participate in the convention. The Nile Provincial Government promised to prosecute, uncompromisingly, the war of liberation for national freedom and complete independence. However, Jaden's ardent supporters solicited some Anya-Nya support without his consent, and declared an Anyidi Revolutionary Government. Meanwhile, other factions such as the Sudan Azania under Ezibon Mondiri, the Sue River Republic and the Anya-Nya organization were established. The last, headed by an Anya-Nya officer, Colonel Joseph Lagu, maintains Anya-Nya independence from the politicians and is the only recognized supreme authority of the "Southern Sudan Liberation Movement". Colonel Lagu was previously the Eastern Commander of the Anya-Nya armed forces and he disagreed with his Commander-in-Chief, Major General A. Taffeng, who headed the Anyidi Government. Colonel Lagu gained ground and eventually united all the Anya-Nya officers under his command, pensioned off General Taffeng and declared the Anya-Nya as the sole authority in the Southern Sudan. The Nile Provincial Government dissolved itself in mid-1970 in the interests of unity, and subsequently, all the rest of the parties followed its example and declared support for Colonel Lagu's leadership. Colonel Lagu has maintained his authority over the Anya-Nya up to the time of writing and has eclipsed all the politicians in exile. This does not, however, mean that all these factions have completely died.

The characteristics of these factions among the Southern politicians outside the Sudan are many. All these politicians are confused and have lost contact with the real issues involved in the North-South conflict. Some of them have no keen interest in the Anya-Nya and have even worked for the disunity of the Anya-Nya to serve their own interests. Sheer personal ambition has led to power struggles resulting in internal divisions, thereby creating a meaningless government purporting to represent the Southern Sudanese. Incompetence and lack of political foresight are common among them. They have refused to see the fact that they lack the ability to put political issues in proper perspective and have assumed certain positions of power which they are unable to shoulder. All these factions suffer from the lack of a serious intention to serve the people they claim to lead, and egoistic pursuits occupy much of their time. The creation of a multiplicity of presidents was motivated by the struggle for financial help from their beneficiaries. Tribalism has also plagued all Southern politicians outside the Sudan. I have already indicated that the formation of the Anyidi Revolutionary Government was basically tribally motivated, and aimed at countering the Dinka dominance in the Nile Government. Another common element among them is that they fall under the category of "ignorant elites".[17] They are not revolutionary, but incredibly reactionary, and it is a simple fact that one cannot claim to lead a revolution if one is not revolutionary.

I have already mentioned the sad fact that Southern politicians outside the Sudan subordinate the general interests of the people of the South to their individual pursuit of power. This has made them regard themselves as indispensable for the welfare of the South. They have turned to blackmailing and exploiting the Southern masses. It must also be mentioned that they have failed to understand the complex operation of the machinery of cold war politics. Some imperialist agents have intensified their connections with them. After many years of Southern demand for justice and rational economic development in the Sudan, and after many massacres in the South without any outside sympathy, there are now people claiming to help the Southerners wage the war to the end. Their aim is certainly not to help the Southern Sudanese. It may be understandable that they are pursuing their national interests, but this should be made clear and not camouflaged by talk of aiding oppressed Southern Sudanese. They want the Southerners to go on fighting to thwart any attempt at solving the Southern Problem. Finally, there is no hope of able and united leadership from the Southern politicians outside the Sudan. As long as outsiders continue to aid them financially, they will refuse to unite and will refuse to view the Southern problem with any sort of objectivity. A fragmentary approach to the Southern Question has marred an objective approach to the whole issue of North-South relations.

What, then, does the future hold for the Southern Sudan? This is a difficult question to answer and I do not pretend to provide any adequate reply. From what has been said about the Southern leadership, it seems that the future of the South depends more on the Southerners inside the country, but cooperation with those outside is imperative for any rapid normalization of the situation. It does not seem feasible for the Southern Sudan to attain secession from the rest of the country. There is no success in the fighting, and if Biafra, which had a sophisticated leadership of international standing, a well-drilled and organized army with modern weapons, and a well co-ordinated machinery of propaganda, could be defeated by the Nigerian Federal Government, then the Anya-Nya, who are insignificant beside the Biafrans in military power, efficiency and seriousness of intention, cannot conceivably dislodge Sudanese government troops from the South. That is the hard reality of the situation and to refuse to accept the facts as they are and to continue fighting can only be completely self-defeating.

It is true that in many countries of the world, particularly in Africa, racial, linguistic or religious differences have not successfully prevented the establishment of unified nations. It could, however, be argued, in the words of Zambia's Reuben Kamanga, that "Whereas it is our ardent desire to foster African Unity, it would be morally wrong to force anybody into unity founded on bloodshed. For unity to be meaningful and beneficial it must be based on the consent of all parties concerned, offering security and justice to all."[18] But if there is a high propensity for unity in the Sudan, then we need tolerance: racial, cultural and religious. The need for reconciliation in the Sudan and a devolution of powers based on a system of regional government, in which the Southern Sudan enjoys a relatively fair share of the national cake, is urgent. Relationships between the North and South should have the following basic characteristics of local autonomy, as elucidated by MacDougall: government according to the will of the people, the absence of internal or external domination, the free pursuit of economic, social and cultural development, the enjoyment of fundamental human rights and equal treatment, and the absence of discrimination on grounds of race, colour, class, creed or political conviction.[19] The future is bright for the Southern Sudan only if the Northern and Southern Sudanese leaders can genuinely dedicate themselves to carrying to its logical conclusion the policy of Regional Autonomy as pronounced by President Nimiery, without fear or hesitation. Arguments against Regional Autonomy for the South are stupid exercises of the reactionary petty bourgeoisie politicians and are a thing of the past. The Sudan must adopt a system that suits its peculiar problems; excessive enthusiasm for national integration must not make us overlook the dualistic cultural traits of the country, As Mohamad Omer Beshir put it:

"The appropriate system of government and administration for any country is that which suits its particular problems, rather than one which conforms to ready-made or neatly labelled models. The present Unitary system with no special arrangements for the South has proved that it is weak and incapable of solving the problem of the Sudan as a whole or the problems of the South. It is rejected because of its unsuitability."[20]

Indeed, the narrow and more centralized system of authoritative decision-making in the Sudan has become less accountable and more remote from day-to-day concerns in the Southern Sudan. This has been true since the country became independent, and as a result, the South has been virtually under martial law with increased coercion and inefficiency. The alternative to the unitary system is therefore to decentralize decision-making, thereby increasing accountability. Decentralization, as Professor David Apter has observed,

"may take the form of a proliferation of decision-making subunits, so that the central pattern of government is extended through a number of local governments and becomes more effective on a regional or territorial level. Decision subunits based on region make it possible for the public to participate in problems that are central to their interests and to develop a tradition of civic responsibility."[21]

It is unnecessary and costly for the Sudanese leaders to continue twisting the facts of the Southern Question. Here we are reminded of the words of President Nyerere of Tanzania:

"Sudanese leaders, and Africa leaders, have a real chance of solving the Southern problem — provided we do not make the same mistake as we made in Nigeria and act as if there is no genuine problem ... The solution, as the present Government in Sudan has rightly foreseen, lies in a constitution which recognizes both the unity of the Sudan, and the legitimate interests of the South."[22]

Mwalima Nyerere goes on to provide a lesson which every African leader must learn from the Biafra-Nigeria war. Because of its relevance to the North-South conflict, it deserves quotation at length:

> "But there is a very serious lesson to be learned from the present tragedy. We should learn that where in any African State there is a dominant group, whether that group is ethnic, religious or otherwise, it must wield its power and influence on behalf of all the elements which go to form that country. In particular, it should be very solicitous of the interests of the minorities because they are the ones which need the protection of the State. If a dominant group does not act in this protective manner, then civil strife and and consequent Biafras become inevitable. That is the lesson Africa should learn from the Nigerian tragedy."[23]

Professor Arnold Toynbee gives counsel to the Sudanese leadership and this also demands extensive quotation.

> "The problem of the Sudan is the problem of the two Africas on a miniature scale: and, therefore, the Sudan holds Africa's destiny, as well as her own destiny, in her hands. If she can succeed in reconciling the two elements in her own population, she will have done a piece of constructive pioneer work for the continent as a whole. If the conflict in the Sudan becomes acute and chronic this will heighten the tension between the two Africas everywhere and sooner or later the Southern Sudan will become a focus for Negro Africa's latent resentment against Northern Africa. If things were to come to this pass, the fission of the African continent might become irremediable. The Northern Sudanese have been saddled by fate with a heavy load of responsibility. Let us hope they will rise to the occasion."[24]

This is the time to test our will in the Sudan to survive as a nation, recognizing the cultural hybrid of our origin. This is the time to test our humanity and to prove our sanity. It is also the time to reflect on whether we have the capacity to govern, which means the capacity to shape our own destiny. Although Arab nationalism and African nationalism, whatever differences there are, appear basically divisive and potentially loaded with conflict, there could perhaps be room for both to flourish in the Sudan, for the Sudan is a microcosm of Africa. The old politicians in the Sudan acted dysfunctionally in terms of their manifest power goals, and failed in their bid for national leadership. A dynamic and vigilant leadership to instil confidence and self-awareness in the people would lessen the accumulated agony which the North-South conflict has produced in the Sudan. The Southern Sudan's economic potential is great. There are resources that are being wasted because of the war. The economic viability of the South points to a bright future if arrangements to guarantee equality to both parts of the country can be affected soon. The South is capable of producing men and women of high ability to run a machinery of regional government and to participate in the central government.

X. CONCLUSION

I have tried to show in this chapter that since independence the Sudan has largely been ruled by the army. It is possible that civilian rule will reassert itself in the future. The present military regime has absorbed some civilians into the council of ministers and this is indicative of a possible return to civilian rule. I have also attempted to show that political trends in the Northern Sudan were dominated by Moslem sectarian divisions between the Ansar and the Khatmiyya. Many attempted military coups also figure in my account.

The Southern Question is in the centre of our discussion. The crisis of integration and legitimacy face any Khartoum government in its relations with the Southern part of the country. The Southern problem, analysed in proper perspective, reveals that the memory of the slave trade; the economic disparity between the North and the South as a result of the Anglo-Egyptian colonial policy in the Sudan, and complicated and perpetuated by the feudal, nepotic and corrupt successive Khartoum governments; the arrogance and mistakes of some inexperienced Northern civil servants in the South; and the lack of a genuine appraisal of the Southern problem by Northern politicians, coupled with the politics of some of the Southerners, have all contributed to the problem.

As events have shown, there is no military solution to the Southern problem. The provisional government of Sir El Khatim El Khalifa realized this and so has the present revolutionary government of El-Nimeiry. The Anya-Nya were determined in their fight, and some of them are still optimistic. Undoubtedly, there has been a deep-rooted mutual suspicion between the Northerners and Southerners: the former have believed that regional autonomy for the South would be used by the Southerners as preparation for subsequent secession; and the Southerners have always thought of the Northerners as cunning and colonialist. The literature of the Southern politicians against successive Khartoum governments is the same as that used by African politicians in other parts of the continent against the colonial powers. This attitude of misunderstanding and distrust has not solved the Southern Question. Most of the present Southern politicians outside the Sudan would appear to be divisive betrayers of the public interest of the South. Initially, the Southerners had demanded federation, but as the civil war intensified, the demand switched to self-determination and separation for the South.

There is no hope of getting genuine help from outside. The Organization of African Unity is incapable of (and is not interested in) solving such issues, as was demonstrated by its failure to resolve the Nigeria-Biafra conflict. George W. Shepherd has correctly observed that the tendency to presume the necessity of national unity and integration within the new states of Africa has influenced African conclusions regarding such problems as that of the Southern Sudan.[25] In other words, multi-ethnic states are certainly the order of the day in Africa, and very few African governments are inclined to encourage ethnic self-determination. Jaramogi Oginga Odinga, of Kenya, had argued against the secessionist movement in the North Frontier District of Kenya among the Somalis on the grounds that the principle of self-determination has relevance where foreign domination is the issue, but not where the point in question is territorial disintegration by dissident citizens.[26] Such a view is undoubtedly widely respected and accepted in Africa, and is successfully used by all Sudanese governments against the Southern demand for separation from the North.

The Southern Question is not insurmountable. The problem must be tackled after genuine recognition and careful study of those components that are the source of the conflict. It needs ability, courage, great self-confidence, determination, power of decision and goodwill on the part of those concerned to bring the situation back to normal, so that all the peoples of the Sudan will enjoy the freedom that their fellows elsewhere in independent Africa have. Africa will have much to gain when the people of the Southern Sudan are given the feeling that they belong to humanity, and to Africa, and can thus enjoy all the benefits that this continent offers to her people. In return they must be prepared to defend it when these benefits are threatened or removed by anyone, either from within or without.

REFERENCES

1 A. A. Mazrui, *Violence and Thought*, Chapter on the Multiple Marginality of the Sudan, pp. 174-6. I am indebted to Professor Mazrui for giving me an earlier version of this chapter. The bibliography was very helpful in my own research.
2 Douglas W. Rae and Michael Taylor, *The Analysis of Political Cleavages* (New Haven and London, 1970), p. 107.
3 Richard Gray, Introduction to *The Problem of the Southern Sudan* by Joseph Oduho and William Deng (London 1963), p. 2.
4 Speech by Aggrey Jaden, Khartoum Round Table Conference on the South, March 1965.
5 Mazrui, ibid.

6 P. M. Holt, *A Modern History of the Sudan from the Funji Sultan to the Present Day* (London, 1961), pp. 173-4.

7 For details of Abboud's takeover, see R. First, *The Barrel of a Gun: Political Power in Afrjca and the Coup d'Etat* (London, 1970), pp. 222, 232.

8 Holt, ibid. For details of attempted coups during the Abboud regime see R. First, ibid., pp. 232-46.

9 Robert W. Crawford, "The Sudan the Revolution of 1964", *Africa Report*, March 1965.

10 Ibid.

11 Ibid.

12 First, ibid.

13 Mazrui, ibid.

14 "Views about the 25 May Socialist Revolution", compiled by the Cultural Office of the Sudanese Youth Union, Bahr el Ghazel Province, Wau, p. 9.

15 Ibid.

16 *Sudan News*, March 29th, 1970.

17 For an excellent discussion on "ignorant elites" see Okello Oculi, "Ignorant Elites: Africa's Great Threat", in *East Africa Journal*, Vol. V, No. 10, October, 1968.

18 Kamanga. Statement on Zambia's recognition of Biafra in *Tanzania Standard*, May 21st, 1969.

19 R. MacDougall, "Rhodesia and the UN", 62, AJIL (1968).

20 M. O. Beshir, *The Southern Sudan: Background to Conflict* (London, 1968), p. 106.

21 See D. E. Apter, *Politics of Modernization* (Chicago, 1965), pp. 458-9.

22 President Julius Nyerere, paper on "The Nigeria Biafra Crisis", pp. 9-10.

23 Ibid.

24 A. J. Toynbee, *Between Niger and Nile, 1965*, cited in Beshir, *The Southern Sudan: Background to Conflict*, p. 107.

25 George W. Shepherd, "The Southern Sudan and National Integration", *Journal of Modern African Studies*, Vol. 4, No. 2, October, 1966.

26 Speech by Jaramogi Oginga Odinga, leader of the Kenya delegation to the OAU Inaugural Summit Conference, May, 1963.

EPILOGUE

In the concluding chapter of this volume, I mentioned that the government of President Nimeiry was making contacts with the Anya-Nya leadership with a view to calling a Round Table conference to discuss the future of North-South relations. Events overtook us while we were going into publication. A conference was convened towards the end of February 1972 in Addis Ababa, Ethiopia, between government and Southern Sudan Liberation Movement delegations. The talks were successfully concluded in what will go down in history as the "Addis-Ababa Agreement on the Problem of Southern Sudan".

The Agreement contains six documents:
1. The basic law for the organization of regional autonomy in the three Southern provinces;
2. The amnesty law for those who participated in the Anya-Nya movement;
3. The administrative arrangement for the interim period till the establishment of the institution of Regional Autonomy mentioned in the basic law;
4. The cease-fire;
5. The temporary arrangements concerning the armed forces;
6. The organization of immigration of the refugees and the resettlement of those dwelling in towns and who had originally come from the countryside in the South.

The basic law has been enacted by President Nimeiry as the "Southern Provinces Regional Self-Government Act, 1972", on March 3rd, 1972. The Regional Autonomy law, as it is known, ascertains the unity of the Sudan and organizes decentralization, granting the Southern Sudan the status of Regional Autonomy. The central government in Khartoum legislates, supervises and executes every policy concerning national defence, foreign affairs, nationality, passports and immigration, economic and social planning, foreign trade, finance and currency, communications and telecommunications, air and river transportation within the country, auditing and education planning including syllabuses and higher education.

All other tasks of administration will be run by the regional government in the South. There will be a "Peoples Regional Council" in the South and it will be responsible for legislation on all spheres which are left to the region. Regional policies will be executed by a "High Executive Council" under a Regional President nominated by the "Peoples Regional Council" and then to be appointed by the President of the Country.

As to language, Arabic remains the official language of the country, but English is to be a working language in the South, besides local languages whose use may be necessitated by convenience and practical circumstances.

Besides the basic law organizing regional government, the "Addis-Ababa Agreement" has been implemented in its entirety by Presidential Order (Legislation) numbers:

(39) dealing with the Revenue of Taxes and Duties (Financial Aid and other Revenues for the Southern Sudan Region of the Sudan Act, 1972).

(40) dealing with the Provisional measures preceding the Election of the Peoples Regional Assembly Act, 1972.

(41) to end military operations in the Southern Region of the Democratic Republic of the Sudan and to establish a joint cease-fire commission.

(42) to institute provisional arrangements for the people's military forces of the Sudan in the Southern Region.

(45) to constitute a commission for the repatriation of the Southern Sudanese refugees now residing in neighbouring countries.

President Nimeiry instituted a regional government in the South under the Presidency of Abel Alier who remains Vice-President of the country, following the ratification of the Agreement on March 27th, 1972 in Addis-Ababa. The leader of the Anya-Nya, Major-General Joseph Lagu, has been appointed Commander of the army in the Southern Region with the same rank.

There is now a greater air of optimism in the Southern Sudan than before. President Nimeiry has certainly won the confidence and trust of the peoples of the South as he has proved himself a man of his own word. For the first time in the history of independent Sudan, the country has found a man of strong personality, blessed with vision and certain ideals which have the merit of being intensely practicable. Many problems lie ahead, but it is my hope that the peoples of the Sudan will learn a lesson from the mistakes of the past and dedicate their efforts to nation-building along the lines of the Addis-Ababa Agreement.

D. M. W.   1972

APPENDIX I
1930 MEMORANDUM ON SOUTHERN POLICY

Civil Secretary's Office,
Khartoum, January 25th, 1930

The Governor, Upper Nile Province, Malakal.
The Governor, Mongalla Province, Mongalla.
The Governor, Bahr al Ghazal Province, Wau.

His Excellency the Governor General directs that the main features of the approved policy of the Government for the administration of the Southern Provinces should be re-stated in simple terms.

In the strictly confidential memorandum which accompanies this letter an attempt has been made to do this, though it will of course be seen that innumerable points of detail arising are not dealt with seriatim.

2.   Your attention is directed to Part II of the memorandum, and I should be obliged if you would forward, as soon as possible, your comments on the criteria suggested and any suggestions you may wish to make for additions to the list.

3.   The carrying out of the policy as described may lead from time to time to various financial implications or commitments though it is hoped that these will not be great. It will be convenient that any such foreseen should be notified to the relevant authority without delay for consideration.

4.   Application of the policy will obviously vary in detail and in intensity according to locality. It is essential however, that the ultimate aim should be made clear to all who are responsible for the execution of the policy, and the memorandum should therefore be circulated to and studied by all your District Commissioners. Sufficient copies for this purpose are sent herewith. Copies are also being sent to such Heads of Departments in Khartoum as are concerned.

CIVIL SECRETARY

CS/I.C.I.
STRICTLY CONFIDENTIAL
Memorandum
Part I

The policy of the Government in the Southern Sudan is to build up a series of self contained racial or tribal units with structure and organization based, to whatever extent the requirements of equity and good government permit, upon indigenous customs, traditional usage and beliefs.

The measures already taken or to be taken to promote the above policy are re-stated below.

A. PROVISION OF NON-ARABIC-SPEAKING STAFF (ADMINI-
STRATIVE, CLERICAL AND TECHNICAL).

a) Administrative Staff

The gradual elimination of the Mamur, whether Arab or black. This has
already begun, and it is intended that the process of reduction shall
continue as opportunity offers.

b) Clerical

It has been the recognized policy for some years that locally recruited
staff should take the place of clerks and accountants drawn from the
North and that the language of Government offices should be English.

In the Bahr al Ghazal Province the change to English has already
been made and a large number of local boys are employed.

The process has to be gradual. It is recognized that local boys are not
fit at present to fill the higher posts in Government offices, and the
supply of educated English-speaking boys depends on the speed with
which the two missionary Intermediate schools in Mongalla Province
and the Intermediate and Stack Schools at Wau can produce them. The
missions must retain a certain number of these boys as teachers for their
Elementary schools (which are an integral part of the educational
system) but since the employment of local boys in Government offices
is a vital feature of the general policy every encouragement should be
given to those in charge of mission schools to cooperate in that policy
by sending boys into Government service. Province officials must aim
at maintaining a steady supply of boys for the Elementary Vernacular
schools which feed the Intermediate schools.

c) Technical

Generally speaking, the considerations mentioned above apply also to
the supply of boys for the technical departments — Agriculture,
Medical, Public Works, etc.; but in certain cases it may not be essential
that boys going to these departments should complete the Intermediate
school course.

B. CONTROL OF IMMIGRANT TRADERS FROM THE NORTH

It is the aim of the Government to encourage, as far as is possible, Greek
and Syrian traders rather than the Gellaba type. Permits to the latter
should be decreased unobtrusively but progressively, and only the best
type of Gellaba, whose interests are purely commercial and pursued in a
legitimate manner should be admitted. The limitation of Gellaba trade to
towns or established routes is essential.

C. FUNDAMENTAL NECESSITY FOR BRITISH STAFF TO
FAMILIARIZE THEMSELVES WITH THE BELIEFS AND
CUSTOMS AND THE LANGUAGES OF THE TRIBES THEY
ADMINISTER.

a) Beliefs and Customs.

The policy of Government requires that officials in the South, especially
administrative officials, should be fully informed as to the social
structure, beliefs, customs and mental processes of pagan tribes. Study
on these lines is of vital importance to the solution of administrative
problems, and it is with this fact in view that a highly qualified expert
has been detailed to work in the South.

b) Language.

The Rejaf Language Conference recommended the adoption of certain 'group languages' for use in schools. It is clearly impossible to develop all the languages and dialects of the Southern Sudan and the development of a limited number of them may tend to cause the smaller languages one by one to disappear, and be supplanted by 'group languages'.

It is, of course, true that the adoption of this system carries with it the implication of the gradual adoption of a new, or partly new, language by the population of the areas in which the 'smaller languages' are used at present. Such a result is, indeed, inevitable in the course of time, for 'smaller languages' must always tend to disappear.

It is also recognised that in such places as Wau itself, Arabic is so commonly used that the local languages have been almost completely excluded. Special concessions may be necessary in these places.

The Rejaf Conference did not regard these factors as seriously affecting the policy of 'group languages', and it was held to be a matter of first importance that books for the study of the 'group languages' should be available for missionaries and officials and that a specialist should be appointed to study the question. A linguistic expert, Dr. Tucker, has therefore been appointed for a period of two years, and his chief function will be to advise as to the production of suitable books. The Secretary for Education and Health has already circulated a memorandum on his duties.

The production of grammars and vocabularies will facilitate the study of the local vernaculars. But this will take time and meanwhile it is the duty of our officers to further the policy of the Government without delay. It cannot be stressed too strongly that to speak the natural language of the people whom he controls is the first duty of the administrator. Arabic is not that language, and indeed to the bulk of the population of the South it is a new, or partly new, tongue. Officials should avoid the error of thinking that by speaking Arabic they are in some way conforming to the principle that the administrator should converse with his people in their own language.

D. THE USE OF ENGLISH WHERE COMMUNICATION IN THE LOCAL VERNACULAR IS IMPOSSIBLE.

The time has not yet come for the adoption of a general lingua franca for the Southern Sudan, and it is impossible to foretell what, if ever that time comes, the language would be.

At the same time there are, without doubt, occasions when the use of a local vernacular is impossible, as, for instance in the case of heterogeneous groupings such as the Sudan Defence Force or the Police.

The recent introduction of English words of command in the Equatoria Corps of the Sudan Defence and their use in the Police Forces in the Provinces concerned is a step in the right direction, but more is required. Every effort should be made to make English the means of communication among the men themselves to the complete exclusion of Arabic. This will entail in the various units the opening of classes in which the men would receive instruction in English, and a concentrated effort on the part of those in authority to ensure that English is used by the men when local vernaculars cannot be. It is believed that in a comparatively short time men of these forces could learn as much English as they now know of Arabic.

It is hoped that those in charge of mission schools will assist in providing instructors for the classes referred to above.

Similarly, an official unable to speak the local vernacular should try to use English when speaking to Government employees and servants, and even, if in any way possible, to chiefs and natives. In any case, the use of an interpreter is preferable to the use of Arabic, until the local language can be used.

The initial difficulties are not minimized. Inability to converse freely at first will no doubt result in some loss of efficiency, and the dislike of almost every Englishman to using his own language in conversing with natives is fully recognized; but difficulties and dislikes must be subordinates to the main policy.

Apart from the fact that the restriction of Arabic is an essential feature of the general scheme it must not be forgotten that Arabic, being neither the language of the governing nor the governed, will progressively deteriorate. The type of Arabic at present spoken provides signal proof of this. It cannot be used as a means of communication on anything but the most simple matters, and only if it were first unlearned and then relearned in a less crude form and adopted as the language of instruction in the schools could it fulfil the growing requiremetns of the future. The local vernaculars and English, on the other hand, will in every case be the language of one of the two parties conversing and one party will therefore always be improving the other.

Incidentally it may be argued that if a District Commissioner serving in the South is transferred to the North, a knowledge of Nilotic Arabic is more of a hindrance than a help to him in learning the Arabic of the Northern Sudan.

In short, whereas at present Arabic is considered by many natives of the South as the official and, as it were, the fashionable language, the object of all should be to counteract this idea by every practical means.

Part II

PROGRESS OF POLICY

His Excellency the High Commissioner in approving this policy has suggested the need for criteria by which progress may be measured.

With this end in view it is intended to tabulate various important features of the policy and to set down the progress made at stated intervals.

It is suggested that the matters to be included in the table should be the following:

a) The number of non-Mohammedans in relation to the total Government staff under headings of administrative, clerical, and technical, with a report on the use of English by Government employees of non-British origin.

b) The number of British officials who have qualified in the local languages.

c) Number of immigrant traders of various nationalities from the North.

d) Number of Mission schools, elementary, intermediate and technical respectively.

e) Number of Government schools.

f) The amount spent on education including:

> Subsidies to mission schools;
> cost of Government schools;
> cost of supervisory educational staff.

g) Introduction of English words of command in military or police forces, with a report as to the extent to which Arabic is disappearing as the language in use among the men of these forces.

h) Notes on the progress of the use of English instead of Arabic where communication in the vernacular is impossible.

i) Progress made in the production of text-books in the group languages for use in the schools, and grammars and vocabularies for use of missionaries and officials.

It is proposed to give information in the Annual Report under these heads for the years 1924, 1927 and 1930 and for each subsequent year.

Civil Secretary's Office,

Khartoum, January 25th, 1930.

APPENDIX II
1946 MEMORANDUM ON SOUTHERN POLICY

CS/SCR/I.C.I.

Subject: Southern Sudan policy   Civil Secretary's Office,
SECRET   Khartoum, December 16th, 1946

Financial Secretary	(2)
Legal Secretary	(2)
Kaid	(3)
Director of Agriculture & Forests	(3)
Director of Economics & Trade	(2)
Director of Education	(3)
Director of Medical Service	(3)
General Manager, Sudan Railways	(2)
Director, Veterinary Service	(2)
Governor, Equatoria Province	(12)
Governor, Upper Nile Province	(10)

Will you please refer to Khartoum Secret Despatch No. 89 of August 4th, 1945, of which copies were sent to you (or to your predecessors in Office) personally under this number.

2. You will see that in paragraph 2 of the despatch there are contemplated three possible political futures for the Southern Sudan. The crucial sentence is:

It is only by economic and educational development that these people can be equipped to stand up for themselves in the future, whether their lot be eventually cast with the Northern Sudan or with East Africa (or partly with each).

3. Since the despatch was written, and since the decisions on policy which it records were taken not only have further decisions on policy for the South been taken (of which a list is attached) but great changes have taken place in the political outlook for the country as a whole. Whatever may be the final effect, inside the Sudan, of the present treaty negotiations, it is certain that the advance of the Northern Sudan to self-government, involving the progressive reduction of British executive authority, and public canvassing of the Southern Sudan question, will be accelerated. It is therefore essential that policy for the Southern Sudan should be crystallized as soon as possible and that it should be crystallized in a form which can be publicly explained and supported and which should therefore be based on sound and constructive social and economic principles. These principles must not only bear defence against factious opposition, but

must also command the support of Northern Sudanese who are prepared to take logical and liberal points of view: while the relief of doubts now in the minds of British political and departmental staff who have the interests of the South at heart is also pressing and important.

4. You will see from the foregoing paragraph that I do not suggest that the future of the two million inhabitants of the South should be influenced by appeasement of the as yet immature and ill-informed politicians of the Northern Sudan. But it is the Sudanese, northern and southern, who will live their lives and direct their affairs in future generations in this country: and our efforts must therefore now be concentrated on initiating a policy which is not only sound in itself, but which can be made acceptable to, and eventually workable by patriotic and reasonable Sudanese, northern and southern alike.

5. Apart from the recent rapid political development in the North the following conclusions have further emerged since His Excellency's 1945 despatch and enclosures were written:

a) with reference to Appendix I to the despatch, Section 7 last sentence of penultimate paragraph. East Africa's plans regarding better communications with the Southern Sudan have been found to be nebulous, and contingent on the Lake Albert Dam. Whatever the possibilities, we have no reason to hesitate between development of trade between the South and E. Africa and development of trade between the Southern and the Northern Sudan. Our chance of succeeding depends I think upon confining ourselves to the one aim of developing trade in the South, and between the North and the South.

b) In Education, I believe that while the South may hope to have a secondary school, it cannot hope to support post-secondary education, and I believe that Southerners should get this at the Gordon Memorial College — Arabic is not essential there, but should I think be taught to Southerners as a subject from intermediate school level upwards.

c) The distinctions in rates of pay and other conditions of government service, the artificial rules about employment of Southerners in the North, attempts at economic separation, and all similar distinctions are becoming more and more anomalous as the growing demand for Northerners to be employed in Southern Development Schemes, the rapidly growing communication and travel between North and South, and the very application of the policy of pushing forward in the South, break down the previous isolation of the Southern Provinces and strain these distinctions further.

6. The preceding paragraphs are an attempt to indicate briefly the reasons which have led me to think that an important decision on Southern policy must now be taken. The biennial report to His Britannic Majesty's Government is due early next year. Subject to your comments on this letter, I propose to advise His Excellency that in His Excellency's next report he asks His Britannic Majesty's Government to approve that two of the alternatives mentioned in paragraph 2 above be ruled out as practical politics at the present time. It may in the future be proved that it would be to the advantage of certain of the most southerly tribes, e.g. of Opari or Kajo Kaji, to join up with their relatives in Uganda. It may

be that the feeling which now exists among a few of the wisest Northern Sudanese, that they should not, when self-governing, be asked to shoulder the financial and communal burden which they believe the South will always prove to be, may become an important political policy among them. But we should now work on the assumption that the Sudan, as at present constituted, with possibly minor boundary adjustments, will remain one: and we should therefore restate our Southern policiy and do so publicly, as follows:

"The policy of the Sudan Government regarding the Southern Sudan is to act upon the facts that the peoples of the Southern Sudan are distinctively African and Negroid, but that geography and economics combine (so far as can be foreseen at the present time) to render them inextricably bound for future development to the middle-eastern and arabicized Northern Sudan: and therefore to ensure that they shall, by educational and economic development, be equipped to stand up for themselves in the future as socially and economically the equals of their partners of the Northern Sudan in the Sudan of the future."

7. Certain changes of detail, in each sphere of Government activity in the South, would I think have to follow the approval and publication of a policy so defined. You will wish to suggest briefly the major points.

8. Will you please consider this matter carefully, consult the senior members of your staffs upon it (particularly of course those who have experience of the South), and let me have your views as briefly as possible. Those of any individual member of your staff which you wish to forward separately with your comments will also be welcome.

The views of senior Sudanese in whose judgment and discretion you have confidence may also be asked for.

9. Finally I ask you to read again the late Sir Douglas Newbold's note to Council No. CS/SCR/I.C.14 of 3.4.44, reproduced as Appendix 'B'(1) to the despatch, and to bear in mind that urgency is the essence of the problem. We no longer have time to aim at the ideal: we must aim at doing what is the best for the Southern peoples in the present circumstances.

J. W. ROBERTSON,
Civil Secretary

Copies to: Governors: Blue Nile.
Darfur.
Kassala.
Khartoum. — 2 copies each.
Kordofan.
Northern.
Sudan Agent, Cairo (2)
Sudan Agent, London (2)

APPENDIX III
PROCEEDINGS OF THE JUBA CONFERENCE ON THE POLITICAL DEVELOPMENT OF THE SOUTHERN SUDAN, JUNE 1947

STRICTLY CONFIDENTIAL

The following were present:

J. W. Robertson, Esq., MBE, Civil Secretary, Chairman

F. D. Kingdon, Esq., Governor Upper Nile

B. V. Marwood, Esq., Governor Equatoria

G. H. Barter, Esq., Director of Establishment

M. F. A. Keen, Esq., Assistant Civil Secretary (Councils)

T. R. H. Owen, Esq., Deputy Governor Bahr al Ghazal

Mohd. Saleh Eff. Shingeiti

Ibrahim Eff. Badri

Kamyangi Ababa

Sgt. Major Philemon Majok

Clement Mboro

Hassan Fertak

James Tembura

Chief Cir Rehan

Chief Gir Kiro

Pastor Andrea Apaya

Chief Ukuma Bazia

Edward Adhok

Buth Diu

Chief Lolik Lado

Chief Lapponya

Father Guido Akou

Siricio Iro

Chief Tete

Chief Luoth Ajak

Hassan Eff. Ahmed Osman

Dr. Habib Abdulla

Sheikh Serur Mohd. Ramli

The meeting opened at 9.30 a.m. on Thursday, June 12th. The Chairman in his opening speech said:

Gentlemen,

I should first of all like to say how glad I am to see you all here today, and on behalf of those of us who are visitors I wish to thank the Governor, Mr. Marwood, and the other residents in Juba, who have welcomed us so hospitably and generously.

The origin of this meeting lies in the recent developments of administration and policy in the Northern Sudan. Last year, the Governor-General, Sir Hubert Huddleston, set up a Conference in the North to seek ways and means of associating the Sudanese more closely with the government of their country. As you know, there has been in the Northern Sudan for the last three years, an Advisory Council, and one of the recommendations made by the Conference is to develop the Advisory Council into a more authoritative and responsible body, with the power of making laws and to some extent, of controlling the work of the administration.

The Advisory Council has not had power to concern itself with the two Southern Provinces of Equatoria and the Upper Nile and there are therefore no Southern Sudanese on the Advisory Council. The report of the Conference however, which has just been published, recommends that the Southern Sudan should send representatives to the new Assembly which it is proposed should be set up, and in paragraphs 12 and 13 of this report you will find its recommendations and the reasons for them.

The reasons are important; the main consideration is that the Sudan, though a vast country in area, is small in wealth and population, and if the Sudan is ever really to become self-governing and self-dependent it must not be divided up into small weak units. Those who prepared the report believe that the sooner Southern and Northern Sudanese come together and work together, the sooner they will begin to coalesce and cooperate in the advancement of their country. This belief is sincerely and genuinely held by many Northern Sudanese, and they hope that by including Southern Sudanese in the future Assembly, the process of unification will be hastened. I am confident that their recommendations are based on the very highest motives, and think they do not seek opportunities of exploiting backward tribes in the South.

The Conference in Khartoum did not include Southern representatives, but I invited the Governors of Equatoria and the Upper Nile to attend in order that they should know what was being proposed, and should be able to inform the Conference of conditions and feelings in the South. This they did.

Now that the report of the Conference has been submitted to the Sudan Government and action on it is expected, I have summoned this meeting here of men both from the North and the South, in order to consider the unification of the two parts of the country. I should like to explain to you present Government policy in regard to the South.

The policy was defined in 1945 as follows:

It is only by economic and educational development that these peoples can be equipped to stand up for themselves in the future, whether their lot be eventually cast with the Northern Sudan or with East Africa, or partly with each.

Since 1945 there have been developments both economically and educationally in the South, and it has begun to be clear, I think, that the

Southern Sudan, by its history and by the accidents of geography, river transport and so on, must turn more to the North rather than to Uganda or the Congo, and I believe that our policy regarding these areas should be restated as follows:

The policy of the Sudan Government regarding the Southern Sudan is to act upon the facts that the peoples of Southern Sudan are distinctly African and negroid, but that geography and economics combine (so far as can be foreseen at the present time) to render them inextricably bound for future development to the Middle East and Arabs of the Northern Sudan and therefore to ensure that they shall by educational and economic developments be equipped to take their places in the future as socially and economically the equals of their partners of the Northern Sudan in the Sudan of the future.

If this to be the Government's policy regarding the Southern Sudan I should like the views of this meeting on one or two points of immediate importance.

You have all received copies of a Memorandum giving the terms of reference of this meeting and I think have already had opportunity to discuss them and form your opinion.

MEMORANDUM

The Sudan Administration Conference in paragraphs 12 and 13 of its report dealing with the future closer association of the Sudanese with the Central Government has made certain recommendations about the Southern Sudan.

In order to study the implications of these recommendations about which I shall have to advise His Excellency the Governor-General, I have decided to hold a meeting in the Southern Sudan at which I wish to discuss the proposals with Southern Sudanese and with officials, who have Southern experience, both British and Sudanese. I have therefore arranged for a meeting to be held at Juba on June 11th, 1947 at which I hope representatives from Equatoria and the Upper Nile Province will attend.

The terms of reference of the meeting will be:

1) to consider the recommendations of the Sudan Administration Conference about the Southern Sudan;

2) to discuss the advisability of the Southern Sudanese being represented in the proposed assembly and if it is decided to be advisable to decide how such representation can best be obtained in the present circumstances; and whether the representation proposed by the Sudan Administration Conference is suitable;

3) to discuss whether safeguards can be introduced into the forthcoming legislation setting up the new Assembly, to ensure that the Southern Sudan with its difference in race, tradition, language, customs and outlook is not hindered in its social and political advancement;

4) to discuss whether or not an Advisory Council for the Southern Sudan should be set up to deal with Southern affairs from which representatives might be appointed to sit on the assembly, as representatives of the Southern Sudan;

5) to consider the recommendations of the Sudan Administration Conference in paragraph 13 of their report which deals with matters

not strictly relevant to the political development of the Sudan, which the Conference recommended as essential if the unification of the Sudanese peoples is to be achieved.

Chief Ukuma Bazia then laid before the meeting a set of written answers to the points raised in the Civil Secretary's Memorandum [see Appendix III, pp. 189-205].

MINUTES OF THE PRELIMINARY MEETING OF THE MEMBERS REFERRING TO CIVIL SECRETARY'S MEMORANDUM

2) No, but to send people who will sit and merely study.

3) To leave the matter of race tradition; language customs and outlook die by itself, through education and civilization. More safeguards to be added.

4) We agree to set up our Advisory Council in the South but in link with the North. Before passing laws for the whole Sudan the Legislative Council in the North should consult the Advisory Council here until such time when the South will be capable to send representatives to voice for itself. Since we consented in para 2 we also welcome people from the North to attend our meetings and advise us. People to be sent should be of legal respect.

5) Permits to trade order 1928 to be cancelled on the following conditions:

  i) Only the people with good capitals should be admitted.
  ii) That these capitalists should build their shops in red bricks and corrugated iron sheets in places permitted by this council.
  iii) That Southern Sudanese should be encouraged to trade and the only way of doing this is by employing agents from the South.

5a) One educational policy to be adopted for North and South. The teaching of language should be in bush schools. English and Arabic in Elementary to Higher Schools.

5b) The improvement of communications between the two parts, encouragement of transfers, the unification of the system of establishment should be the same and should be started NOW.

Mohamed Saleh Eff. Shingeiti referring to answer No. 2 asked if the Southerners could explain why the South should be unable to send representatives to the Central Legislative Assembly just as the other outlying tribes and areas of the North, for instance the Bejio, the Kababish, etc. If Southerners were going to attend the Assembly why should they not take part in it, and speak for their own people? Since the more distant tribes of the Northern Sudan were to be represented in the proposed assembly why should not the South?

Kamyangi Ababa replied that Southerners were like recruits compared with old soldiers and the Southerners wanted more training before they could take part in an assembly with Northerners. The other tribes which the last speaker mentioned had already had some experience in the Advisory Council which Southerners had not had. They did not wish to close the door to Southern representation in the Legislative Assembly, but the time was not yet ripe.

The Chairman referred the meeting to the basic question as to whether they considered that the South was essentially to be one with the North.

James Tembura said that education had not advanced far enough in the South to allow for full representation.

Mohd. Saleh Eff. Shingeiti returned to the point that many of the Northern tribes were as backward as anyone in the South and had not previously had Councils of their own. We suggested that there should be Province Councils in each of the Southern Provinces which should send representatives.

Chief Ukuma Bazia asked why the South had not been included in the Advisory Council.

Mr. Kingdon said that Sir Douglas Newbold had answered that question at the time when the Advisory Council was first started. He said Southerners had not reached a standard of education which would enable them to represent their compatriots in such a Council.

Chief Ukuma Bazia asked if, when Sir Douglas Newbold gave this explanation, the Northern Sudanese were satisfied with it.

Mohd. Saleh Eff. Shingeiti replied emphatically that the Northern Sudanese were not satisfied.

Sgt. Major Philemon stated that the Southerners were like children in their relations with the grown-up Northerners and that, as children must drink milk before they eat kisra, so the Southerners must first study self-government before participating in governing.

Chief Cir Rehan said that the South was distinct from the North. If he went to the North, would the Northerners listen to his words as the pre-representative of the Southern peoples?

Mohd. Saleh Eff. Shingeiti said they would.

Chief Cir Rehan replied that the Southerners should go on learning under their British Administrators and in due course they would acquire understanding. He could not see that at the present time, Northerners could understand the needs of Southerners.

Mohd. Saleh Eff. Shingeiti said that he was understanding them now and that if they came to the North then the Northerners and the Southerners would have the opportunity of understanding each other even better.

Chief Cir Rehan was still dissatisfied and said that the Southerners must have training in Councils before they could represent their people.

Dr. Habib Abdulla remarked that in his opinion all the Southerners present were labouring under the misconception that all Northerners have great training and Southerners was much less than they thought, in fact it was negligible. The Southerners should not be afraid of being at disadvantages vis à vis the Northerners in matters of self government.

Sgt. Major Philemon admitted that that was in fact what he was afraid of, and could not see why the Northerners should not simply invite them North to enable them first of all to observe the procedure. He added that the Southerners could not ignore past history.

Hassan Fertak, replying to Judge Shingeiti, said that everything had to have a beginning. The North had had its Advisory Council for four years and was now ready for the next steps, a Legislative Assembly. They were like pupils who had been through class I and now were going into class II. The South had not yet been through class I, and it would be absurd to put them straight into class II.

Mohd. Saleh Eff. Shingeiti explained that members of the Advisory Council had not all been in the same stage, some were more advanced than others and the less advanced has learnt a lot from the more advanced.

Hassan Fertak pointed out that the less advanced had at any rate many contacts and much in common with the more advanced members.

Mohd. Saleh Eff. Shingeiti drew attention to the fact that the Conference in which they were engaged was very similar to a meeting of the Advisory Council, and if Southerners could speak for themselves in this Conference why should they not do so in a legislative Assembly?

Mr. Marwood stressed the difference between an Advisory Council and a Legislative Assembly which would have powers to make laws and would have some control over the administration. Judge Shingeiti had not yet given any convincing reason why the first step of an Advisory Council which had been found necessary in the North should not be equally necessary in the South.

Sheikh Serur Mohd. Ramli wished to return to the basic point of whether the Sudan was to be a single united nation. Before details of representation were discussed it was necessary to have that point settled.

Mr. Marwood nominated a speaker to reply but objection was taken to this by Mohd. Saleh Eff. Shingeiti who said that if anybody wanted to speak they should do so without prompting from the Governor.

The Chairman asked whether anybody present had any objections to the Unity of Sudan.

Mohd. Saleh Eff. Shingeiti complained that this was outside the meeting's terms of reference but the Civil Secretary refused to admit this. The Civil Secretary again addressed the meeting and said that if nobody spoke on this subject, then they would assume agreement on the principle of the Unity of the Sudan.

Chief Lapponya stated that the principle of unity could only be decided later when the Southerners were grown up, by which time they would be in a position to decide whether to join the North or go to the Belgian Congo or Uganda.

The Chairman explained that people could not get up and go where they like just like that.

Mr. Owen addressed the Northern Sudanese present and explained that they were still suffering from the sins of Zubeir Pasha and the slavers. "The sins of the Fathers shall be visited upon their children even unto the third and fourth generation". He said that the South had not forgotten the days of oppression even if the North had done so, and even today the Southerners would never willingly join the North until the latter should prove by their acts, not merely by their words, they they had undergone a change of heart.

Mohd. Saleh Eff. Shingeiti stressed that Northerners had no desire to dominate the South. They maintained that the country was one and the policy of this country was made in Khartoum, so the Northerners wanted the Southerners to join with them in the formation of policy for a whole country. Mr. Owen had referred to the slave trade . . . but he felt bound to point out that the British had in their time been the biggest slave traders in history. The West Indies were populated by Africans who had been enslaved in the past by the British but with the growth of public opinion the British had come to realize the evils of the slave trade. What had happened in England had now happened in the Northern Sudan where it was fully realized that slavery was barbaric and harmful. It has happened that, under this Government, slaves had been introduced into the Sudan from Abyssinia. He had himself been a Sub-Mamur in the White Nile at that time and had personally taken part in the freeing of these slaves. This trade had been discovered by the vigilance of Sudanese Officials. Northerners had no evil intentions towards the South. If they had they would not have been prepared to put up the money for the Zande Scheme.

Chief Lapponya said that when British and Northerners had first come to their country in 1914 the Northerners had despised and insulted Southerners. Southerners were also envious of the Northerners because they were paid at higher rates.

Chief Gir Kiro admitted that the Sudan was a single country but said that this was the first time they had ever taken part in a conference of this kind how could they be expected to send representatives to an assembly in Khartoum. The Northerners were their older brothers and were inviting them to swim across the river with the Northerners.

Chief Cir Rehan said that he and Chief Gir Kiro were answerable to their people and must speak for them. At the Gogrial and Tonj Councils their people had said they had no objection to live as brothers with the Northerners but they wanted first to wait and learn before joining them. That is what he and Chief Gir Kiro were saying now.

Mohd. Saleh Eff. Shingeiti said that the Southerners could best learn in the course of the work they would do in the Province and District Councils.

The Chairman summed up at this point and said that so far the discussion boiled down to two facts. Firstly, that most Southerners present (Shingeiti Eff. "All of them.") were agreed that the Sudan was one country. Secondly, that the Southerners were not yet advanced enough to take part in the legislative Assembly but would in their opinion be able to participate after a period of educational training in Southern Councils.

The meeting then adjourned for fifteen minutes.

The Chairman referred to note 2 of the Minutes of the Preliminary Meeting. If it was proposed to send people to the Legislative Assembly as learners, how many would they wish to send and how would they be chosen? The administration Conference had recommended that there should be fifteen representatives from the South.

Chief Ukuma Bazia said that this point had not been discussed as they did not know if the suggestion would be accepted. They would certainly wish to select them themselves rather than they should be appointed by Government.

Siricio Iro said that they would wish at first to send a large number, probably more than the number suggested.

Mr. Kingdon asked what language or languages would be used in the Legislative Assembly. If there were too many it would cause serious delay in the proceedings.

Mohd. Saleh Eff. Shingeiti said that the proceedings would be in English and Arabic, but there would be no difficulty in having them translated into the language of any member who did not understand either of these.

Mr. Kingdon pointed out that the absence of a large number of the leading personalities for prolonged periods would cause a serious delay in the advance of local Government.

Mohd. Saleh Eff. Singeiti said that the Government of the people must be representative and that the foundation of Representative Government lay in the Town, Rural District, and Province Councils. Thus he considered that in the South there should be town councils in places like Juba, and Wau, Rural Councils in the Districts, and a Province Council formed from the leaders of the Town and Rural Councils. This he considered could be achieved in one year in the South. Some three or four of the Southern representatives of the Legislative Assembly could be chosen from the Province Council. The Province Governor could nominate others, being guided only by the interests of the Province. In due course these nominated members to the Legislative Assembly would be replaced by Members selected or elected from the Province Council, which in the normal course of its deliberations would automatically effect the necessary training and education of its members. All this had already taken place in the North, and he saw no reason why the same should not happen in the South.

Clement Mboro asked what would happen if the Legislative Assembly were to meet before these Province Councils are set up.

The Chairman pointed out that it was hoped that the Legislative Assembly would be set up fairly soon, but there might be some delay.

Mohd. Saleh Eff. Shingeiti presumed that Governors would nominate representatives in that case, but emphasized that Southern representation was essential or the North would have everything its own way.

Clement Mboro thought that considerably more than thirteen should be sent from the South, even though they did not take part in the debates, in order to study the art of government.

Mohd. Saleh Eff. Shingeiti pointed out that the place to learn the art of government was in Local Government.

Clement Mboro pleaded for patience till the Southerners were sufficiently advanced to play their part in the Assembly.

Mohd. Saleh Eff. Shingeiti said that the North could not wait until the South caught up. If Southerners could take part in an Advisory Council they could take part in a Legislative Assembly.

Clement Mboro again stressed the essential difference between an Advisory Council and a Legislative Assembly. The number of representatives to be sent to the North should be more than thirteen. When asked by the Chairman to explain his reasons for this, he said it would form a wider field for selection when the time came to appoint the thirteen members to the Legislative Assembly proper.

Mr. Owen asked Clement Mboro if these Southerners would go to the North to study the Legislative Assembly only, or would they have to report back to a Southern Advisory Council.

Clement Mboro said they would have to report back to the Southern Advisory Council?

Mohd. Saleh Eff. Shingeiti protested that the Conference was useless as long as Southern Members present came with fixed ideas which they had conceived before the Conference began.

The Chairman replied that the Conference was quite open and that what was taking place now was an elucidation of the Southerners' reasons for the various decisions they had come to.

Mohd. Saleh Eff. Shingeiti repeated that the Southerners' ideas had already been fixed and that therefore the Conference was fruitless.

The Chairman summed up the previous discussion as follows: first, that the Southerners were agreed to send a number of representatives to the North in order to observe the process of Government, to broaden their minds, and to report back to the Southern Advisory Council. Secondly, that no fixed numbers had been agreed upon but that more than thirteen should go. He went on to ask how these representatives were to be selected.

Clement Mboro replied that the Government should begin now with Local Councils which in due course would be able to send representatives, but in the meantime the Government should nominate representatives.

Dr. Habib Abdulla deprecated the separatist tendency that would be fostered by any proposals to treat the Southern Sudan on a different footing from the North.

Father Guido Akou said that the North wanted immediate Southern representation in an Assembly which would legislate for the whole Sudan. Southerners were afraid of this because they felt that, through lack of understanding, their representatives might agree to laws which would prove harmful.

Edward Adhok considered that there was no-one from Upper Nile capable of representing his people in such an assembly. The Shilluk Council had not been a success so far owing to lack of experience of members. He himself did not feel qualified to represent his own people or take the responsibility of committing them to laws which, owing to a lack of understanding on his part, might not be for the benefit of his people.

Ibrahim Eff. Badri said that when a man thinks he is backward it is difficult to persuade him that he is not, and that the Northern Sudanese must appreciate this difficulty.

Chief Lolik Lado regretted that he was not ready for these discussions as he had not been able to consult his people before coming to Juba. He said however, that a girl who has been asked to marry a young man usually wants time to hear reports of that young man from other people before consenting; likewise before coming to any fixed decisions about their relations with the Northerners. The ancestors of the Northern Sudanese were not peace-loving and domesticated like cows. The younger generation claim that they mean no harm, but time would show what they would in fact do. He agreed to unification with the North but insisted on the Southerners' need for protection and for further time to consider the matter in conference with the elders of the people. An immediate decision could not be taken now.

Sheikh Serur Mohd. Ramli thought that Southerners need have no fear of laws which interfered with their customs for they could be administered with discretion. He quoted the law against pharaonic circumcision which had been passed by the Sudan Government at the request of the Advisory Council. This law was only enforced on the express direction of the Governor who took into account all the circumstances. Any laws passed by the Legislative Assembly which ran counter to Southern customs could doubtless make similar provision.

Chief Tete said that Northerners still despised and frequently insulted Southerners. A child must be brought up gradually and Southerners must learn to walk before they try to run.

The Chairman then referred to para 3 of the Memorandum and the minute of the preliminary meeting, and asked what safeguards the Southerners had in mind.

Chief Ukuma Bazia instanced the customs of his people to draw their teeth and feared that Northerners who think this a barbarous custom might try to stop it by law.

Dr. Habib Abdulla said that the best safeguard was that Southerners should be members of the Legislative Assembly.

Chief Buth Diu said that Northerners claim to have no desire to dominate the South, but this was not enough and there must be safeguards. There should be no settlement by Northerners on land in the South without permission. Secondly there must be no interference from the North in Local Government in the South. Thirdly there should be a law to prevent a Northerner calling a Southerner a slave.

Mohd. Saleh Eff. Shingeiti pointed out that such an insult was in fact punishable under the penal code.

James Tembura said, on the subject of safeguards, that they must ensure that Northerners who have children by Southern women must not desert them when they go back to the North.

Mohd. Saleh Eff. Shingeiti replied that this was the Government's fault since the Government bids these wives and children to go North.

James Tembura in reply to a question by the Chairman asserted that he was referring to cases where Northerners were properly married to Southern women both by local custom and by Muslim law.

Dr. Habib Abdulla thought that the reason for these cases of desertion were to be found in the variety of laws governing marriage in the Sudan, and that this could be rectified by future legislation.

The Chairman thought that further discussion on this point would not be profitable as it had little to do with the safeguards they were at present discussing.

o

Mr. Marwood said that one sort of safeguard he had in mind was that laws affecting local customs could only be enforced at the discretion of the Governor.

The Chairman then referred to the suggestion to set up an Advisory Council for the Southern Sudan and the Minute from the Preliminary Meeting on this point. In particular he asked what was meant by the expression "people of legal respect".

Clement Mboro said that they had intended by this phrase men who had experience of Local Government and of the working of Councils and people who know and sympathize with Southerners.

Mohd. Saleh Eff. Shingeiti asked how long such an Advisory Council would last.

Clement Mboro thought that it would be like the Advisory Council for the Northern Sudan and last a few years only, but that it might possibly be necessary to keep it in existence after Southern representatives had taken their place in the Legislative Assembly.

Hassan Eff. Ahmed Osman felt that this would mean separation of North and South.

The Chairman deplored the tendency to regard any suggestion that Southern problems should be treated in a different manner from those in the North as a conspiracy to divide North from the South.

Dr. Habib Abdulla thought that there would be some delay in setting up the Legislative Assembly and that if in the meanwhile real progress should be made with the advancement of Local Government and Local Councils, Southerners might feel that a suitable form of representation could be worked out by them in which they could have confidence.

Hassan Fertak thought that a Southern Advisory Council would have the merit of providing a reserve of potential representatives to the Legislative Assembly.

The Chairman pointed out in reply that this could equally well be done by Province Councils once they started.

Sheikh Serur Mohd. Ramli considered that the differences between North and South would no longer present any difficulty once Local Government developed in the South.

The meeting then adjourned until 9.30 a.m. on June 13th, 1947.

The Conference reopened at 9.30 a.m. on Friday, June 13th.

The Chairman explained that the nature of the conference was exploratory only and that no decisions were being taken. They were all there to learn each others' ideas. The decisions, if any, would be taken later by the Central Government. He deplored the mutual suspicion which seemed to exist between Northerners and Southerners. The Northerners on the one hand were suspecting the Southerners of wanting to separate from the North (and the Government of desiring this separation). The Southerners on the other hand were suspecting that the Northerners wished to dominate them.

It was essential to get away from these suspicions so that they would all talk together.

Summing up the discussion of the day before the Chairman said that the following conclusions had been arrived at:

Firstly, that the Southerners want a unified Sudan;

Secondly, that they want to participate in the proposed Legislative Assembly, but that

Thirdly, they were not sufficiently advanced to do so immediately.

Fourthly, it was important to hasten the establishment and the development of Local Government in the South.

Fifthly, that at first Southerners should attend the Legislative Assembly as observers. These should be more than the thirteen eventual members.

Questions were asked about safeguards but they had been misunderstood. Southern spokesmen had referred to these specific hurts they wished to be defended from rather than the general method to be adopted to protect them from these hurts.

The Chairman referred to para 4 the Southerners' answers to the Questions put in his Memorandum. Some reference had been made to it the day before but the discussion had not been complete. He personally thought that a Southern Advisory Council was unnecessary, and the Province Councils would be adequate. In Province Councils there would be great opportunity for more people to meet and discuss and thereby learn the art of Government. He also thought that this would be more agreeable to the people of the North. The Chairman invited comments on this subject.

Dr. Habib Abdulla referred to the differences of opinion and suspicions between the North and South which had been mentioned by the Chairman, and asked permission to go over the ground of yesterday's debate to bring out certain important points. There were certain essential things which must be agreed before other matters could be discussed. Firstly, the Sudan is one country because of geographical condition. Secondly, there was no reason why laws made for the Sudan as a whole should be harmful to one part of it. There were two kinds of laws, laws which protected person and property which were welcome to everybody, and laws relating to taxation, etc., which nobody liked. Reference had frequently been made to political backwardness of Southerners. This was purely a relative matter. There were some 200 tribes in the Sudan, each with its own customs and conditions. They were all of the same economic standard for they were all poor and in need of economic advance.

Religion might differ, but each had his own. There was no reason to say that any one section was more backward than another. It was true that some Southerners went naked, but some Northerners never wash. No one wished to upset the Government. The Government wished to teach the Sudanese to govern themselves and told them they could not learn to do so without taking responsibility. Finally he wished to know why the Southern members had asked for an Advisory Council for the South.

The Chairman pointed out this had been answered the previous day when the Southerners had said that the North had had practice in an Advisory Council for four years, that a baby had to drink milk before it could eat kisra. This appeared to be a full answer to the question. The point now before the meeting was whether there should not be Province Councils instead of a single Advisory Council.

Siricio Iro thought that Province Councils would be a good thing and that Southern Members to the Legislative Assembly could later be drawn from these councils. There was no wonder or mystery about these councils. It was a matter of common sense and the councils would be comparable to the present Chief's courts. The experience gained in these councils would assist the Southerners in their deliberation with the Northerners.

Kamyangi Ababa referred to the difference between Northern and Southern rates of pay for work which was, in effect, the same, and to the reasons given for this by his District Commissioner, that is to say, lack of education in the South, and lower rates of taxation in the South. He referred also to the higher standard of housing enjoyed by Northern officials, and concluded that although they were the sons of one father it seemed to him that father was treating his brother better than himself.

Clement Mboro stated that since the conference of the day before he had fundamentally changed his mind and now considered that the best way to which the Southerners could protect themselves would be to go to Khartoum now to Legislate together with the Northerners. Any Councils formed in the South would be defenceless before the Legislative Assembly. An Advisory Council was advisory only and its advice could easily be rejected by the Legislative Assembly or similar body. It was best for the Southerners to go and legislate now in spite of their backwardness; since the Southerners could speak for themselves in the present conference there was no reason why they could not speak for themselves in a Legislative Assembly. If any law was proposed which was not agreeable to the South they could stand up and object. The Southerners must defend themselves and speak and think for themselves.

Mr. Owen asked Clement Mboro what his safeguard would be if in spite of the Southern objections in the Legislative Assembly a law was passed which was against the interests of the Southerners.

Clement Mboro replied that the Government would protect them.

Mohd. Saleh Eff. Shingeiti protested against Mr. Owen's question. His protest was over-ruled.

Clement Mboro went on to say that if the Government could not protect them there must be rules and legislation in the Legislative Assembly which would do so. Meantime the Government must press on without delay with the estabishment of Province, District, and Town Councils in the South.

Chief Cir Rehan said that in their country they had originally been given courts, and when they had learnt to use them the Government had set up a Council of about forty men with three officials who were responsible for the work of the court, and for the chest. They had found this very different from the Court work and had it not been for the help of the D.C. they could not have made work at all. They had found this conference different again. When they discussed amongst themselves the first day they took five hours to reach their decisions. He was certain that Northerners would have completed the business in one hour (laughter).

What they had said yesterday was not their own opinion only but that of their people. They had agreed to join the North in a Government for the whole Sudan only if they were given time. Was he to go back and tell his people that the Northerners insisted on their coming in at once or not at all? He did not feel that it showed a brotherly feeling to try to force them.

James Tembura said that he agreed emphatically with what Clement Mboro had said with regard to immediate representation in the Legislative Assembly.

The Chairman asked him why he had changed his mind since the previous day.

James Tembura replied that Judge Shingeiti had said that if they did not do so they would have no say in the future Government of the Sudan, and he had thought this over very carefully the previous night after considering what had been said during the day.

Chief Tete said he wanted to study in the South until he was clever enough to go to the North. One could not begin to do work which one did not understand.

Sgt. Major Philemon Majok said that they were speaking on behalf of their people and that they, as spokesmen, could see more clearly than the people. He thought that if the Southerners adopted a "go slow" policy now they would never reach the required level. The Southerners could speak their mind in a Legislative Assembly just as a Chief could speak to Chief's Court or as a Major Court member could speak to D.C. presiding. In a Legislative Assembly there would be somebody to defend them and guide them. In spite of his statement the day before he now thought that there was no danger in sending Southerners to the North to join in the Legislative Assembly as soon as it was formed.

Chief Lolik Lado said that the day before they had spoken for their people and could not change their words today. The Southerners wanted to send representatives to the North but so far they had found nobody to send. The Government would later select the right people to go to speak on their behalf.

Chief Lapponya thought that if representatives were to be sent to a Legislative Assembly they should have had previous experience in councils of their own. It was impossible to send untrained recruits into battle. When the Governor thought they were sufficiently trained he would send them into the firing line.

Hassan Fertak said that they were all, or nearly all, agreed that the Sudan was one country and that was the most important decision that had to be made. They were also agreed that Province Councils should be formed. He wanted to know when the Legislative Assembly was likely to be set up.

The Chairman said they hoped it would be very soon but he could not say exactly when.

Hassan Fertak could see no reason why their representatives should not, for the time being, watch the proceedings in order to learn, without being full voting members.

The Chairman said that there seemed to have been a change of mind among some of the Southern members but that the discussion had been a useful one. He would now like to return to the question he asked at the beginning of the session. Did they wish to have one Advisory Council for the south or a Province Council for each Province. From what had been said, it appeared that they favoured Province Councils, and that these Councils should send representatives to the Legislative Assembly. There was some difference of opinion whether these representatives should be full voting members from the start, or whether they should at first watch the proceedings until they had some experience of procedure.

Chief Buth Diu thought the Southerners should send representatives to the North not only to study but to participate in legislation, finance, and administration. He referred to para 2 of the Civil Secretary's Memorandum, and thought that the best way of representing the South would be to send people who had been attached to outstations for three or four years, and also those who had served a long time with the Government. The Government could appoint the best representatives. Four representatives from Upper Nile Province were enough. Of the ten members to be nominated by the Governor General, two could be from Upper Nile Province. An Advisory Council for the South would be the first step towards separation. It was much better to have Province Councils. Laws made by the Legislative Assembly should not be enforced without the consent of the Governor or the Governor-General.

The Chairman explained that in any case according to the report of the administration Conference all laws made by the Legislative Assembly would be referred to the Governor-General for his comments.

Chief Luoth Ajak agreed with Buth Diu.

The meeting adjourned for fifteen minutes. When the conference reopened the Chairman referred the Members to para. 5 of his Memorandum, and said that some of the subject matter therein had already been discussed by the Southerners at their own meeting held prior to the opening of the present conference. With regard to Permits to Trade the Southerners had expressed their opinion in their para. 5 sub-para. 1, 2 & 3. The Council referred to in para. 5, sub-para. 2 was presumably a Local Council, District or Province.

Sheikh Serur Mohd. Ramli said that if the conditions stipulated by the Southerners were necessary it would be matter for the Local Council to decide.

The Chairman asked whether the condition laid down by the Southerners had reference to Northern traders only or to all non-Southern traders.

Chief Ukuma Bazia and others explained that they referred to all non-Southern traders.

Mohd. Saleh Eff. Shingeiti explained that the licensing authority would probably be the Local Council who would have power to attach what conditions they like to the licence. It was not necessary to define these conditions now. If the Local Councils were given adequate power the conditions attached to trader's licences could safely be left to them.

The Chairman asked Mohd. Saleh Eff. Shingeiti if he was speaking on behalf of the Legal Secretary or for himself only.

Mohd. Saleh Eff. Shingeiti said that he was speaking for himself only.

The Chairman explained that his reason for asking that question was that the Legal Secretary adhered firmly to the view that licences should be bought over the Merkaz counter and that there should be no restrictions.

Mr. Marwood pointed out that Local Government Authorities were not, in law, the issuing authority for traders' licences. If Judge Shingeiti's proposal to hand over this authority to Local Governments and to enable them to impose what conditions they liked were adopted, it would presumably apply in the North as well as in the South.

Mohd. Saleh Eff. Shingeiti said that in the North there were no restrictions (apart from certain temporary restrictions resulting from the war) attached to the issue of traders' licences. It was open to the conference however, to recommend that Local Authorities be empowered to make such restrictions.

The Chairman explained that in the South there were two licences which a non-Southern trader had to take out. One was the ordinary trader's licence without restrictions, and the other a special licence under the Permits to Trade Order. The reason for this was that in the past many Gellaba with little capital and a tendency to exploit the unsophisticated came to the South and the Permits to Trade Order was brought in to protect the tribesmen from this type of trader. If the Permits to Trade Order was cancelled, how was the South to be protected from a possible influx of such people?

Chief Buth Diu said that at the preliminary meeting they had decided to recommend that the Permits to Trade Order be cancelled under certain conditions. The reason for this was that the Sudan Administration Conference had felt strongly that the Permits to Trade Order was a hindrance to the unification of the Sudan. The majority at that meeting were against the cancellation of this Order, but the minority had persuaded the majority to agree, provided certain conditions were laid down.

Chief Luoth Ajak emphasized the fear of the Southerners that a crowd of hungry Gellaba would invade the South and swamp them and cheat the people.

James Tembura said that the feeling at the preliminary meeting was that rich traders from the North and elsewhere should be restricted to the big towns, leaving the bush shops for Southerners who wished to learn shop-keeping.

Mr. Owen asked James Tembura if he thought there were enough Southerners who wanted to open bush shops, as in his experience there were disappointingly few who wished to do so.

James Tembura replied that he thought that there were enough.

Chief Lolik Lado was sure that many Southerners wanted to open shops.

Chief Tete agreed and added that many ex-soldiers wanted to open shops with their gratuities.

The Chairman thought that what the Southerners wanted was a safe-guard that Northerners should not come and open shops in the villages but that village shops should be reserved for Southerners. He asked Mohd. Saleh Eff. Shingeiti if the Legal Secretary would agree to that. Mohd. Saleh Eff. Shingeiti thought that he would.

The Chairman thought there was little difference between this and the old Permits to Trade Order.

Hassan Eff. Ahmed Osman thought that the difference lay in this: that although Local Authorities should have power to refuse a licence disappointed applicants would still have the right of appeal against their decision.

Mr. Marwood thought that present legislation in the Sudan was deficient. A permit to trade was merely a piece of financial machinery, but there was no Ordinance governing the proper conduct of trade in the Sudan. Some legislation was necessary to ensure the proper conduct of trade, and this legislation should apply to the whole of the Sudan. The proposed Legislative Assembly might consider this in due course.

Clement Mboro explained that what the Southerners had intended was that adequate opportunity should be left to the Southerner to become a trader.

Mohd. Saleh Eff. Shingeiti explained Mr. Marwood's point that before conditions could be attached to the issue of a trader's licence a law must be enacted to that effect.

The Chairman said this seemed to imply a Permit to Trade Order for the whole Sudan in fact (laughter).

Chief Ukuma Bazia thought that 1928 Order should stand until they heard what the Legislative Assembly had to say about it.

Hassan Eff. Ahmed Osman thought that there was no basic difference of opinion between Northerners and Southerners with regard to the need for protecting villagers against adventurers of whatever nationality.

The Chairman considered that that was what the Permits to Trade Order was, in effect, doing at present. There was a good deal of muddled thinking about this Order in the North.

Mohd. Saleh Eff. Shingeiti agreed that this may be so, but explained that the Northerners considered that the Permit to Trade Order was being applied in such a way as to hinder economic development in the South. The best remedy lay in ensuring that disappointed applicants should have right of appeal to a Court of Justice.

Mr. Marwood thought there was a common misconception that his office was full of rejected applications to trade. Up till very recently he had received no application from people outside the province. In the past three or four months only one or two had come in. In one of these cases he had asked the trader where he wanted to trade, and what capital he had to build shops and buy lorries for transport etc. He awaited his reply. The Permits to Trade Order had been interpreted exactly as this meeting would have liked it to be interpreted. Small traders with a capital of only £10 or so were not wanted. Responsible traders with capital are wanted. The last thing he wanted to do was to hinder economic development.

The Chairman summed up and thought they were all agreed that it was necessary to improve trade and that merchants with capital were wanted to improve and develop the country, and that people should be protected against adventurers and exploiters. He thought that the Southerners wanted to stress that there should be enough places left in the villages to give Southerners the opportunity to set up as traders and in due course build up bigger businesses of their own. When they returned to Khartoum they would consider the recommendations of this meeting.

The next point for discussion was the question of unification of educational policy in the North and South, and the teaching of Arabic.

Mr. Owen asked for a clarification of the phrase "one educational policy".

Mr. Kingdon thought that the reply to this question by the preliminary meeting of the Southerners in their minute 5a was self-contradictory.

Hassan Eff. Ahmed Osman thought that this meant merely that the curricula in Northern and Southern schools should be the same. He did not find any contradiction in the recommendation that education in bush schools should be in vernacular and that English and Arabic should be taught in Elementary and Higher schools.

James Tembura said that the Southerners felt strongly that a boy should first learn to read and write in his own language and could later go on to other languages.

Mohd. Saleh Eff. Shingeiti felt that it should be left to the educationalist to say if a boy could learn two foreign languages in the elementary stage.

The Chairman pointed out that the essential difference in practice between North and South was that in the North a boy learnt in Arabic to the end of the elementary stage and did not start to learn a foreign language before then. The meeting felt that Arabic should be taught as soon as the boy was able to learn it, but that it should be left to the educationalist to say when this stage was reached.

Pastor Adrea Apaya asked if the introduction of Arabic would apply to Mission Schools.

The Chairman thought that this was the general opinion of the meeting.

Dr. Habib Adballa thought that Southerners were still thinking of education in terms of preparation for government service, an idea still held by many Northerners, and he thought that the reasons Southerners were so anxious for the same education as the Northerners was to strengthen their claim to receive the same rates of pay as the Northerners.

The Chairman referred to the great shortage of teachers in the North and doubted if Northerners would be prepared to restrict their educational expansion to send Arabic teachers to the South.

Mohd. Saleh Eff. Shingeiti felt that the available teachers should be equally distributed between North and South, and even more generously to the South to help them catch up. If the Northerners were not willing to do this they should not claim that the Sudan was a single country.

Buth Diu thought that there must be no delay in the introduction of Arabic to Schools to enable them to catch up with the North.

Chief Lolik Lado thought that there might be some difficulties caused by introduction of Arabic. He had found that Catholics and Protestants did not readily cooperate, and he feared that this would be a new complication.

Pastor Andrea Apaya said that both English and Arabic were difficult languages and doubted if boys at the elementary stage could assimilate both. He was not against the introduction of Arabic, and in fact welcomed it, but doubted if it was feasible at that stage.

The Chairman felt that it must be left to the Director of Education to say at what stage a pupil could start learning a second language.

Father Guido Akou asked for an explanation of the phrase "single educational policy".

Mohd. Saleh Eff. Shingeiti thought that it meant firstly that the standards of equivalent schools should be roughly equal, and secondly that a boy leaving a Southern Intermediate School should be able to go straight to a Northern Secondary School. In addition pupils of both parts of the country should have a similarity of outlook.

Father Guido Akou asked if this unification of policy was to be implemented at once.

The Chairman thought that there was a misunderstanding in the use of this phrase, in that the bush schools corresponded to Sub-Grade Schools in the North, elementary schools in both areas were on the same footing, and so were Intermediate schools and from this point of view educational policy was in fact the same in North and South.

Mr. Marwood said that for the last ten years the Education Department had been exercising more and more supervision in Mission Schools and the Inspector had devoted much time and energy to working with the Mission School authorities to ensure that curricula and standards should approach those of the North as closely and quickly as possible.

Hassan Eff. Ahmed Osman was grateful to Mr. Marwood for dispelling much of the misunderstanding which existed on the question of unified education. He thought it not irrelevant to request that the sending of Southern boys to Uganda should be discontinued. The medium of instruction in the North is English in Higher and Secondary education, and Arabic was studied only as a subject. Southern boys should therefore go North for Higher and Secondary education.

The Chairman said that the sending of boys to Uganda had been a temporary expedient since the schools in the North were too full to take them. In due course there would be a Secondary School for the South and Southerners would go to Gordon College for higher education.

The Chairman then raised the question of improvement of communications. The meeting was generally in favour of an improvement of communications between North and South.

The Chairman went on to consider the question of transfer of officials, and thought that this could be best discussed in a small committee with the Director of Establishment as it did not concern all the Members present.

Mr. Marwood thought that the Chiefs were concerned in so far as the proposed Local Council would require educated staff and must find money to pay this staff. In the North he believed that at present most local Councils employed seconded government officials on government rates of pay, but that the time will come when the Council would employ staff independently of the government. In the south the local Councils would have to decide how much they could afford to pay for their staff, and choose between a highly paid government official and a local boy requiring lesser remuneration.

The Chairman wanted to know what the Southerners meant by the term "encouragement of transfers". A transfer was a transfer and brooked no discussion. He referred to instances where some Northerners had attempted to evade service in the South on medical grounds.

Mohd. Saleh Eff. Shingeiti admitted that such instances had occurred. but said that most Northerners who came South wanted to stay on there.

Buth Diu thought that Northerners were unwilling to come South not only because they were afraid of losing their children through malaria, but also because they were afraid of lions. He suggested that better housing would remove this unwillingness. The Southerners on the other hand were unwilling to go North because of the extensive use of Arabic in offices.

Clement Mboro referred to para. 5b of the minute of the Southerners' preliminary meeting, and he said he wished to stress how strongly they adhered to the unification of the system of establishment. This must be decided in this conference. And not in separate committee. Refusal to unify establishments was in his opinion the greatest obstacle in the way of a unified Sudan.

The Chairman considered that it was not easy to discuss such an intricate matter at this conference. He noted the Southerners' view. But thought a small committee was best fitted to consider the matter in detail. Mohd. Saleh Eff. Shingeiti asked if they could not agree on the broad lines.

The Chairman replied that the Southern members present were already agreed on the broad lines.

The Chairman in closing the conference thanked the members for coming and felt that the deliberations has been of considerable value to Southerners, to Northerners, and to the Government. He could not promise that every suggestion would be carried out, nor when it would be carried out, but he thanked them for their advice and recommendations which were of definite value.

Mr. Marwood said that this was the first opportunity that Southerners had had to come together from all over the Southern Provinces to discuss these things. He himself had felt, after the report of the Sudan Administration Conference, that it was essential that Northern Sudanese and members of the Central Government should hear from their own lips what Southerners felt about these proposals. He was very grateful to the Civil Secretary and the other members who had come from the North for affording them this opportunity.

Mohd. Saleh Eff. Shingeiti on behalf of the Northern Sudanese Members thanked the Civil Secretary and the two Governors. The Civil Secretary as Chairman had given everyone complete freedom to speak his mind. This was an essential feature of such a conference. He thanked Mr. Marwood for giving them this opportunity to meet the Southerners and hear their point of view. He had been much impressed with what the Southerners had said and the way they had said it, and wished them then every success in the Local Councils so that they would be able to send representatives to take a full part in the Government of Sudan.

APPENDIX IV
RESOLUTIONS OF THE ROUND TABLE CONFERENCE ON THE SOUTH, KHARTOUM, MARCH 16-25, 1965

We the Delegates of the following Political Parties and Organizations:
1 Islamic Charter Front
2 National Unionist Party
3 People's Democratic Party
4 Professional Front
5 Sudanese Africans National Union (SANU)
6 Sudan Communist Party
7 Southern Front
8 Umma Party

attending the Round Table Conference on the South meeting in Khartoum at the House of Parliament from March 16th-25th, 1965, having considered all aspects of the Southern Question, are convinced:

1 that national conciliation is imperative, and
2 that the differences in views are not beyond solution, and
3 that only through peaceful means can these differences be settled;

and do hereby resolve:

1 That the following steps be taken by the Government in order to normalize the situation in the South:

i) The implementation of the agreement between the Governments of Uganda and the Sudan concerning refugees and thereby re-settling them.

ii) Approaching the Governments of other neighbouring countries with a view to reaching similar agreements over refugees.

iii) Resettlement of those inside the country whose homes and property have been destroyed.

iv) To request the Government
  a) to alleviate famine in those parts of the South affected thereby;
  b) to investigate the inherent causes of famine and floods in the South and take the necessary steps.

v) Retransfer of all Southern Schools from the North to the South.

2 that the following lines of policy be adopted:
  i) Selection of more Southerners for training as:
    a) Police and Prison Officers;
    b) Administrators;
    c) Military Officers;
    d) Public Health Officers and Medical Assistants;
    e) Forest Officers;
    f) Game and Fisheries Officers.
  ii) The Southernization of Administration, Police, Prisons and Information Service whenever qualified Southerners are available. Where they are not available steps should be taken to accelerate their training and promotion.
  iii) Equality of opportunities for employment and equality of wages. There will be no discrimination by reason only of religious beliefs or language or race.
  iv) Freedom of Religion and freedom of Missionary activity within the laws of the land.
  v) Allowing of private persons or bodies to open schools as long as these persons and bodies conform to the laws of the land.
  vi) Freedom of movement.
  vii) Establishment of a University in the South
  viii) Opening Girls' Secondary Schools and an Agricultural School in Malakal.
  ix) Re-establishment of Yambio Agricultural School, Juba Training Centre and Malakal Veterinary Centre.
  x) All Southern Schools to be headed by qualified Southerners. Ignorance of Arabic language shall not bar promotion to the post of Head Master.
  xi) Finding jobs for the unemployed.
  xii) The establishment of a national economic council for economic development with a subsidiary agency for economic development in the South. This will consider the detailed schemes presented by the team of investigation of 1954 and any other schemes in all aspects of development and plan their implementation. The Government should also consider the revival of the Azande Scheme.
  xiii) Giving priority and facilities to the local population in the exploitation of land.
3 That the delegates who participated in the Conference are determined on the rectification of these grievances and the execution of these policies and that they are prepared to go into a peace campaign to tour the South, to pacify and normalize and see to it that they will employ all their resource to end all hostilities in two months' time.
4 i) That the Conference considered some patterns of Government for the Sudan and could not reach a unanimous resolution as required by the rules of the Conference.
  ii) We have, therefore, appointed a twelve-man committee to dwell on the issue of the issue of the constitutional and administrative set-up which will protect the special interest of the South as well

as the general interest of the Sudan. The committee shall in addition have the following terms of reference.

    a) To act as a watch committee on the implementation of the steps and policies agreed upon.

    b) To plan the normalization of conditions in the South, and consider steps for the lifting of the state of emergency and the establishment of law and order.

  iii) The findings of the committee shall be presented to the Conference which shall be called by the Government within three months.

5 We consider that in addition to these achievements the Conference was successful in:

    i) Affording an opportunity to political leaders from the North and South, for the first time in six years, to meet in an amicable atmosphere and exchange views on the Southern problem.

    ii) Affording an opportunity to the sister African countries invited to the Conference to acquaint themselves with the problem and enlisting their sympathy and support for its solution.

    iii) Allaying doubts and suspicions between political leaders of North and South and establishing a firm basis for understanding and cooperation.

    iv) Providing an opportunity for our people in the South and the North and South to know the facts and thus appreciate the problem and see it in its true perspective.

We believe that only through such an appreciation can our people forge ahead and utilize their energies and resources in building the future; only through this can our great ideals of peace, love, and confidence be a reality.

6 We express deep gratitude:

    i) To the Chairman of the Conference for the skill and impartiality with which he conducted the meetings of the Conference, thus contributing to its success.

    ii) To the Observers, their Governments and peoples for taking great interests in the affairs of the Sudan and for their ceaseless efforts to see that National conciliation be realized; and for their invaluable contribution to the ultimate success of the Conference.

    iii) To the Secretary General and Secretariat for the devoted and tireless efforts exerted by them before and during the Conference and thus making it a success.

    iv) To the Sudan Government for taking the initiative and adopting a forward policy that resulted in the holding of the Conference and for the support, moral and material, which it generously extended.

APPENDIX V
REPORT OF THE TWELVE-MAN COMMITTEE

Introduction:

1. The Southern Problem has been living with us ever since we stood on the threshold of our independence more than ten years ago. It has challenged the efforts of successive governments until it reached the extent of being the primary and direct factor leading to the victorious popular uprising of October which called for a peaceful solution to the Problem.

2. And to implement this enlightened popular will the October Transitional Government made commendable efforts the result of which was the Round Table Conference in March, 1965 which was attended by observers from sister African countries.

That Conference after considering all aspects of the Southern Question declared:

    i) that national conciliation is imperative, and

    ii) that the differences in views are not beyond solution, and

    iii) that only through peaceful means can these differences be settled.

3. Acting on these principles the Conference after considering some patterns of government for the Sudan and having failed to come to a unanimous resolution upon the matter appointed a Twelve-Man Committee to carry out the following functions:

    i) to dwell on the issue of the constitutional and administrative set-up which will protect the special interest of the South as well as the general interest of the Sudan.

    ii) to act as a watch committee on the implementation of the steps and policies agreed upon.

    iii) to plan the normalization of conditions in the South, and consider steps for the lifting of the state of emergency and the establishment of law and order.

4. The Conference agreed to reconvene the Conference after the Twelve-Man Committee has finished its work and submitted its report.

5. The Committee began its life with faltering steps.

It was not constituted until nearly two months after the Conference due to the engagement of the Government and Parties in the General Elections;

and the controversies about the representation of some Southern Parties in the Committee occupied several meetings.

Differences over condemnation of acts of violence as to who is responsible for them also occupied more meetings.

There upon the People's Democratic Party and the Communist Party decided to withdraw from the Committee.

And here the Committee faced the most critical period in its life but in the end it decided to concentrate on its primary term of reference: the constitutional and administrative set-up.

The Proposed Constitutional and Administrative Set-Up

6.   Although the Round Table Conference could not reach a unanimous resolution on the pattern of government which should be adopted it did resolve that two forms of solution — separation and the present status quo (Centralized Unitary Government) — should not be considered by the Committee.

The Committee, therefore, after receiving the schemes submitted by the members set aside those schemes which were outside its terms of reference.

Then it found that the Constitutional and Administrative formula which it was trying to work out was of two main parts: the distribution of powers between the Centre and the Region and the relationship between the two and further that its objective would be facilitated if the distribution of powers was considered first.

Therefore, lists containing the powers proposed to remain in the Centre and those proposed to be transferred to the Region were worked out from the schemes accepted by the Committee, and the study began.

7.   The result was that the Committee were agreed that the following powers shall be exercised by the Central Government:

(1)	National Defence	(5)	Foreign Trade
(2)	External Affairs	(6)	Nationality
(3)	Currency	(7)	Customs
(4)	Communications and Telecommunications	(8)	Inter-Regional Trade

8.   The following powers were to be concurrent between the Centre and the Region in the following manner:

   i) *Security Forces:*

   1) The National Legislature shall by enactment, organize the security forces. This will include:

   a) Recruitment and use of the national police force which carries out the functions assigned to such forces,

   b) The recruitment and use of the local police forces.

   2) The Head National Executive shall be the ultimate authority as regards the security forces and can in certain circumstances place any of these forces under his direct command.

   Subject to 1) and 2) above the Region shall recruit and use the local police force.

   ii) *Education:*

   1) The policy of education shall be national and in the hands of the Centre. Policy has been defined to include at least the following:

   Syllabuses, National Planning of Education, Definition of Standard and Qualifications.

But as there are some regional peculiarities that reflect on education this fact must be given its due consideration in formulating the policy.

2) That the administration of education up to the intermediate level should be the responsibility of the Region.

3) And that it should be concurrent in the secondary stage so that the Centre and the Region may each establish such schools and administer them.

4) That higher education (post-secondary) should be in the hands of the Centre.

iii) *Public Health:*

The Centre should retain:

1) The general policy and planning.

2) Education and training of doctors, the registration of doctors and all the other professions attached to the medical profession.

3) Control and supervision of assisted projects.

4) National policy for nutrition.

5) Control over drugs and poisons.

6) Medical research and control of epidemics.

7) Registration of births and deaths.

8) Hospitals: The licensing and supervision for maintenance of the standards is the province of the Centre — but the administration is concurrent, so that the Centre and the Region may each administer the hospitals established by it.

And the following to be transferred to the Region:

1) Control of endemic diseases.

2) Environmental health services.

3) School health services.

4) Health education.

5) Maternity and child-welfare services.

6) Control of markets.

7) Training of village Midwives.

8) Training of medical assistants and opening of dispensaries.

iv) *Antiquities:*

Both the Centre and the Region may carry out its excavations.

v) *Labour:*

1) The Centre shall lay down the policy.

2) The execution of the policy as laid down in the legislations should be by the Region.

9. The Committee agreed to transfer the following powers to the Region:

1) Regional and local government administration.

2) Regional public information.

3) Promotion of tourism.

4) Museums and zoos.

5) Exhibitions.

6) Projects: Establishment of local roads, maintenance of main roads — Town and village planning.

7) Protection of forests, crops and pastures — according to national legislations.

8) Protection and development of animal resources — according to national legislations.
9) Land utilization and agricultural development in accordance with the national plan for development.
10) The study and development of the languages and the local culture.
11) Commerce and industry and local industries — organization of markets — trade licences, formation of co-operative societies.

THE GOVERNMENT OF THE REGION:

A Legislative Assembly and an Executive Machinery:

a) *The Legislative Machinery:*

Each Region shall have its legislative body in form of an assembly elected directly on the same conditions as to qualification as that applied to the Central Parliament. This assembly exercises its right of enacting Regional law and supervising the local executive machinery as well as setting down the policy for it.

The constitution defines the powers granted to the Regional Legislative Council as agreed on.

b) *The Executive Machinery:*

1. The Legislative Council elects the members of the Executive Council for the Region.

These are responsible to the Legislative Council which can dismiss them.

2. It was agreed that the Head Executive should be from amongst the inhabitants of the Region and that he should be responsible for the Central Agencies and units in the Region by delegation from the Centre as well as for the Regional Executive Machinery. This is to guarantee co-ordination and unity of leadership.

It was also agreed that this necessitates that he should be appointed through a joint process. But there was difference over the exact procedure to be followed.

There is a view that the Regional Assembly should offer two candidates and the Central Government should choose from between them.

And another view that the Central Government appoint him after consultation with the Region.

THE RELATIONSHIP BETWEEN THE CENTRAL AND REGIONAL AUTHORITIES:

We had to consider here how to strike a balance between preserving the sovereignty of the National Parliament to protect the vital interest of the Nation and at the same time securing the autonomy of the Regions and protecting them against any persistent and unwarranted interference by the Centre in their sphere of powers.

We would like to clarify that when our agreed system of Government is adopted as part of the Constitution, there can be no withdrawal of the Regional powers except by a constitutional amendment with a two thirds majority. Further it is conceded that the Central Parliament being sovereign — subject to the Constitution — may overrule any Regional legislation or take the initiative in legislating within the sphere of the Regional powers. But in order to protect the Regions against any unwarranted encroachments by the Centre we recommend that:

a) A declaration be written into the constitution to the effect that this sovereignty is granted to Parliament:

1) to protect the vital interests of the country; and
2) to guarantee the co-ordination of Regional legislations and to provide leadership and initiative.

b) Before any such legislation is passed by Parliament there must be full consultations with the Regions concerned.

Emergency:

1) We were agreed that in the case of a public security emergency occasioned by an external or internal threat the Centre may either suspend any of the Regional powers or dissolve the Regional Assembly provided that in the latter case elections must take place within one month after the Emergency.

and 2) a declaration of emergency has to be approved by a resolution of Parliament within two weeks of its announcement.

The Regional Geography:

After it has finished with the distribution of powers and the relationship between the Centre and the Region the Committee went on to consider the geographical location of the Regions.

1. The Southern Members suggested dividing the country into 4 Regions:
   a) South (Constituting the present Southern Provinces);
   b) East (Constituting Blue Nile and Kassala);
   c) West (Constituting Kordofan and Darfur);
   d) North (Constituting Khartoum and Northern Province)

or to adopt the present division in the Northern Provinces making six Regions out of them and making the three Southern Provinces into one Region.

2. The Northern members suggested adopting the present administrative boundaries for the Provinces creating nine Regions out of them.

3. The Southern members gave the following reasons:

a) Any division must start by the North and the South as two units because of the differences between them in culture, religion, language and race.

b) The South considers itself as a unit and the Southern citizens have expressed their wish to remain as a unit and there is nothing in this demand that is detrimental to the public interest. Also our basic duty is to solve the Southern Problem and this necessitates giving this fact due consideration and not treating the South as the other parts of the country where no such problem has arisen or not to the extent of the Southern Problem.

c) The guarantees agreed upon for the protection of the autonomy of the Regions will not be sufficient unless we enlarge the Regions geographically so that the public opinion in them will carry such a political weight that the centre shall have to pay that fact due consideration.

In fact this was put as a condition by the representative of the Southern Front for his agreement to the relationship between the Centre and the Region agreed to above.

    d) The present administrative divisions are inherited from the Colonial Administration and are based on the tribal system and our duty is to adopt a system that weakens tribalism and so help Sudanese nation building.

4. The Northern members based their view on the following reasons:

    a) It is preferable to begin by the present administrative divisions. This facilitates administrative activities as the main advantage of Regional Government is that it limits administrative units to smaller areas thus avoiding administering large units from a far Centre. The South from an administrative aspect is too large to be administered from one Regional Capital.

    b) It is true that we are primarily interested in the solution of the Southern Problem but we must take note of the repercussions of any solution that we propose. In view of existing claims for regional autonomy any scheme that we develop is bound to solve (serve?) as an example.

    c) In substance the demand of the Southern Parties has been for a constitutional set-up that would enable local initiative for the advancement of their region. This submission should be satisfied whether the three Southern Provinces are united or separate.

    d) If the South is made into one Region this will perpetuate the sense of confrontation between North and South which we are trying to end through these efforts. As there may be some sentimental feeling that urges this demand, and as sentimental feeling can be legitimate and beneficial it may be met in this case by allowing any number of Regions to pool any of their services.

    e) There is no objection to any adjustment of regional boundaries later on if experience indicates such a change.

Both sides maintain their stands on this point.

CONCLUSION

These are the broad lines of the proposed system of government. The public opinion — which has been patient and understanding on our difficult task through a whole year during which we tried silently and persistently to find points of agreement, and during which we fluctuated between feelings of hope and despair — is entitled to know that a breakthrough has been made and to be assured that the remaining differences of opinion are not fundamental and can be solved.

When we have finished preparing our report within the next two weeks and submitted it to the Government so that it calls the Round Table Conference in accordance with the Resolutions of that Conference we will devote ourselves to our other terms of reference relating to the normalization of the situation in the South. We hope that we will find the sufficient understanding and cooperation from the Government that will enable us to carry out this duty and that the public opinion will give us its support and encouragement.

Citizens in the North and the South:

The problem which we are trying to solve is a complex human problem and we have tried to the best of our human capacity to reconcile the different views and to put into consideration laying down the foundations of Sudanese Nation building, taking the lesson from the experiences of the developing nations. We tried to be human without being sentimental.

We hope that our proposals will be a rational basis for reaching the peaceful solution which we seek.

FORMATION OF THE TWELVE-MAN COMMITTEE

Umma Party	Mohd. Dawood El Khalifa
National Unionist Party	Abdel Latif El Khalifa
Islamic Charter Front	Doctor Hassan El Turabi
S. A. N. U.	William Deng — Andrew Wieu
	Nikanora Agweir
	"Alternate Members"
	Joshwa Malwal — Ambrose Wol
Southern Front	Hillary Logali — Lubari Ramba
	Abel Alier
Professional Front	Sayed Abdalla El Sayed

APPENDIX VI
PRESIDENT GENERAL NIMEIRY'S POLICY STATEMENT ON THE SOUTHERN QUESTION, 9th JULY, 1969

Dear Countrymen,

Warm congratulations and greetings to you on this historic occasion of your revolution.

No doubt you have heard of the broad aims of the revolution outlined in my speech and in that of the Prime Minister which was broadcast on the 25th of May. Our revolution is the continuation of the October 21st, popular revolution. It works for the regeneration of life in our country, for social progress and the raising of the standard of living of the masses of our people throughout the country. It stands against imperialism, colonialism and whole-heartedly supports the liberation movements of the African and Arab peoples as well as other peoples throughout the world.

A HISTORICAL BACKGROUND

Dear Countrymen,

The revolutionary Government is fully aware of the magnitude of the Southern problem and is determined to arrive at a lasting solution.

This problem has deep-going historical roots dating back to the last century. It is the result of the policies of British Colonialism which left the legacy of uneven development between the Northern and Southern parts of the country, with the result that on the advent of independence Southerners found themselves in an unequal position with their Northern brethren in every field.

The traditional circles and parties that held the reigns of power in our country since independence have utterly failed to solve the Southern Question. They have exploited state power for self-enrichment and for serving narrow partisan interests without caring about the interests of the masses of our people whether in the North or in the South.

It is important to realize also that most of the Southern leaders contributed a great deal to the present deterioration of the state of affairs in that part of our beloved country. Over the years, since 1950 to the present day they have sought alliances with the Northern reactionary circles and with imperialism whether from inside or outside the borders. Personal gain was the mainspring of their actions.

Dear Countrymen,

The enemies of the North are also the enemies of the South. The common enemy is imperialism and neo-colonialism, which is oppressing and exploiting the African and Arab peoples, and standing in the way of their advance. Internally, our common enemies are the reactionary forces of counter-revolution. The 25th May Revolution is not the same as the Coup d'état of November, 1958. That was a reactionary move staged by the imperialists in alliance with local reaction in and outside the army. It was made to silence the demands of the masses of our people in both the North and the South for social change and genuine democracy.

The Revolution of May 25th, is the very opposite of the Coup d'état of 1958. Our revolution is, we repeat, directed against imperialism, the reactionary circles and corrupt parties that destroyed the October Revolution and were aiming at finally liquidating any progressive movement and installing a reactionary dictatorship.

Dear Countrymen,

The revolutionary Government is confident and competent enough to face existing realities. It recognizes the historical and cultural differences between the North and South and firmly believes that the unity of our country must be built upon these objective realities. The Southern people have the right to develop their respective cultures and traditions within a united Socialist Sudan.

In furtherance of these objectives the Revolutionary Council and the Council of Ministers held joint meetings and after a full discussion of the matter resolved to recognize the right of the Southern people to Regional Autonomy within a united Sudan.

REGIONAL AUTONOMY PROGRAMME

Dear Countrymen,

You realize that the building of a broad socialist oriented democratic movement in the South, forming part of the revolutionary structure in the North and capable of assuming the reigns of power in that region and rebuffing imperialist penetration and infiltration from the rear is an essential pre-requisite for the practical and healthy application of Regional Autonomy.

Within this framework and in order to prepare for that day when this right can be exercised the revolutionary Government is drawing up the following programme:—

1) The continuation and further extension of the Amnesty Law.
2) Economic, social and cultural development of the South.
3) The appointment of a Minister for Southern Affairs and
4) The training of personnel.

The Government will create a special economic planning board for the South and will prepare a special budget for the South, which aims at the development of the southern provinces at the shortest possible time.

Dear Southern Countrymen,

In order that we may be able to carry out this programme it is of the utmost importance that peace and security should prevail in the South and that life return to normal. It is primarily the responsibility of you all whether you be in the bush or at home to maintain peace and stability. The way is open for those abroad to return home and cooperate with us in building a prosperous Sudan, united and democratic.

APPENDIX VII

THE ADDIS ABABA AGREEMENT
ON
THE PROBLEM OF SOUTH SUDAN

CONTENTS

DRAFT ORGANIC LAW TO ORGANIZE REGIONAL SELF GOVERNMENT IN THE SOUTHERN PROVINCES OF THE DEMOCRATIC REPUBLIC OF THE SUDAN

In accordance with the provisions of the Constitution of the Democratic Republic of the Sudan and in realization of the memorable May Revolution Declaration of June 9th, 1969, granting the Southern Provinces of the Sudan Regional Self-Government within a united socialist Sudan, and in accordance with the principle of the May Revolution that the Sudanese people participate actively in and supervise the decentralized system of the government of their country.

It is hereunder enacted:

Article 1:

This law shall be called the law for Regional Self Government in the Southern Provinces. It shall come into force on a date within a period not exceeding *thirty days* from the date of Addis Ababa Agreement.

Article 2:

This law shall be issued as an organic law which cannot be amended except by a three-quarters majority of the People's National Assembly and confirmed by two-thirds majority in a referendum held in the three Southern Provinces of the Sudan.

CHAPTER II
DEFINITIONS

Article 3:

i) Constitution refers to the Republican Order No. 5 or any basic law replacing or amending it.

ii) "President" means the President of the Democratic Republic of the Sudan.

iii) "Southern Provinces of the Sudan" means the Provinces of Bahr El Ghazal, Equatoria and Upper Nile in accordance with their boundaries as they stood on January 1st, 1956, and any other areas that were culturally and geographically a part of the Southern complex as may be decided by a referendum.

iv) "Peoples Regional Assembly" refers to the legislative body for the Southern Region of the Sudan.

v) "High Executive Council" refers to the Executive Council appointed by the President on the recommendation of the President of the High Executive Council and such body shall supervise the administration and direct public affairs in the Southern Region of the Sudan.

vi) "President of the High Executive Council" refers to the person appointed by the President on the recommendation of the Peoples Regional Assembly to lead and supervise the executive organs responsible for the administration of the Southern Provinces.

vii) "Peoples National Assembly" refers to the National Legislative Assembly representing the people of the Sudan in accordance with the constitution.

viii) "Sudanese" refers to any Sudanese citizens as defined by the Sudanese Nationality Act, 1957, and any amendments thereof.

CHAPTER III

Article 4:

The Provinces of Bahr El Ghazal, Equatoria and Upper Nile as defined in Article 3 (iii) shall constitute a self-governing Region with the Democratic Republic of the Sudan and shall be known as the Southern Region.

Article 5:

The Southern Region shall have legislative and executive organs, the functions and powers of which are defined by this law.

Article 6:

Arabic shall be the official language for the Sudan, and English the principal language for the Southern Region without prejudice to the use of any other language or languages which may serve a practical necessity or the efficient and expeditious discharge of executive and administrative functions of the Region.

CHAPTER IV

Article 7:

Neither the Peoples Regional Assembly nor the High Executive Council shall legislate or exercise any powers on matters of national nature which are:

  i) National Defence
  ii) External Affairs.
  iii) Currency and Coinage.
  iv) Air and Inter Regional River Transport.
  v) Communications and Telecommunications.
  vi) Customs and Foreign Trade except for border trade and certain commodities which the Regional Government may specify with the approval of the Central Government.
  vii) Nationality and Immigration. (Emigration).
  viii) Planning for Economic and Social Development.
  ix) Educational Planning.
  x) Public Audit.

CHAPTER V
LEGISLATURE

Article 8:

Regional Legislation in the Southern Region is exercised by a Peoples Regional Assembly elected by Sudanese Citizens resident in the Southern Region. The constitution and conditions of membership of the Assembly shall be determined by law.

Article 9:

Members of the Peoples Regional Assembly shall be elected by direct secret ballot.

Article 10:

  i) For the First Assembly the President may appoint additional members to the Peoples Regional Assembly where conditions for elections are not conducive to such elections as stipulated in Article 9, provided that such appointed members shall not exceed one quarter of the Assembly.

ii) The Peoples Regional Assembly shall regulate the conduct of its business in accordance with rules of procedures to be laid down by the said Assembly during its first sitting.

iii) The Peoples Regional Assembly shall elect one of its members as a speaker, provided that the first sitting shall be presided over by the Interim President of the High Executive Council.

Article 11:

The Peoples Regional Assembly shall legislate for the preservation of public order, internal security, efficient administration and the development of the Southern Region in cultural, economic and social fields and in particular in the following:

i) Promotion and utilization of Regional financial resources for the development and administration of the Southern Region.

ii) Organization of the machinery for Regional and Local Administration.

iii) Legislation on traditional law and custom within the framework of National Law.

iv) Establishment, maintenance and administration of prisons and reformatory institutions.

v) Establishment, maintenance and administration of Public Schools at all levels in accordance with National Plans for education and economic and social development.

vi) Promotion of local languages and cultures.

vii) Town and Village planning and the construction of roads in accordance with National Plans and programmes.

viii) Promotion of trade; establishment of local industries and markets; issue of traders licences and formation of co-operative societies.

ix) Establishment, maintenance and administration of public hospitals.

x) Administration of environmental health services; maternity care; child welfare; supervision of markets; combat of epidemic diseases; training of medical assistants and rural midwives; establishment of health centres, dispensaries and dressing stations.

xi) Promotion of animal health; control of epidemics and improvement of animal production and trade.

xii) Promotion of tourism.

xiii) Establishment of zoological gardens, museums, organization of trade and cultural exhibitions.

xiv) Mining and quarrying without prejudice to the right of the Central Government in the event of the discovery of natural gas and minerals.

xv) Recruitment for, organization and administration of Police and Prison services in accordance with the national policy and standards.

xvi) Land use in accordance with national laws and plans.

xvii) Control and prevention of pests and plant diseases.

xviii) Development, utilization and protection of forests, crops and pastures in accordance with national laws.

xix) Promotion and encouragement of self-help programmes.

xx) All other matters delegated by the President or the Peoples National Assembly for legislation.

Q

Article 12:

The Peoples National Assembly may call for facts and information concerning the conduct of administration in the Southern Region.

Article 13:

i) The Peoples Regional Assembly may, by a three-quarters majority and for specified reasons relating to public interest, request the President to relieve the President or any member of the High Executive Council from office. The President shall accede to such request.

ii) In case of vacancy, relief or resignation of the President of the High Executive Council, the entire body shall be considered as having automatically resigned.

Article 14:

The Peoples Regional Assembly may, by a two-thirds majority, request the President to postpone the coming into force of any law which, in the view of the members, adversely affects the welfare and interests of the citizens of the Southern Region. The President may, if he thinks fit, accede to such request.

Article 15:

i) The Peoples Regional Assembly may, by a majority of its members, request the President to withdraw any bill presented to the Peoples National Assembly which, in their view, affects adversely the welfare, rights or interests of the citizens in the Southern Region, pending communication of the views of the Peoples Regional Assembly.

ii) If the President accedes to such request, the Peoples Regional Assembly shall present its views within fifteen days from the date of accession to the request.

iii) The President shall communicate any such views to the Peoples National Assembly together with his own observations if he deems necessary.

Article 16:

The Peoples National Assembly shall communicate all Bills and Acts to the Peoples Regional Assembly for their information. The Peoples Regional Assembly shall act similarly.

CHAPTER VI
THE EXECUTIVE

Article 17:

The Regional Executive Authority is vested in a High Executive Council which acts on behalf of the President.

Article 18:

The High Executive Council shall specify the duties of the various departments in the Southern Region provided that on matters relating to Central Government Agencies it shall act with the approval of the President.

Article 19:

The President of the High Executive Council shall be appointed and relieved of office by the President on the recommendation of the Peoples Regional Assembly.

Article 20:

The High Executive Council shall be composed of members appointed and relieved of office by the President on the recommendation of the President of the High Executive Council.

Article 21:

The President of the High Executive Council and its members are responsible to the President and to the Peoples Regional Assembly for the efficient administration in the Southern Region. They shall take an oath of office before the President.

Article 22:

The President and members of the High Executive Council may attend meetings of the Peoples Regional Assembly and participate in its deliberations without the right to vote, unless they are also members of the Peoples Regional Assembly.

CHAPTER VII

Article 23:

The President shall from time to time regulate the relationship between the High Executive Council and the central ministries.

Article 24:

The High Executive Council may initiate laws for the creation of a Regional Public Service. These laws shall specify the terms and conditions of service for the Regional public service.

CHAPTER VIII
FINANCE

Article 25:

The Peoples Regional Assembly may levy Regional duties and taxes in addition to National and Local duties and taxes. It may issue legislations and orders to guarantee the collection of all public monies at different levels.

Article 26:

a) The source of revenue of the Southern Region shall consist of the following:

i) Direct and indirect regional taxes.

ii) Contributions from Peoples Local Government Councils.

iii) Revenue from commercial, industrial and agricultural projects in the Region in accordance with the National Plan.

iv) Funds from the National Treasury for established services.

v) Funds voted by the National Assembly in accordance with the requirements of the Region.

vi) The Special Development Budget for the South as presented by the Peoples Regional Assembly for the acceleration of economic and social advancement of the Southern Region as envisaged in the declaration of the June 9th, 1969.

vii) See Appendix B.

viii) Any other sources.

b) The Regional Executive Council shall prepare a budget to meet the expenditure of regional services, security, administration and development in accordance with National Plans and programmes, and shall submit it to the Peoples Regional Assembly for approval.

CHAPTER IX
OTHER PROVISIONS

Article 27:

   i) Citizens of the Southern Region shall constitute a sizeable proportion of the Peoples Armed Forces in such reasonable numbers as will correspond to the population of the Region.

   ii) The use of the Peoples Armed Forces within the Region and outside the framework of national defence shall be controlled by the President on the advice of the President of the High Executive Council.

   iii) Temporary arrangements for the composition of units of the Peoples Armed Forces in the Southern Region are provided for in the Protocol on Interim Arrangements.

Article 28:

   The President may veto any Bill which he deems contrary to the Provisions of the National Constitution, provided the Peoples Regional Assembly, after receiving the President's views, may reintroduce the Bill.

Article 29:

   The President and members of the High Executive Council may initiate laws in the Peoples Regional Assembly.

Article 30:

   Any member of the Peoples Regional Assembly may initiate any law provided that financial Bills shall not be presented without a sufficient notice to the President of the High Executive Council.

Article 31:

   The Peoples Regional Assembly shall strive to consolidate the unity of the Sudan and respect the spirit of the National Constitution.

Article 32:

   All citizens are guaranteed the freedom of movement in and out of the Southern Region, provided restriction or prohibition of movement may be imposed on a named citizen or citizens solely on grounds of public health and order.

Article 33:

   i) All citizens resident in the Southern Region are guaranteed equal opportunity of education, employment, commerce and the practice of any profession.

   ii) No law may adversely affect the rights of citizens enumerated in the previous item on the basis of race, tribal origin, religion, place of birth, or sex.

Article 34:

   Juba shall be the capital of the Southern Region, and the seat of the Regional Executive and Legislature.

APPENDIX (A)
FUNDAMENTAL RIGHTS AND FREEDOMS

The following should be guaranteed by the Constitution of the Democratic Republic of the Sudan.

1. A citizen should not be deprived of his citizenship.

2. Equality of citizens.
   i) All citizens without distinction based on race, national origin, birth, language, sex, economic or social status, should have equal rights and duties before the law.
   ii) All persons should be equal before the courts of law and should have the right to institute legal proceedings in order to remove any injustice or declare any right in an open court without delay prejudicing their interests.
3. Personal liberty.
   i) Penal liability should be personal. Any kind of collective punishment should be prohibited.
   ii) The accused should be presumed innocent until proved guilty.
   iii) Retrospective Penal Legislation and punishment should be prohibited.
   iv) The right of the accused to defend himself personally or through an agent should be guaranteed.
   v) No person should be arrested, detained or imprisoned except in accordance with due process of law, and no person should remain in custody or detention for more than twenty-four hours without judicial order.
   vi) No accused person should be subjected to inducement, intimidation or torture in order to extract evidence from him whether in his favour or against him or against any other person, and no humiliating punishment should be inflicted on any convicted person.
4. Freedom of religion and conscience.
   i) Every person should enjoy freedom of religious opinion, conscience and the right to profess them publicly and privately and to establish religious institutions subject to reasonable limitations in favour of morality, health or public order as prescribed by law.
   ii) Parents and guardians should be guaranteed the right to educate their children and those under their care in accordance with their choice.
5. Protection of labour.
   i) Forced and compulsory labour of any kind should be prohibited except when ordered for military or civil necessity or pursuant to penal punishment prescribed by law.
   ii) The right to equal pay for equal work should be guaranteed.
6. Freedom of minorities to use their languages and develop their culture should be guaranteed.

APPENDIX (B)
DRAFT ORDINANCE ON ITEMS OF REVENUE AND GRANTS IN-AID FOR THE SOUTHERN REGION

1. Profits accruing to the Central Government as a result of exporting products of the Southern Region.
2. Business Profit Tax of the Southern Region that are at present in the central list of the Ministry of Treasury.

3. Excise Duties on alcoholic beverages and spirits consumed in the Southern Region.
4. Profits on sugar consumed in the Southern Region.
5. Royalties on forest products of the Southern Region.
6. Royalties on leaf tobacco and cigarettes.
7. Taxation on property other than that provided in the Rates Ordinance.
8. Taxes and Rates on Central and Local Government Projects, (5% of net profits of factories, cooperative societies, agricultural enterprises and cinemas).
9. Revenue accruing from Central Government activities in the Southern Region provided the Region shall bear maintenance expenses, e.g. Post Office revenue, land sales, sale of forms and documents, stamp duties, and any other item to be specified from time to time.
10. Licences other than those provided for in the Peoples Local Government Act, 1971.
11. Special Development tax to be paid by Residents in the Southern Region, the rate of which should be decided by the Peoples Regional Assembly.
12. Income Tax collected from officials and employees serving in the Southern Region both in the local and national civil services as well as in the Army, Police and Prisons, Judiciary, and Political establishment.
13. Corporation Tax on any factory and/or agricultural project established in the Region but not run by Regional Government, (5% of the initial cost).
14. Contributions from the Central Government for the encouragement of construction and development; for every agricultural project, industrial project and trading enterprise, (20% of the initial cost as assessed by the Central Government).
15. New Social Service Projects to be established by the Region or any of its Local Government units, and for which funds are allocated, shall receive grants from the National Treasury in the following manner:
    Educational institutions: 20% of expenses.
    Trunk and through Road and Bridges: 25% expenses.
    Relief and Social amenities: 15% expenses.
    Tourist attraction projects: 25% expenses.
    Security: 15% expenses.
    Grants for Post Secondary and University education within the Sudan: 20% of grants; outside the Sudan: 30% of grants.
    Contribution for Research, Scientific Advancement, and Cultural activities: 25% of expenses.

AGREEMENT ON THE CEASE-FIRE IN THE SOUTHERN REGION

Article 1:
This Agreement shall come into force on the date and time specified for the ratification of the Addis Ababa Agreement.

Article 2:
There will be an end to all military operations and to all armed actions in the Southern Region from the time of cease-fire.

Article 3:
All combat forces shall remain in the area under their control at the time of the cease-fire.

Article 4:
Both parties agree to forbid any individual or collective acts of violence. Any underground activities contrary to public order shall cease.

Article 5:
Movements of individual members of both combat forces outside the areas under their control shall be allowed only if these individuals are unarmed and authorized by their respective authorities. The plans for stationing of troops from the National Army shall be such as to avoid any contact between them and the Southern Sudan Liberation Movement combat forces.

Article 6:
A Joint-Commission is hereby created for the implementation of all questions related to the cease-fire including repatriation of refugees. The Joint-Commission shall include members from all the countries bordering on the Southern Region, as well as representatives of the International Committee of the Red Cross, World Council of Churches, All Africa Conference of Churches, and United Nations High Commissioner for Refugees.

Article 7:
The Joint-Commission shall propose all measures to be undertaken by both parties in dealing with all incidents after a full inquiry on the spot.

Article 8:
Each party shall be represented on the Joint-Commission by one senior military officer and a maximum of five other members.

Article 9:
The headquarters of the Joint-Commission shall be located in Juba with provincial branches in Juba, Malakal and Wau.

Article 10:
The Joint-Commission shall appoint local commissions in various centres of the Southern Region, composed of two members from each party.

PROTOCOLS ON INTERIM ARRANGEMENTS

CHAPTER I
INTERIM ADMINISTRATIVE ARRANGEMENTS:
(POLITICAL, LOCAL GOVERNMENT AND CIVIL SERVICE)

Article 1:

The President of the Democratic Republic of the Sudan shall, in consultation with the South Sudan Liberation Movement (SSLM) and branches of the Sudan Socialist Union in the Southern Region, appoint the President and members of an Interim High Executive Council.

Article 2:

The Interim High Executive Council shall consist of the President and other members with portfolios in:

a) Finance and Economic Planning;
b) Education;
c) Information, Culture and Tourism;
d) Communications and Transport;
e) Agriculture, Animal Production and Fisheries;
f) Public Health;
g) Regional Administration (Local Government, Legal Affairs, Police and Prisons);
h) Housing, Public Works and Utilities;
i) Natural Resources and Rural Development;
j) Public Service and Labour;
k) Minerals and Industry, Trade and Supply.

Article 3:

The Interim High Executive Council shall, in accordance with national laws, establish a Regional Civil Service, subject to ratification by the Peoples Regional Assembly.

Article 4:

The President shall, in consultation with the Interim High Executive Council, determine the date for the election to the Peoples Regional Assembly, and the Interim High Executive Council shall make arrangements for the setting up of this Assembly.

Article 5:

In order to facilitate the placement in and appointment to both central and regional institutions, the South Sudan Liberation Movement shall compile and communicate lists of citizens of the Southern Region outside the Sudan in accordance with details to be supplied by the Ministry of Public Service and Administrative Reform.

Article 6:

The Interim High Executive Council and the Ministry of Public Service and Administrative Reform shall undertake to provide necessary financial allocations with effect from 1972-73 Budget for such placements and appointments.

Article 7:

The Mandate of the Interim High Executive Council shall not exceed a period of 18 months.

CHAPTER II
TEMPORARY ARRANGEMENTS
FOR THE COMPOSITION OF UNITS
OF THE PEOPLES ARMED FORCES
IN THE SOUTHERN REGION

Article 1:

These arrangements shall remain in force for a period of five years subject to revision by the President of the High Executive Council acting with the consent of the Peoples Regional Assembly.

Article 2:

The Peoples Armed Forces in the Southern Region shall consist of a national force called the Southern Command, composed of 12,000 officers and men, of whom 6,000 shall be citizens from that region and the other 6,000 from outside the Region.

Article 3:

The recruitment and integration of citizens from the Southern Region within the aforementioned Forces shall be determined by a Joint Military Commission taking into account the need for initial separate deployment of troops with a view to achieve smooth integration in the national force. The Commission shall ensure that this deployment shall be such that an atmosphere of peace and confidence shall prevail in the Southern Region.

Article 4:

The Joint Military Commission shall be composed of three senior military officers from each side. Decisions of the Joint Military Commission shall be taken unanimously. In case of disagreement, such matters shall be referred to the respective authorities.

CHAPTER III
AMNESTY AND JUDICIAL ARRANGEMENTS

Article 1:

No action or other legal proceedings whatsoever, civil, or criminal, shall be instituted against any person in any Court of Law for, or on account of, any act or matter done inside or outside the Sudan as from the 18th day of August, 1955, if such act or matter done in connection with mutiny, rebellion or sedition in the Southern Region.

Article 2:

If a civil suit in relation to any acts or matters referred to in Article One is instituted before or after the date of ratification of the Addis Ababa Agreement, such a suit shall be discharged and made null and void.

Article 3:

All persons serving terms of prisons or held in detention in respect of offences hereinbefore specified in Article One shall be discharged or released within fifteen days from the date of ratification of the Addis Ababa Agreement.

Article 4:

The Joint Cease-Fire Commission shall keep a register of all civilian returnees which register shall serve to certify that the persons therein named are considered indemnified within the meaning of this Agreement provided that the Commission may delegate such power to the Diplomatic Missions of the Democratic Republic of the Sudan in the case of citizens from the Southern Region living abroad and to whom the provisions of this Agreement apply.

Article 5:

In the case of armed returnees or those belonging to combat forces, the Joint Military Commission shall keep a similar register of those persons who shall be treated in the same manner as provided for in Article Four.

Article 6:

Notwithstanding the provisions of Articles Four and Five above, a Special Tribunal with ad hoc judicial powers shall be established to examine and decide on those cases which in the estimation of the authorities do not meet the conditions for amnesty specified in Article One of this Agreement. The Special Tribunal shall be composed of a President appointed by the President of the Republic and not more than four members named by the Cease-Fire Commission.

Article 7:

Cases referred to in Article Six shall be brought to the attention of the Special Tribunal by request of the Minister of Justice.

Article 8:

The Amnesty Provisions contained in this Agreement as well as the powers of the Special Tribunal shall remain in force until such time as the President after consultation with the commissions referred to in this Agreement, decide that they have fulfilled their functions.

CHAPTER IV
REPATRIATION AND RESETTLEMENT COMMISSION
I. REPATRIATION

Article 1:

There shall be established Special Commissions inside and where required outside the Southern Region charged with the responsibility of taking all administrative and other measures as may be necessary in order to repatriate all citizens from the Southern Region who today are residing in other countries and especially in the neighbouring countries. The headquarters of the Commission shall be in Juba.

Article 2:

The Commissions shall be composed of, at least, three members including one representative of the Central Government, one representative of the Southern Region, and one representative of the UN High Commissioner for Refugees. For those commissions operating outside the Sudan, a representative of the host Government shall be included, plus the central Government representative, who shall be the Ambassador of the Sudan or his representative.

Article 3:

The control of repatriation at the borders shall be assumed by the competent border authorities in cooperation with the representatives of the Resettlement Commission.

Article 4:

The Repatriation Commission shall work very closely with the Commission for Relief and Resettlement to ensure that the operation and timing of the returning of refugees from across borders is adequately co-ordinated.

II. RESETTLEMENT

Article 1:

There shall be established a Special Commission for Relief and Resettlement under the President of the Interim High Executive Council with headquarters in Juba and provincial branches in Juba, Malakal and Wau. The Commission, its branches, and whatever units it may deem fit to create in other localities in order to facilitate its functions, shall be responsible for co-ordination and implementation of all relief services and planning related to Resettlement and Rehabilitation of all returnees, that is:

a) Refugees from neighbouring countries
b) Displaced persons resident in the main centres in the Southern Region and other parts of the Sudan.
c) Displaced persons including residual Anya-Nya personnel and supporters in the bush.
d) Handicapped and orphans.

Article 2:

Although resettlement and rehabilitation of refugees and displaced persons is administratively the responsibility of the Regional Government, the present conditions in the Southern Region dictate that efforts of the whole nation of the Sudan and International Organizations should be pooled to help and rehabilitate persons affected by the conflict. The Relief and Resettlement Commission shall co-ordinate activities and resources of the Organizations within the country.

Article 3:

The first priority shall be the resettlement of displaced persons within the Sudan in the following order:

a) Persons presently residing in overcrowded centres in the Southern Region, and persons desirous to return to their original areas and homes.
b) Persons returning from the bush including Anya-Nya supporters.
c) Handicapped persons and orphans.

Article 4:

The second priority shall be given to returnees from the neighbouring and other countries according to an agreed plan. This plan shall provide for:

a) Adequate reception centres with facilities for shelter, food supplies, medicine and medicaments.
b) Transportation to permanent resettlement villages or places of origin.
c) Materials and equipments.

Article 5:

The Relief and Resettlement Commission shall:

a) Appeal to International Organizations and Voluntary agencies to continue assistance for students already under their support particularly for students in secondary schools and higher institutions until appropriate arrangements are made for their repatriation.

b) Compile adequate information on students and persons in need of financial support from the Sudan Government.

Article 6:

The Relief and Resettlement Commission shall arrange for the education of all returnees who were attending primary schools.

This Agreement is hereby concluded on this twenty-seventh day of the month of February in the year one thousand nine hundred and seventy two, A.D. in this City, Addis Ababa, Ethiopia, between the Government of the Democratic Republic of the Sudan on the one hand and the South Sudan Liberation Movement on the other.

It shall come into force on the date and hour fixed for its ratification by the President of the Democratic Republic of the Sudan and the Leader of the South Sudan Liberation Movement.

It shall be ratified by the said two Leaders in persons or through their respective authorized Representatives, in this City, Addis Ababa, Ethiopia, at the twelfth hour at noon, on the twelfth day of the month of March, in the year one thousand nine hundred and seventy two, A.D.

In witness whereof, We the Representatives of the Government of the Democratic Republic of the Sudan and the Representatives of the South Sudan Liberation Movement hereby append our signatures in the presence of the Representative of His Imperial Majesty, the Emperor of Ethiopia and the Representatives of the World Council of Churches, the All Africa Conference of Churches, and the Sudan Council of Churches.

For the Government of the Democratic Republic of the Sudan

1. Abel Alier-Wal Kuai
     Vice President and Minister of State for Southern Affairs.
2. Dr. Mansour Khalid,
     Minister for Foreign Affairs.
3. Dr. Jaafar Mohammed Ali Bakheit,
     Minister for Local Government.
4. Major General P. S. C. Mohammed El Baghir Ahmed,
     Minister of Interior.
5. Abdel Rahman Abdalla,
     Minister of Public Service and Administrative Reform.
6. Brigadier P. S. C. Mirghani Suleiman.
7. Colonel Kamal Abasher.

For the South Sudan Liberation Movement:

1. Ezboni Mondiri Gwonza,
     Leader of the Delegation.
2. Dr. Lawrence Wol Wol,
     Secretary of the Delegation.
3. E. Mading DeGarang,
     Spokesman of the Delegation.
4. Colonel Frederick Brian Maggott,
     Special Military Representative.
5. Oliver Batali Albino,
     Member.

R

6. Angelo Voga Morjan,
    Member.
7. Rev. Paul Puot,
    Member.
8. Job Adier de Jok,
    Member.

Witnesses:
1. Nabiyelul Kifle,
   The Representative of His Imperial Majesty, the Emperor of Ethiopia.
2. Leopoldo J. Niilus,
   Representative of the World Council of Churches.
3. Kodwo E. Ankrah,
   Representative of the World Council of Churches.
4. Burgess Carr,
   General Secretary, All Africa Conference of Churches.
5. Samuel Athi Bwogo,
   Representative of Sudan Council of Churches.

Attestation:
I attest that these signatures are genuine and true.

Burgess Carr,
Moderator.

INDEX

Amnesty Law, 173, 220, 240–41
Anglo-Egyptian Agreement, 18, 22,
    116;
  failure to consult South, 98
Anglo-Egyptian Condominium, *see*
    British Colonial rule
Angudri convention, 102
Animal husbandry, 9, 10, 92
Ansar sect, 146, 147, 153, 158
Antiquities, Twelve-Man Committee
    proposals, 213
Anuak tribe, 9, 14, 125
Anya-Nya, 2, 161, 163, 166;
  amnesty law for, 173;
  formation, 102, 149, 164;
  popular support, 103
Anyidi Revolutionary Government,
    102, 163, 164, 165
Apaya, Pastor Andrea, Southern
    representative, 203
Apter, Professor David, 167
Aptheker, Herbert, historian, 62
Arab-Israeli War, 127–9
Arab League, 127
Arab society,
  ascending miscegenation, 54–7,
    65–9;
  biocultural assimilation, 73–4;
  intermarriage, 61, 70–72
Arabic,
  Juba Conference discussion, 203;
  official status, 226;
  Round Table Conference, 208;
  Southern Policy restrictions, 15,
    176–8, 182
Arabism, 158;
  characteristics, 43
Arabization, 2, 15–16, 51–2, 62, 68–9,
    108, 135, 148;
  history in the Sudan, 31–2;
  and nationalist movement, 38–9;
  see also Biocultural assimilation;
    Islamization
Arabs,
  acceptance as natives of Africa,
    50–51;
  pigmental differences between, 55;
  racial definition, 54–5;
  in Zanzibar, 54, 55, 67, 74–6
Armed Forces, 212;
  under Addis Ababa agreement, 230,
    240;
  corruption, 149

recruitment, 20, 106
Asaf Fyzee, *see* Fyzee
Ashanti separatism, 87
Atot, Dinka sub-tribe, 10
Atta, Major Hashim el-, Communist
    revolutionary, 160
Aukaya tribe, 10
Awadalla, Bahikel, Vice President,
    161
Azande tribes, 10, 89, 125
Azania Liberation Front, 163
Azhari, Ismail El, politician 19, 152,
    154, 156

Badri, *see* Ibrahim Badri
Baggara Arabs, 32
Bahr al-Ghazal Province, 7, 15, 176,
    225;
  racial mingling, 55
Baker, Samuel, explorer, 12, 13
Bakheit, Dr. Jaafar Mohammed Ali,
    243
Baldo, Governor Ali, 100
Bari tribe, 10, 12, 14, 89, 125
Bashir, *see* Mohammad Omer Bashir
Beja Congress, 112
Beja tribes, 99, 111
Belanda tribe, 125
Biafra, 87, 94, 111, 115, 118, 119, 124;
  propaganda, 134
Bilad al-Sudan, 33
Bio-cultural assimilation, 47–52;
  as solution to Southern Problem,
    69–73
Black Africa, Conference of
    Independent States, of, 133
"Black Block", 112
Blyden, Edward, Liberian intellectual,
    56, 57
Bor, Dinka sub-tribe, 9, 10
Bourgeoisie, role in independence
    movements, 85–6
Brazil, miscegenation, 52, 53, 63–4
British Colonial rule, 3–4, 13–20,
    36–7, 88, 176;
  see also Southern Policy
Bugunda, 87
Burun tribe, 9
Buth Diu, Chief, Southern politician,
    147, 195, 200, 201, 203, 205
Cairo, 50
Canada, racial questions, 59–60, 107
Capitalism, and self-determination, 87

Mahdia, 11–12, 36;
  Southern resistance to, 13
Mahdists, influence on nationalist
  movement, 37–8
Mahgoub, Muhammed Ahmed,
  politician, 40–41, 99;
  overthrow, 152, 153;
  and Southern Problem, 152–3
Mahgoub, Khalid, Communist
  official, 160
Majok, Chief, 155
Majok, Philemon, 162, 190, 199
Makerere University, 139, 154
Malakal, 242;
  paper project, 110
Malawi, 132, 138;
  educational policy, 142
Malwal, Joshwa, SANU member, 217
Marwood, B. V., Governor, 191,
  196, 202, 204
Matrilineal races, and miscegenation,
  48
May Revolution of 1969, 25–7, 101,
  150;
  Government, 16
Mayanja, Abu, 114
Mayen, Gordon M., Southern
  politician, 164
Mazrui, Professor Ali, 115, 131–2, 150
Mboro, Clement, Southern politician,
  151, 193, 194, 196, 198, 202
Melo, Francisco Manuel de, 53
Middle East, risk of Sudanese
  involvement, 127
Military Government of 1958, 99
Mineral resources, Southern Sudan, 9
Mirghani, Sayyid 'Ali al-, religious
  leader, 35
Mirghani Suleiman, Brigadier, P. S. C.,
  243
Miscegenation,
  ambivalent, 52, 76;
  ascending, 54–7, 65–9, 71–2, 76,
  78–9;
  attitude of white women to, 60–61;
  descending, 52, 62–5, 77–8;
  divergent, 54, 64, 77;
  symmetrical and asymmetrical,
  48–9
Missionaries, Christian, 12, 130;
  criticized by Khartoum
  Government, 127;
  failure to assimilate, 57;

Round Table Conference proposals,
  208
Missionaries, Muslim, cultural
  assimilation, 57
Missionary Societies Act of 1962, 16,
  20
Mohammed, *see also* Muhammad
Mohammed Ali, Viceroy of Egypt,
  11, 33
Mohammed Aggad, slave trader, 14
Mohammad Dawood El Khalifa,
  Northern politician, 217
Mohammad Omer Bashir, politician,
  167
Mohammed El Baghir Ahmed,
  Major-General P. S. C., 243
Mohammed Saleh Shengeiti, *see*
  Shengeiti
Moller, Herbert, 59–60
Mondiri, Ezibon, Southern politician,
  151, 164
Mongalla sugar project, 110
Monrovia Conference, principles for
  African states' relations, 133–4
Morjan, Angelo Voga, Southern
  politician, 244
Moru tribe, 10, 125
Moru-land, 102
Moslem Brothers, 158
Muhammad Ali Pasha, Viceroy of
  Egypt, 11, 33
Muhammed Mifta al-Faytoury, *see*
  Faytoury
Muhammad Sa'id al- 'Abbasi,
  Sheikh unionist, 40
Mulla, D. F., Islamic jurist, 70
Mundari tribe, 10
Murle tribe, 125
Muslim conquests, 51
Mutiny of 1955, 3, 19, 23, 98, 147;
  see also Cotran Commission of
  Inquiry

NPG, *see* Nile Provisional
  Government
NUP; *see* National Unionist Party
Nadler, L. F., 34
Nasser, Gamal Abdul,
  pan-Africanism, 50
National sovereignty, and secession,
  114
National Unionist Party, 147, 148,
  152, 207, 217